SOUN

Chapters

Sound Example CDs

INTRODUCTION

In 2005 I was invited to a music festival in Cagliari, Sardinia, by Lucio Garau. Whilst there, Lucio asked if I had any teaching materials he might use in the music course at the University in Palermo, especially as he felt pieces like *Imago* were too complex to analyse and discuss with students without some help. For some years I have been giving presentations about my musical works and therefore it seemed sensible to gather together all the notes, together with the sound examples I use, into a new book, so that the structural ideas used in the pieces might be more widely disseminated. The music of sounds is perhaps more difficult to analyse and teach about, as there is (usually) no score to act as a guide. Without a score it can take more time and effort to tease out the structural ideas in such pieces; this can be done only by listening over and over again, and this is a difficult option for students on a music or general arts course who have lots of other demands on their time. So I hope these chapters will offer a guide to the pieces.

More importantly, I'm anxious to propagate an idea about structure in sonic art. In the studio it is very simple to both generate new sounds, and to join those sounds together in sequence. As technology has advanced, making high quality recordings of the real world has also become both simple and inexpensive. As the sounds we gather and use may have nothing in common with traditional instrumental sounds, and may lie outside conventional frameworks of pitch (tempered scales, chord structures) or timbre (the timbral 'consistency' of traditional instruments), the question of how to structure those sounds to make a satisfying work becomes paramount.

Two traditions have grown up in the world of sonic arts (and these are not mutually exclusive, as I hope some of my pieces demonstrate). The first derives from the work of John Cage, and is most prevalent amongst visual and media artists. Here, the traditional notions of musical 'language' are abandoned in favour of the direct montage of materials. These materials are often chosen for what they represent (what they are a recording of, what the recording reveals about its origins) and with an aesthetic slant which foregrounds the *idea behind* using the particular sound, or juxtaposition of sounds.

The second approach, originally growing out of work at the *GRM* in Paris in the mid twentieth century, concerns itself more with the *heard relationships* amongst the sounds themselves, and is therefore more akin to the instrumental musical tradition. However this approach originally grew up in the context of the high modernism of mid twentieth century music, with its complex musical structures. The resulting sophistication of form, combined with the absence of written scores, meant that works could be difficult to penetrate analytically and for teaching purposes. This meant that a common language for approaching sounds *as sounds* grew more by a process of osmosis, or by the learning of common studio techniques, than by the detailed analysis and study of existing works. In the later twentieth century, the arrival of digital recording and computer analysis of sound greatly increased our knowledge of, and ability to manipulate, those sounds. The knowledge and insights that had grown out of studio practice could now be greatly extended in a rational way by the application of computing power to sound.

4

In this book I will describe a particular approach to the formal structuring of sounds based on the idea of *sound metamorphosis*. I have developed this approach in most of my own work, and feel it is sufficiently general to provide a framework in which others might approach sonic organisation, without having to adopt my musical style. It can be seen as a *generalisation* of the traditional notions of variation and development in instrumental music, but applied to the *sound as a whole*.

For me it was necessary to step back from the parameterised vision of the musical world inspired by analytic musical notation (where pitch, time and 'colour' are represented as *distinct* features of musical events, and these events themselves pre-selected to conform to notions of the 'timbral consistency' of instruments, or the given set of pitch values in the tempered scale). Once we deal with *any* sound as a possible source for music-making we discover that the sounds of instruments are a very particular subset of the world of sounds in general, with instruments physically constructed, and musical writing systems specifically designed, to restrict sounds within given boundaries. Although many traditional composers have explored the outer limits of instrumental possibilities, this approach still centres on the notion of the *perceptual coherence of the instrument* – the new sounds are extreme extensions of a familiar source-object originally designed to work well in the traditional context. The new sounds clearly originate in the same physical object (and therefore from the same performer or concert platform) but this in itself provides a situational or social context, rather than a *sonic logic*, for their use.

In the world at large, most sounds simply do not conform to those traditional criteria. In particular, many sounds are characterised by the way they *change* their spectral and temporal characteristics. Human speech is a good example of this. To organise such sounds we cannot appeal to pre-ordained frameworks of pitch, or 'timbral consistency' to organise them. What we can do, however, is to establish relationships between them by the process of *transformation* of one sound into another. The special nature of this transformation space is discussed in *On Sonic Art* and techniques for achieving these transformations are described in *Audible Design*.

This new book attempts to describe the musical organisation that can arise from structuring sounds in this way. It does not provide a *complete* description of the works, merely a guide to some of their more prominent feature. It is also not meant to be a substitute for listening. You must decide for yourself whether the formal relationships described *work* in some sense in your musical experience of the pieces. And some aspects of composing are not talked about in any detail here. In particular I will not say much about the important role of extra-musical ideas in many of the pieces (and the ways these are subsumed in a musical-formal way of dealing with the sound materials), nor about the way I often develop the musical instruments (software) to achieve the transformations that I need during the course of composing (in fact, often perfecting them only *after* completing the pieces). However, the book's stress on the formal organisation of the pieces should not be taken to imply that I am 'merely' interested in form (and, by implication, not in ideas, emotions or sensual pleasure!). On the contrary I believe that the power of music lies in the way it harnesses formal procedures to produce powerful emotional or sensual responses, and the way these can resonate with other experiences in our lives.

Finally, this book is derived from a collection of pre-existing talks created at different times, usually soon after the completion of the piece being discussed, so I must apologise in advance for any inconsistencies in style, and repetitions of ideas from one to the next. I have also added a chapter about *Anticredos*, and resurrected a presentation about the *Vox cycle* given at the University of York in 1988. Although not concerned with pure electro-acoustic composition, I hope these will illustrate the continuity of my thinking about the organisation of sound, and how this has also influenced the composition of live works using vocal sounds as their materials.

MACHINE

&

JOURNEY INTO SPACE

MACHINE & JOURNEY INTO SPACE [1]

My initial interest in sound metamorphosis grew out of personal experience and my wish to engage with the world. As an M.A. student I was busy analysing the orchestral works of Xenakis and composing a large orchestra work employing several 12-tone rows plus texture-generation with random-number tables. At that moment, my father, a factory worker in Leeds, died. Apart from being deeply affected by his loss, I became conscious that the music I was pursuing was very far removed from his world and the world I experienced around me. I had strong memories of the dark cavernous factory where he had to work, and which I visited just once a year for the children's party laid on by the Union. I naively wanted to make some critical connection with that 'reality', whatever this might mean, so bought a cheap low-quality portable mono tape recorder with an attached microphone (the best I could afford) and set off to record the sounds of machinery in factories and power-stations around Nottingham and Leeds, applying to do further study at the University of York as it was one of the few departments in the UK with a sound-studio. At York I gradually learned the mysteries of sound-manipulation in the analogue studio (and how different they were from my experience of composing with notes on paper) and developed an approach called 'musicmontage' that involved loosely scored, improvised performances that were recorded and used as source-material for further processing in the studio[2].

I had taken my factory recordings to York without a clear idea of what might be done with them, having only the vague notion of commenting upon or 'humanising' them in some way. One of the projects developed (*Machine-2*: see score extracts below) involved a small choir imitating the sounds of specific machine sounds (trapped on tape-loops) and then gradually changing their sounds towards something less mechanical and more clearly human in character. The chorus was recorded on one channel of a stereo tape-recorder, and the machine-loop on the other, so I always had the possibility of synchronously remixing the two when I finally took the materials to the studio. The score provided some suggestions about how to achieve changes from one sound type to another, plus an organisational strategy for devolving leadership from one conductor to many conductors, and hence a way for several streams of development to grow from a single stream. The resulting sounds became an important part of my earliest studio work *Machine, an electronically-preserved dream*. In retrospect this was the first time that I used the notion of sound metamorphosis in my work.

After completing this hour-long piece, I worked on a second, even longer, work called *Journey into Space*[3]. This involved the merging of three journeys, a journey in the real world, a journey into space (the Apollo 11 launch is heard on the car radio) and the personal dream-journey of the imagined protagonist, over a slowly evolving, 80 minute time-frame. The piece contained some evocative sound landscapes (**Sound Example 1)**[4] plus my first attempts at sound-metamorphosis in the analogue studio and the use of sounds as symbols (the sounds of doors), ideas later fully developed in *Red Bird* (see next chapter) **(Sound Example 2)**.

---

[1] Chapter written specifically for this book. For material contemporary with the composition of the pieces, see *Journey into Space, an Antiscore.*
[2] This linked with my parallel interest in free improvisation and performance art.
[3] This piece has a cult following, but I now find it embarrassing in many respects!
[4] This recording involved the use of several 20 foot scaffolding pieces I hired from a local builder and dragged to the campus through traffic on a 6 foot trolley, plus cheap toy musical boxes, toy trumpets, steel combs, bicycle and other bells, and old car-horns powered by air in a hand-squeezed rubber sac.

from 'MACHINE 2'

INTRODUCTION

Machine-2 involves prerecorded machine-sounds and a choir. The general conception of the piece is as follows. A tape-loop of a machine-sound that has some distinct and constant characteristics (e.g. a rhythm, a pitch, a consonant-quality) is played into the performance area via a loudspeaker and via headphones to the various choir leaders. The choir gradually takes up the sound (imitating it), being initially led by one or more choir-leaders, and then **gradually** changes it into something else, something essentially human; human articulation arises from the Machine-sounds. The latter, on the main loudspeaker(s) may be faded out gradually, or quickly, or constantly varied in level to interact with the choir sounds.[5] However. The choir-leaders will always have a constant-volume reference signal on their headphones......

CONTROL INSTRUCTIONS (general description)

Layout of the choir. The choir is arranged in a series of distinct columns. At the head of each column, and *facing the other members of the column*, is a choir-leader (designated by '@' in the diagram below). The two central choir leaders are designated "A" and "B" below, and will be referred to as the principal choir-leader and the secondary choir-leader respectively. If only a limited number of headphones are available, these should be made available to the principal (and secondary) choir leader(s) before anyone else. They thuscan always hear the original machine-tape. All the choir-leaders should be visible to *all* members of the choir.

(columns	1	2	3	4	5	6	7	8	.......)
	@	@	@	A	B	@	@	@	
(1st line)	x	x	x	x	x	x	x	x	
(2nd line)	x	x	x	x	x	x	x	x	
(3rd line)	x	x	x	x	x	x	x	x	
(4th line)	x	x	x	x	x	x	x	x	
etc....									

The choir always begins by imitating the sound made by the principal choir leader, *unless* s/he shares this initial leadership (by using a "SHARE" card ... see below) before s/he begins. After this. Leadership may devolve to the other choir leaders by passing suitable cards (see below).
The other choir leaders do not become *active* leaders until they have been passed an appropriate card by the principal leader or by some other already active leader. Hence, in the first diagram (below) the principal and secondary leaders are the only active leaders, whereas in the 2nd diagram, the leaders at the heads of columns 2 and 7 are also active, and in the 3rd diagram, all choir leaders are active.

The choir members will always imitate the sounds being made by the *active* leader *nearest* to them, *looking towards the centre* (see diagrams). The choir members will thus never be silent unless *all* choir-leaders are silent.

Devolution of leadership may take place at any stage, according to the discretion of the then-current leaders. It will take place in the sequence indicated by the succession of diagrams on the following page. It may be conditional e.g. one might pass on a mandate for a pitch variation but *not* a rhythm variation, ad so on. Leadership may finally devolve to the individual choir members in any or all the columns by the display of certain cards (DISCOORDINATE-1 and DISCOORDINATE-2 described below) and thismay also be conditional.

Choir-leaders may voluntarily centralise leadership by imitating other choir-leaders. Choir-members may similarly decide to imitate other members in their columns.

---

[5] For use in the final tape-piece, the machine-sound was faded out quite quickly, but the machine-sound was fed to the 2nd channel of a stereo recording tape, with the choir being recorded on the other.

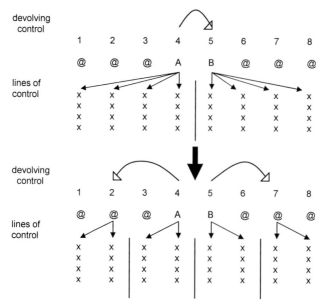

These two devolutions need not occur simultaneously

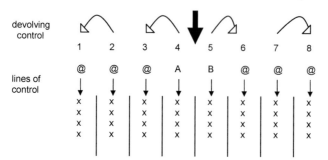

These four devolutions need not occur simultaneously

Transition Instructions

Any new sounds must *not* begin abruptly but must merge with the total already-present sound before emerging from it. The initial sound is first adopted by each choir member before *very quietly* crescendoing to a normal level. All leaders must then only change their own strategies *very gradually.*

When a leader receives a mandate (in the form of a card) from another leader, s/he may diverge from the other's strategy, *but only gradually.*

If a section of the choir is assigned a new leader who adopts completely new pitches, they must take up these pitches *very quietly* aand *very gradually* crescendo to a normal level. If the leader adopts any new strategy, they will adopt this new strategy simultaneously with the leader.

11

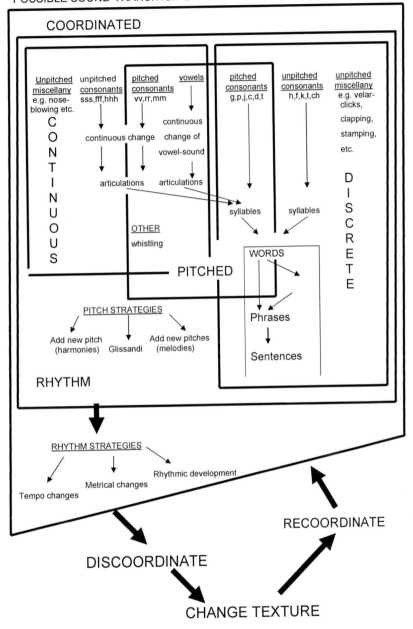

RED BIRD

RED BIRD

One evening I was motorcycling through countryside close to York when I came across a small nature reserve, a wood in the grounds of a hospital, with tall, thin trees protruding above a dense undergrowth of rhododendron bushes. It was dusk - the light was failing - so I was able to walk along the narrow pathways between the bushes almost unseen. However, from time to time I approached too close to a blackbird hidden in the bushes. At this moment it burst from cover with a loud and startling rustling of leaves and twigs, disappearing into the semi-darkness. This experience was repeated over and over again in the deepening gloom. The aural connection between the commonplace rustling of the pages of a book and this mysterious and frightening rustling of leaves and wings struck me at once.

Red Bird, was composed in the analogue studio of the University of York, after completing *Machine, an electronically-preserved dream* and *Journey into Space*. In those pieces I developed from scratch an approach to working with sound-materials (which I called 'musicmontage') using recorded environmental sounds and structured improvisations to generate source material that was later used in the studio. There was a link here too with my involvement in Free Improvisation and street Performance Art activities. *Red Bird* differs from later digital pieces in using *classes* of recognisable sounds as metaphors in a mythic sound-landscape. (Later pieces focus on the metamorphosis of the sounds themselves).

At that time, the studio had few sophisticated technical tools. One could change the speed of most of the (stereo) tape-recorders over a continuous range of 2 octaves, edit the tape with a razor blade and splicing block, filter the sound using the EQ controls on the mixing desk and some limited analogue filters, and mix down from up to 5 tape-recorders (often using a group of helpers and a pre-timed mixing score) assembling more complex sounds by mixing the mixes (always with an ear for the build-up of analogue tape noise on the one hand, and analogue distortion on the other).

After 4 years experience I had begun to master these simple techniques, knew how to get the best from them, and had a more developed idea of how to use environmental sounds in a sound composition[6]. I therefore decided to embark on a more (technically) ambitious project, in which *sound transformation*[7] or metamorphosis would be central to the workings of the piece.

---

[6] Some of these theoretical ideas (especially the idea of *sound landscape*) are discussed in my 1985 book, *On Sonic Art*, subsequently published in a new edition , by Harwood Academic (later Taylor & Francis), edited by Simon Emmerson. The intellectual ideas behind the specific 'symbolism' in *Red Bird* are discussed in *Red Bird, a document*, produced soon after the piece was completed, from which much of the text of this chapter is taken.

[7] Sound transformation, in a precise and detailed way became much more feasible with the advent of digital sound. A discussion of digital sound transformation techniques can be found in later chapters, and in the *Sound Transformation* overview on my website (2011).

Origins of the Project: The Source Material

Unlike previous and subsequent works, Red Bird grew from an exploration of the possibilities of transforming sound-materials *in the abstract*, plus the collection of a large body of source material from which to select possible usable sounds. Rather than work from specific recorded sounds, I grouped sounds into categories (in terms of what they represented e.g. Birds, Machines) and explored how these various categories of sounds might be inter-transformed and organised. The original conceptual search took several months. Notions of what I would like to do with the sounds would have to be drastically trimmed to the possibilities of the particular sounds I collected (I therefore collected a very large body of sources) and, much more significantly, to the general limitations of the analogue studio. Bird and animal sources were collected from all available vinyl recordings, and vocal sources generated through guided performance and recording.

The ideas behind Red Bird

In '*The Raw and The Cooked*' Levi-Strauss attempts to demonstrate that diverse myths, though superficially different (e.g. they refer to different creatures, different journeys etc.), reveal underlying *structural* parallels, and particularly the notion of metamorphosis. To emphasize this concern with the abstract structure, he named the chapters of his book after musical forms. In Red Bird I decided to reverse this notion, to sonically structure and metamorphose recognisable real-world sounds into the form of a contemporary myth having several parallel interpretations, political, philosophical and environmental, and in some ways a commentary, in music, on rationality itself. It's therefore worth quoting the following line from *Red Bird, a document* the original documentation of the piece.

> This verbal document is therefore only a commentary on what is an essentially and irreducibly musical experience[8].

---

[8] The original text from which this is taken, (not necessarily my current viewpoint) is as follows..

"A conventionally accepted wisdom is that rational language constitutes a precise and articulate medium, the only 'objective' means with which to approach the elucidation of reality, be it physical, 'mental' or social. Music, in contrast, is usually regarded as a peripheral activity, purely epiphenomenal to the core of social reality, at best an ill-defined means of articulating vague 'emotional' attitudes. *Red Bird*, however, is constructed on the assumption that, as far as global structures and their dynamics are concerned, language is a longwinded (circumlocuitous!) and ultimately inadequate medium, and that only a system of reference which itself partakes of a global structural dynamic is adequate to the task. Music is such a medium. Further, *Red Bird* deals with a conflict of 'mental' (and hence social) structures. The philosopher who attempts to analytically write about the consequences of analytic modes of thought is trapped in a logical paradox. Philosophical language remains a mystery towards which he has contributed. *Red Bird* aims, among other things, to use the dynamic-relational structuring of music (and speech) *as aural experience*, to comment upon the linear-analytic-causal mode of thought and its consequences. This verbal document is therefore only a commentary on what is an essentially and irreducibly musical experience. No 'explanation', either in terms of 'what the symbols mean' or 'how the sounds are put together' in a one-to-one correspondence with the sequence of sounds in the piece, will be offered. In particular the notion that to understand how the sounds are put together constitutes understanding the music is a fallacy propagated through the visually-distanced logic of some avant-garde music......this document will unfortunately not reveal what the music 'really is'... Music is not translatable."

Politics

The myth of Red Bird was influenced by reading Albert Camus' "*The Rebel*", a damning indictment of Stalinist tyranny, but with strong resonances for our industrial world.

"The irrational escapes calculation and calculation must reign in the empire."
"To ensure man's control of the world it is necessary to suppress ... everything that does not come under the reign of quantity."
"In this new Jerusalem, echoing with the roar of miraculous machinery, who will still
 remember the cry of the victims."
"Nothing is less determined on conquest than reason."

Philosophy and Language

Red Bird was also a reaction against the (then dominant) school of *Linguistic Philosophy*, which suggested that problems that could not be clearly formulated in language were therefore not problems at all. The phrases "Listen to Reason" and the word "Reasonable" are developed in such a way that their explicit verbal meaning become just one dimension of a larger space of meaning-articulation. Utterances are fragmented into words e.g. isolating the word 'listen' ('Listen!!'), opening new fields of suggested reference: words segmented into phonemes, like "rr" and "ll" which are transformed by *tone of voice*, investing meaningless syllables with semantic import – "Li??", "Li!!", "Li [sneered]": or a phrase completely transformed in significance through different emphases – "**Listen** to reason??", "Listen to **Reason**??", "**Listen to Reason**!!!!".

Combining these processes we can place the straightforward written meaning of the utterances in a larger space of meaning, and in this way perhaps comment upon the 'rational' interpretation of speech utterance.

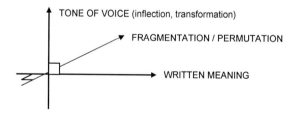

The Environment

The sounds in Red Bird are also organised to suggest various images of the body, and of machinery (and these sound constructions often use the sounds of language). The body has been viewed as the seat of an extra-rational reality of desire, creation and death, but also, with the emergence of modern materialistic rationalism, as (merely) a complex machine. These conflicting notions - the Eco-logical and the Deterministically Rational - resonate in our relationship with the natural world and the world of cities and industry. The sounds of animals and birds (and the fly) in Red Bird may thus represent the natural world, or act as metaphors in a symbolic drama. Symbol–sounds (see below), and their metamorphoses, in Red Bird are thus open to a multi-layered interpretation.

A Contemporary Myth

All these aspects of Red Bird can be regarded as facets of the underlying *myth structure*. The connection with myths is not entirely intellectual. Quoting again from *"Red Bird, a document"*...

> "In listening ... we are cast adrift in an entirely aural world ... sounds may again take on some of the 'magical' power they must have had for pre-literate ... peoples ..... If we permit ourselves, we may re-enter the state of perception in which Myths have their power, where the environment is vibrant with significant sounds.."

Red Bird is a drama of processes and transformations, rather than of fixed objects in a visual space. To articulate the underlying mythic structure it uses *categories* of sounds (rather than specific sounds themselves) with symbolic resonances. The sounds are chosen to be as accessible as possible (in their significance) to the potential audience. (The idea of esoteric reference contradicts the whole notion of myth as a carrier of meanings 'universal' to the group). However, the connections and metamorphoses of these symbol-sounds may be quite involved.

The four symbolic sound-categories used in Red Bird are....

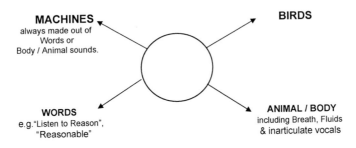

MACHINES
always made out of
Words or
Body / Animal sounds.

BIRDS

WORDS
e.g."Listen to Reason",
"Reasonable"

ANIMAL / BODY
including Breath, Fluids
& inarticulate vocals

In addition a number of subsidiary symbol-sounds are used ….

THE BOOK   the pages of the open book transform into the fluttering of wings. The sound of the slammed book transform into slammed doors.

THE CLOCK   (rational industrial time ?) emerges from the syllable 'Rea' of 'Reason'

THE FLY, THE WELL, THE DOOR etc

Symbol-sounds are open to many simultaneous interpretations e.g.

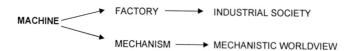

And complex webs of connectedness are established ….

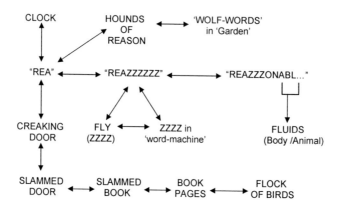

In addition, entire environments (such as the 'Garden' and the 'Universal Factory') act as larger scale sound-symbols.

Musical Form

The detailed structure of Red Bird aims to constantly develop the meaning of the symbol-sounds. This development is set within a larger time-structure which we may divide, for descriptive convenience, into a number of sections. *The section names used are only for descriptive convenience, to help the listener identify them. They are not definitions of what is heard, and were not used in composing the piece.*

There are three major areas, the Opening Area, the Central Area and the Final Area. (see diagram 1 below).

Opening Area

Exposition of various sound-symbols: defining of the situation. The introductory metamorphosis (*Scream → Bird*) encapsulates the nature of the piece. These ideas are briefly developed but we are already in the first section of the exposition, the chief constituents of which are a sequence of Body and Attack-type sounds (*Torture, Breath-as-Wind*) and a sequence of *Transfigured Words*. This section is characterised by a sense of (sometimes terrifying) urgency. It leads, via a transitional area (*Philosopher*) into the second section of the exposition, the *Garden*, which has a totally contrasting musical dynamic.

Central Area

This section is introduced by a tense section with long periods of silence punctuated by loud commands (*Empty*), and then presents various sound-images in a more extended format and with new interactions between the sound-symbols, and concludes with the sound of the Clock (*Death → Clock*).

Final Area

This area begins with a cadenza for birdsong (*Bird Cadenza*) which is abruptly interrupted by a condensed recapitulation of the piece forced into the format of the *Universal Factory*. This section is finally contradicted by the ensuing, contrasting Coda (*Well → Bird*).

I also had to consider the time-structure as both a *symbolic narrative* and as a *piece of music*. In reality, the distinction between these two approaches fell away and I found myself working seamlessly with the materials.

Musical and possible narrative synopses of the opening and ending of Red Bird can be found on subsequent pages. The narrative synopses were not used in *making* the piece, but are a possible reading of the events we hear. (See diagrams 2 and 3).

Diagram 1: Section names (merely for purpose of identifying them when listening) and *some* of the anticipations & recapitulations of materials used.

OPENING AREA	CENTRAL AREA	FINAL AREA
Introduction Whispermix (from *Philosopher*) Doors (*Book & Fly*)	**Empty** Flocking Words (*Poet*)	**Bird Cadenza** Bird behind Breathwind (*Breath as Wind*) Machine-squeak bird (*Empty*) beat-up sequence (*Torture*)
Torture Lis→Birds (*Eros*) Word-Machine (*Universal Factory*) Clipped Door (*Empty*) Book (*Book & Fly*)	**Eros** Lis → Birds (*Torture*)	**Universal Factory** ...numerous, ending with Scream down Well (*Scream down Well*)
Breath as Wind Creaking Door (*Death*) Hounds of Reason (*Prison Courtyard*)	**Book & Fly** Body-Machine (*Eros*) Philosopher,book,whispermix (*Philosopher*) Distant Birds, Animals (*Garden*)	**Well → Bird** (*Coda*) Bird (from Scream→Bird) (*Introduction*)
Transfigured Words Bird (from Scream→Bird in *Introduction*) "LL" texture like water (end of *Poet*)	**Book Pages → Poet** Whispermix (opening of *Garden*)	
Prison Courtyard Hounds of Reason (various) Doors (*Book & Fly*) Interrogator's voice (*Universal Factory*)	**Death → Clock** Multi-screamed 'rea' (*Scream down Well*) Philosopher's voice (*Philosopher*) Breath-Wind, Creaking Door (*Breath as Wind*)	
Scream Down Well Body /Machine (*Eros*) Multi-screamed 'rea' (*Death*) Scream down well (*Well → Bird*)		
Philosopher Book (*Book & Fly*) Whispermix (*Introduction*)		
Garden Fly (*Book & Fly*)		

Diagram 2: OPENING: Musical and possible narrative synopses

MUSICAL SYNOPSIS	INTRO Dramatic Opening motif	EXPOSITION (part 1) Torture / Prisoner	TRANSITION Book of Reason	EXPOSITION (part 2) Garden
	Scream→bird motif Listen-to-reason *(whisper)*	(A) <u>Body-a/Animal + Sharp</u> → Body-b with :- *Lis → birdsong* with anticipations:- *Word-Machine* *Creaking voice door-slam* *(= Philosopher)* *Hounds of Reason* *Bird-behind-breathwind* *(anticipates cadenza)* (B) <u>Words and their transformations</u>.. with anticipations:- *Doors* *Interrogator's voice* *Body-Machine* and recapitulations:- *Opening bird* *Opening scream* *Scream→Bird (new)* *Sharp* group also introduces *Door* and *slammed-book* *Body-a* anticipates **Eros** section *Body-b* links *breath* with *Breath-wind* and **Death** section.	(C) <u>Book</u> pages + slam with :- *Philosopher* recapitulation:- *Whispermix* (from opening, extended)	(D) <u>Bird + Animal + Buzz</u> etc. etc.
MUSICAL DYNAMIC		Rapid Rate Of Events Constant surprise; often sense of enforced progression. Within this scheme, variety sectionwise & instant to instant.		Constant variety of juxtaposed events *without* sense of forced progression; 'Polymorphous diversity'
POSSIBLE NARRATIVE SYNOPSIS	Motif *scream→bird* shorthand for entire piece, and is also final symbol-sound in piece. Victim is being tortured (but some of sharp sounds are books (book of reason), doors (slammed), and word-machine). Seems to find release from tightly ordered violence as body-landscape travels through erotic and animal-like to sounds of breath becoming wind, violently interrupted by assault of words. Words appear now ridiculous, now violent, transforming finally into sound of opening bird, only to be cut off by antithesis, hounds of reason (baying in prison courtyard? heavy doors). Victim, fleeing interrogator's voice, lets out cry (of opening) falls headlong into well of the body, only to find it transforming into machine. Whole preceding section has feel of a prisoner's nightmare. Philosopher now states his case, attempting to suppress whispered voices by slamming book of knowledge. Instead they transform into image of.... The Garden...			

22

Diagram 3: ENDING: Musical and possible narrative synopses

	LINK PASSAGE (from Cadenza)	CONDENSED RECAPITULATION Material from the entire piece re-presented in highly condensed, highly unified format.	CODA With return to opening
MUSICAL SYNOPSIS			
	Telescoped recapitulation of opening Torture sequence.	Material is recapitulated … 1) as elementsof the machine-cycles (as 'machine squeaks') and allowed it to then emerge. 2) superimposed over machines. 3) interrupting the machine cycles. Numerous specific recapitulations of materials, often in a new context or transforming in a different direction.	Long variation of the intro motif, *scream→bird* Linking it with *scream→well* Recapitulation of Opening motif, at end of piece. Suggests cyclic form.
MUSICAL DYNAMIC		Overbearing sense of inevitability and interminability of one mode of organisation. Cannot sustain this merely by repetition. Hence constant interruptions, machine-speed changes, emergence of sounds from transformation of machine squeaks etc. to maintain musical dynamic.	Total contrast: Quiet, slow transformation (i.e. sense of change, release)
POSSIBLE NARRATIVE SYNOPSIS	Joyful display of bird-symbol is shot out of sky and initial torture scene taken up with a vengeance, Victim thrown into *Torture-Chamber* of Reason, victim's world annihilated, *Universal Factory,* triumph of mechanistic world-view as all elements of piece are absorbed into mechanical landscape. Many specific recapitulations e.g. *book* (which transformed to doors) which tried unsuccessfully to swat the *Fly*, now hammers after the victim. Uniting of image of apparent defeat (*Scream→well*) and image of escape (*scream→bird*) in final transformation (*scream down well → bird*) negates interrogator's victory. However, as piece ends with same bird as at opening, suggests entire struggle about to begin again.		

Context and Illusion

The structure of Red Bird depends on the recognition of sounds that are, themselves, often ambiguous[9]. We often need to create a context for the interpretation (or misinterpretation) of the sounds. Thus, by the time we arrive at the *Universal Factory,* the interpretation of the *Word-Machine* and *Body-Machine* as machines is clear and provides a context for us to interpret the fragments of human cries or bird calls as (initially) squeaks of that machinery (first sound in **Sound Example 3**). However, as the *Word-Machine* is merely a construct of spoken words, when we first hear a fragment of it, in the opening *Torture* sequence, we have little time to establish what it is. So here the mechanical illusion is reinforced by a low-level background recording from a metal-working factory, also heard in some later occurrences **(Sound Example 4)**. Similarly, after the *Scream → Well* event, the *Body-Machine* emerges by changing the context of a loop of breath-sounds, gradually adding reverberation (suggesting a large resonant building or factory), introducing the metalworking sounds, and concluding with a metallic hammer-blow.

---

[9] E.g. 'machine' sounds are constructed entirely from vocal, and other natural, sounds.

Such ambiguity is already encountered in the opening *Torture* scene. The prisoner is assailed with heavy 'blows', but careful listening reveals that some of these are the (often edit-curtailed) sounds of books or doors being slammed and other sounds heard in full later in the piece **(Sound Example 5)**.

The *Garden* landscape clearly uses recordings of birds and animals, but in many ways is also an illusion. For example, many of the large birds we hear are imaginary creatures, created by large downward transpositions of recordings of small birds, or upward transposition of animal noises. 'Insects' are 'frogs' may similarly be transpositions of other creatures. Cries are selected in pitch and placed in time so they provide musical continuity without masking one another, and musical transition, the sound types moving gradually from more raucous cries to more 'relaxed' calls and then into the static, cycling sounds of 'crickets' and 'frogs' - the landscape is an impossible and imaginary ecology. The ambience of a 'forest' is created in the studio. Woodland acoustics (unlike savannah acoustics) have the special character that reverberation increases with distance because the further a sound is from the listener, the more trees can provide sound-reflections before it reaches the listener's ear. This link between distance (loudness) and reverberation level is created in the studio. Sounds in the *Garden* were organised into 8 sets and assigned to 8 separate positions; appropriate loudness and reverberation were assigned using the mixer pan control and reverb sends and returns.

SPATIAL LAYERS IN 'GARDEN'

1: CLOSE: LEFT	2: CLOSE: CENTRE	3: CLOSE: RIGHT
4: MIDDLE DISTANCE: HALF-LEFT	5: MIDDLE DISTANCE: HALF RIGHT	
1: DISTANT: LEFT	2: DISTANT: CENTRE	3: DISTANT: RIGHT

Separate 8-layered mixes of animals and of birds were made, and then mixed, together with some pre-panned moving elements **(Sound Example 6)**.

Sound Transformation in the Analogue Studio

My interest in sound-metamorphosis grew out of my musical aesthetic, rather than from any potential latent in the tools available to me. Morphs are of two types:

1) *Sequential morph*: a sound is repeated, with small changes in its spectral characteristics, until it becomes a sound with an apparently different origin[10].

---

[10] How we assign an origin to the sounds we hear is discussed in more detail in *Audible Design*.

2) *Continuous morph*: a sound plays and, as it does so, seamlessly changes into something else, suggesting a different origin.

With the digital representation of sound and the analytical powers of the computer, it became possible to take a systematic and rational approach to sound-morphing, for example using windowed Fourier analysis of two sources and interpolating between the frequencies and amplitudes of their partials. In the analogue studio, however, no such access to the inner details of a sound was possible, and various pragmatic approaches had to be adopted[11].

Source Matching

Most successful digital morphs still rely on the aural matching of the two sounds involved. Sounds with very different characteristics simply cannot be morphed into each other. In the analogue studio, a close matching of the sources is all we have to work with. We cannot achieve a true morph. However, the spectral flexibility of the human voice enables us at least to imitate other sounds with varying degrees of success. Most of the 'morphs' in Red Bird are thus to or from voice sounds.

The most successful continuous morph, the transformation '*Lis*' → *birdsong*, is made in this way (**Sound Example 7**). It begins with a vocal '*Lis*' moving into sss-whistling with rapidly fluctuating pitch, vaguely similar to the rapidly bubbling line of the skylark into which if morphs. With a rapidly changing or complex source, a mix of several similar (but not identical) copies will blur the spectral details. We can then crossfade between such layered versions of our two matched sources and hope to fool the ear into accepting that a true spectral morph has taken place. The skylark source was chosen because it most closely matched the vocal whistling and it was adjusted in (average) pitch to match the vocal sound. The first layered mix is made to gradually emerge out of a single line of the original source, while a single line of the final source emerges out of its own, layered version.

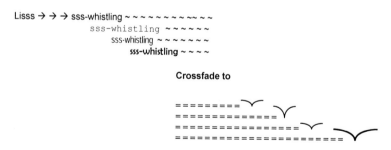

Lisss → → → sss-whistling ~ ~ ~ ~ ~ ~ ~ ~ ~~ ~ ~

         sss-whistling ~ ~ ~ ~ ~ ~

       sss-whistling ~ ~ ~ ~ ~ ~ ~

        sss-whistling ~ ~ ~ ~

Crossfade to

---

[11] In fact, I was far from satisfied with the majority of attempted morphs in Red Bird, but it led me on to explore the newly available world of digital sound processing becoming available at IRCAM in Paris, and subsequently to develop many different kinds of sound transformation software.

The sequence *Book* → *Door* is an example of a sequential morph **(Sound Example 8)**. It moves from the sound of a book being slammed on a surface to the sound of a door being slammed. Here the origins of two sources have themselves to be established as, especially in this unreal context, their origins are not readily apparent. So we first hear the *pages* of the book being turned; then the *Fly* enters and the book tries to swat the fly. As the transformation proceeds, the door landscape[12] is established by the sound of the door-handle preceding the bare slam, and we finally move into a sequence of several different doors. The book and door slams have different pitches. The transition therefore involves gradually lowering the pitch of the book-slam until it is near the door-slam rage; the door-slam begins raised in pitch then moves down into its normal range. As we move down, more and more of the handle-sound is added to the start of the door-slams, to establish the door origin. The two sources, however, also have a different sound quality which we have no way of matching. So the two sets of pitch-changing sounds are interleaved so that there is a confusion of their origin (especially as both are now changed in pitch from the originals), and the sequence of pitch is not direct (i.e. it does not simply go gradually downwards). In this way we are already hearing door-derived slams among the book-slams before the handle-sound focuses our perception on what they really are.

BOOK / DOOR SEQUENCE

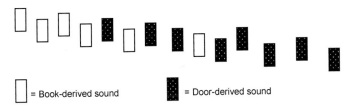

☐ = Book-derived sound   ▓ = Door-derived sound

In some cases, the performers who generated the vocal sources[13] were asked to imitate a particular bird call as best they could, and at a pitch they could reach. The vocal recording could then be gradually raised in pitch and appropriately filtered to approach the original bird sound. Creating a texture that moved gradually from one to the other then achieved a transformation between the two sources. This can be heard in the transition from vocal 'Li' to high bird cries in the following example **(Sound Example 9)**.

Context

In the 'morph' *Clock-alarm* → *Birds* **(Sound Example 10)**, the transformation depends on establishing a context for the initial sound. The preceding ticking of a clock predisposes us to hear the ensuing high frequency, mechanically looped sound as a clock-alarm[14]. However, it is simply a single sound from a birdsong line that has been lowered in pitch, strongly filtered and looped. By subsequently removing the filtering, then raising the pitch, then allowing more of the original bird line to emerge we make a transition from clock to birdsong.

---

[12] For more on the concept of sound landscape, see *On Sonic Art*.
[13] See next chapter.
[14] At the same time the alarm-sound helps contextualise the clock tick.

Similarly, at the end of the *Garden* a strange aggressive voice is heard to attack a *Bird*. The voice here is slowed-down human speech delivered in an aggressive manner. This voice emerges out of wolf-like sounds heard in the background of the Garden-landscape much earlier **(Sound Example 11)**. But these sounds are merely the same slowed human voices using less aggressive (less plosive consonants, more continuous[15]) delivery, and with the high frequencies (which convey much of the information allowing us to comprehend speech) filtered out. In particular the context, a long section of animal, bird and insect sounds, predisposes us not to recognise these first sounds as human voices[16]. By gradually removing the filtering (so the speech-like quality becomes clearer, and changing the character of the speech (more plosive, silence-gapped and aggressive) the voices can emerge from the original sound **(Sound Example 12)**.

The final contest between voice and bird is orchestrated by using small intercut segments of voice and bird, and choosing bird cries which are more strident. The final transition to the *Glasscrash* cuts the two sets of sounds together so rapidly that they transform into something more 'abstract'[17] **(Sound Example 13)**.

On a larger scale, sound-images that are already ambiguous can have their interpretation changed by gradually changing the sounds that surround them. In this example, the *Body-Machine* sound-image (made up of breath and water materials) is at first contextualised as a machine (it emerges from behind the *Word-Machine*). But, after the 'steam-blowoff' (derived from the 'sss' of 'Listen'), the *Word-Machine* is replaced by erotic cries and birdsong and the image is reinterpreted as belonging to the body **(Sound Example 14)**.

Quickness, and mouth action

Occasionally a transition can be made simply by a very rapid crossfade between related materials. In the transformation *Reasonabllll* → *Water* **(Sound Example 15)**, the very end of the vocal source (a rapid articulation of the tongue similar to the 'bl' syllable which initiates it) is somewhat similar to the bubbling water that immediately follows it. The transition is aided by the 'ejective' character of the sound - the word is made to emerge rapidly in a crescendo from a reverberant acoustic to a close acoustic, and the final syllable 'bursts' (a plosive opening of the mouth releasing air), releasing the flow of water. The speed of the transition (especially in the busy context) helps us to accept it.

---

[15] i.e. the 'speech' is not intersected by any tiny silences separating syllables or words.

[16] Though, once it is pointed out, it becomes difficult not to notice their human origin!

[17] The *Glasscrash* itself is a metaphorical illusion. We imagine the shattering of the *Garden* landscape itself rather than merely the breaking of a sheet of glass.

Metaphor

The *Poet* section contains a number of phrases where an initial, clearly heard syllable is then massed into a texture that diverges and spreads in pitch from the original (a *wedge*). The sources themselves were selected for their particular character, and sometimes studio-modified (e.g. by plucking the tape as it passed the heads, introducing random vibrato effects; the voice 'wobbles'). The gradual massing and pitch divergence metaphorically and sonically allude to the swarming of (vocalising) birds, though it does not attempt to imitate massed bird sounds **(Sound Example 16)**.

Association by Juxtaposition

Sometimes no more than connection-by-association can be achieved. In this example, the vocal 'rrr' sounds become more aggressive and bark-like as real dog barks are mixed into the texture **(Sound Example 17)**.

Extended transformations

Some transformations in Red Bird take a long time to develop. *Screamed 'Rea'* → *Clock* begins with a strongly filtered, screamed 'rea' which is quickly developed into a knot of 3 slightly transposed versions of the sound, then to a bigger knot **(Sound Example 18)**. (It is then extended into a much denser extended texture, but this is not on the route to the extended transformation sequence being described).

When the knot recurs at the start of the *Death* section it has been extended in time and pitch-depth. More importantly, it now has an imposed envelope beginning with a sudden attack followed by an initially steep decay. As this new version recurs, the envelope is successively shortened, so that we begin to hear *only* the percussive attack, while reverberation is gradually added which, combined with the spectral characteristics of the sound, produce a metal-hammer-like sound.

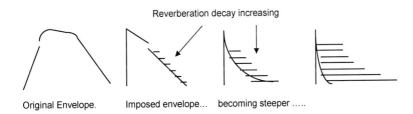

Reverberation decay increasing

Original Envelope.   Imposed envelope...   becoming steeper .....

Later in the sequence, this is mixed synchronously with the sound of a single clock-tick; initially the clock-tick level in the mix is very low, but gradually the tick comes to dominate until the metal-hammer disappears and we are left with just the tick[18]. At the same time the sequence of attacks becomes completely regular, like the ticking of a clock **(Sound Example 19)**.

---

[18] Later, in the digital domain, absolute synchronisation of attacks, and the process of gradual mixing of sources to make a metamorphosis (*Inbetweening*) were developed in the CDP software.

Complex structure: Universal Factory

The *Universal Factory* section, just before the end of the piece, is based around the two machine sound-images *Word-Machine* and *Body-Machine*, each cycling at a different rate. The balance between these two is constantly changing so that one or other of the cycles comes into prominence, and each may change in speed[19]. This tends to happen immediately after an interruption (see below), and also towards the end of the section, where both cycles tend to speed up as the material reaches its culmination. Furthermore, the breathe-like sounds in the *Body-Machine* may be interpreted as faster or slower breathing and therefore, by association, as states of fear, pain, anticipation and so on, so speed-changes in this cycle are organised with this in mind.

The basic machine-cycles are supplemented by "machine-squeaks", materials edited and treated to appear as much as possible like the creaking and squeaking of the machinery. The materials accompanying the *Word-Machine* are derived from animal and bird sounds, mainly from elsewhere in the piece, and those accompanying the *Body-Machine*, the sound of human screams. Each machine cycle contains up to seven such "squeaks" at any time, and the squeaks in any one machine change in level with respect to one another[20].

At certain points these "machine-squeaks" emerge from the machinery, i.e. a shortened fragment of a cry in the machine gets gradually louder on each repetition and finally extends to its full length, revealing its true human origin, then is immediately taken back into the machine-image **(Sound example 3)**. Or the rest of the machinery (apart from the "squeaks") may suddenly stop to reveal the animal contents **(Sound Example 20)**.

The cycling machines are interrupted by other events. These interruptions may be of two types: interruptions to just on of the machine cycles, or interruptions to both.

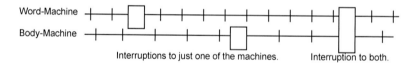

Interruptions to just one of the machines.   Interruption to both.

Interruptions may be complete or partial; in the latter case certain elements of the interrupted machine continue to cycle behind the interrupting material. Complete interruptions to both streams disrupt the flow of the music in a radical way, while any interruption type may cause the speed of the associated machine to change.

Interruptions may or may not be introduced or ended by a loud, staccato sound. These sounds are themselves recapitulations of events heard earlier in the piece. In particular the 'metal-hammer' emerging earlier from screamed 'Rea' (see above) occurs repeatedly, and finally cadences the whole section, rising by a 5th (and falling a 4th to make the octave).

---

[19] …achieved by edit-shortening the tape-loops

[20] In the analogue studio, this involved making synchronous loops of different materials, recording the looping materials, and then mixing them with the looped machine-sounds.

The interruptions themselves may be recapitulations of material from elsewhere in the piece, often transformed, thus changing their metaphoric significance. Thus the whole *Universal Factory* section begins with the *Torture* sequence from the opening of the piece **(Sound Example 5)** recapitulated in a time-contracted form, soon followed by an even more contracted version **(Sound Example 21)**. In the middle of the section a door opens onto the *Garden* landscape (as at the end of the slammed *Book → Door* sequence earlier in the piece) and towards the end we get a tantalisingly brief glimpse of the *Garden* far in the background of the sound landscape **(Sound Example 22)**. The slammed *Book → Door* sequence itself appears, also time-contracted, but in this case pursuing the prisoner, rather than the *Fly* **(Sound Example 23)**.

In the *Poet* section, the syllable 'Lis' introduced a 'flock' of rising bird-like vocal cries. This recurs in the *Universal Factory* but now the vocal cries turn downwards, becoming screechy and resonant and crowded out by the machinery **(Sound Example 24)**. From the bird-cadenza, the descending texture of bird-sounds followed by a rising interval between two 'pure' pitches recurs, but the final pitch is immediately grabbed as a constituent of the *Word-Machine*, while the bird 'multichord', originally falling slightly in pitch into a quiet texture behind the continuing birdsong, now plunges into the bass register as the machine sounds overwhelm it **(Sound Example 25)**. In this way, elements from the entire piece are absorbed to form both a condensed recapitulation and a consistent overall metaphorical landscape for the *Universal Factory*.

.. and finally

Red Bird was made in the analogue tape-music studio at the University of York between 1973 and 1977. The female voice materials were performed by Pippa Pierce and Poppy Holden, the male voice material by Hugh Bernays, Graham Treacher and myself, and the opening vocal sequence (whispering → gunshots) by members of the 'Clap' music-theatre group. Robert Fletcher provided the tame bluebottle for the bluebottle recordings, and Martin Mayes helped with the 'well' recordings. As I had completed my studies and was no longer an official member of the University, I was only able to create the piece through the generosity of the studio director, Richard Orton, who ensured the studio was available to non-University composers whenever it was not needed by students. I worked in the studio between 4am and 10am each day of the week during this 4 years.

The precomposition of

RED BIRD

THE PRECOMPOSITION OF RED BIRD

This chapter is concerned with my approach to composing Red Bird, not with how it might be perceived by the listener. The categories I used to classify sound types, or to describe vocal expressions to the performers, are just that. They don't necessarily relate to anything heard directly in the final piece (many of the resulting sounds, or proposed transformations were not used).

Devising the form

I began by classifying the potential sound-material into 11 broad categories.

Sound Categories

(BIRD)	1. BIRD	(MACHINE)	8. MACHINE
	2. BLACKBIRD	(OTHER)	9. BUZZ
(WORD)	3. WORD		10. BOOK
(BODY / ANIMAL)	4. BODY-a		11. SHARP
	5. BODY-b		
	6. WATER		
	7. ANIMAL		

Birdsong were loosely divided into extended articulate birdsong (*'Blackbird'*)[21] and simple elements of birdsong (notes, glissandi, trills, repeated melodic units) (*'Bird'*). Body sounds were divided between the vocal (screams, sighs) (*'Body-a'*) and the visceral (breath, pulsations, associated fluid sounds) (*'Body-b'*). *Buzz* was the sound of the fly. *Sharp* defined very short, very loud sounds suggesting violence (e.g. akin to gunfire, thumps, etc.) often derived by distorting, or editing-short other sounds. This categorisation, and the following approach to working with it, evolved out of initial unsuccessful attempts to come to grips with the diverse materials.

Next I needed a systematic way to explore the filed of possibilities. The scheme I'll describe is a way of *forcing the imagination*, a way to ensure that a very large number of possibilities are considered (rather than the ones that happen to spring to mind). But (unlike a 12-tone music permutation procedure) it is not a way to define what happens in the piece. It simply *helps* to generate possibilities, with are then assessed using other musical criteria.

Thus, we may consider each of these 11 sound-categories individually, or in combination with any of the others (giving 2047 combinations in all). And there are many ways in which we might imaginatively consider the potential of these combinations. Each may be considered from a purely musical point of view (M), or purely in terms of a sonic landscape[22] (L) or from both points of view simultaneously (ML). (This does not imply that the material is organised in different ways at different times but merely that looking at the materials from different, narrowed perspectives may throw up different possibilities at this stage). And under each of these headings

---

[21] When working with a lots of source material, I adopt relevant ad-hoc names to differentiate the classes of materials, and which I can remember.
[22] The concept of *Sound Landscape* is discussed in more detail in *On Sonic Art*.

we may define further criteria relating to e.g. Duration, Internal Dynamic of the musical activity, Density of Events, presence or absence of Sound Metamorphosis, and so on. A complete set of separable musical parameters might seem logical, but, even if it were hypothetically possible, would produce many millions of possible permutations to be considered. However, with this type of complex material, a complete 'parameterisation' of the sources would be impossible. Instead it's important to find a small, but reasonably productive set of categories that will throw up a large number of diverse possibilities.

Note that each of these permutations does not lead to a definition of a musical event, but only to a different vantage point from which the imagination can seek to *invent* musical possibilities.

The final set of categories used was ….

Organisation-1	Organisation-2	Duration	Internal Dynamic	Density
as Music M	Gestalts preserved e	Long +	Dramatic **X**	Dense ::
	Gestalts elaborated e¤	Medium .	Static O	Sparse .
	Gestalts transformed e→	Short -		
~~	~~~~~~~~~~~~~~			
as Landscape **L**	Reason landscape **R**			
	Reason gestalts **R** predominate **g**			
	Mixed **GR**			
	Garden gestalts **G** predominate **r**			
	Garden landscape **G**			
	Viewed as **W** Real-world landscape			
~~	~~~~~~~~~~~~~~~			
Other **ML**	Landscape transformed **L→** Elements transformed **e →**			
	Landscape preserved **L** Elements transformed **e→**			
	Landscape transformed **L→** Elements preserved **e**			

A typical permutation might read {**Body-a** + **Book** + **Word   M   e   .   X   ::**} and we would attempt to dream-up musical instances satisfying these criteria.

The next task was to devise a form plan for the piece. Initially a set of crude sections was defined in which one or more sound-categories predominated. I then looked at how to anticipate and recapitulate materials from other sections within these preliminary sections so that the formal texture was woven together. Also, each sound-symbol (or symbolic landscape) had to be given a clear statement (where the individual element was not too involved with other elements) as an *exposition* of *that* material. Then ways needed to be found of using similar material evolving (through transformation) in different ways in different areas of the piece (see the diagrams of musical form in the previous chapter).

Collecting and Generating the Sounds

Having developed an idea of the structure of the piece, we have to *find* suitable sound-sources with which to realise this preconceived idea structure. In reality, particularly because sound transformations are so difficult to make in the analogue studio, the final structure had to be provisional (open to revision) while sound ideas were tested (having spent one whole week making the short, transforming sound-event with which Red Bird opens, I almost abandoned the project).

Bird and Animal sounds

Bird and animal sounds for Red Bird were collected from all the wildlife recordings on vinyl[23] that I could find. Most materials collected were bedevilled by other ambient sounds at the recording location and by disk surface noise. Birdsong causes a particular problem as the most prominent noise bands appear in the same frequency range as the signal and so cannot simply be filtered out.

The preliminary approach was to use Dolby-A (often cascaded) as an active filtering device, and to edit out small, unwanted sounds (e.g. surface clicks) where possible. The next important approach was to mask the unwanted sounds. This was done by carefully editing each sound of (say) a birdsong line, replacing the gaps between bird sounds (however short) by leader tape of the same duration. In the retained segments, the ambient background was masked by the bird sound, and the intervening ambient sound was replaced by the silent leader-tape. The resulting song, however, had an unnatural quality, so reverberation was added to restore the continuity of the line.

In addition most of the resulting animal and bird sounds used are transformed in some way. They might be shortened (by editing out constituent events) or extended (by copying constituent events and editing them into the original sequence). The whole line, or some constituents, might be changed in pitch (by altering tape-speed). In particular, whole phrases might be used at double, or half, or even one sixteenth of their original speed (changing the speed in octaves is particularly straightforward on a 2 or 3-speed analogue tape-recorder). This is particularly effective because smaller birds generally have a smaller vocal apparatus, and therefore higher pitched songs. Slowing down a song by a factor of two (down an octave) effectively produces an imaginary bird twice as big.

For the *Fly*, recording a real fly seemed impractical, particularly because any real fly would spend very little time close to the mike, so the signal to noise ratio would be

---

[23] CDs were not invented at the time.

extremely low. What was needed was a buzzing sound that could then metamorphose into the 'zzz' of 'reazzzon'. Superficially this seemed a simple problem - produce a vocal imitation of a buzzing fly, and then use filtering and speed changes to get a more realistic result. Gradually removing those changes should then produce the required metamorphosis *fly → voice*. Unfortunately this failed to work, partly due to the limitations of available filters, but more to the fact that the human ear is attuned to recognising human voices under the most unlikely conditions (just as the eye is attuned to seeing faces) and no amount of filtering or shifting of the original sound could convince my ear that this 'fly' was not *already* a sound of vocal origin. Hence, no convincing transformation from *Fly* to voice was possible.

A different approach was to use a synthesizer, but with the equipment available no convincing fly-imitation could be made. Having run out of ideas, I discovered a biology research student working on bluebottles (large buzzing flies). These flies have touch-sense receptors only on their feet. Thus a rod can be glued to their back, and later removed, without distressing them. In addition, the signal for a bluebottle to fly is that it receives *no* touch signals from any of its feet. Thus by touching the feet and letting go, the bluebottle is triggered to 'fly' – but, being attached to the rod, it remains 'flying' in a fixed location, making the recording task straightforward. Nevertheless, even this ideal recording failed to sound like a real fly. We recognise the sound of a fly partly by the fact that it moves around the space, its sound consequently varying in loudness, quality (and slightly in pitch) as it does so. Hence the 'ideal' recording had to be varied in loudness, spatial position and pitch to produce a convincing fly sound.

Finally, despite all this effort, there proved to be no way to make a convincing morph from the fly to the voice in the analogue studio, and in the piece the change is made by a sleight of hand - in the *Empty* section, a very loud attack triggers the sound to switch from *fly* to vocal 'zzz'.

Vocal materials

The vocal materials were generated through performance and recording. Different approaches were used for different purposes. The most complicated involved asking the performer to imitate as closely as possible a bird (or animal) sound on a recording, and then move their sound (through several repetitions) towards normal verbal or sung articulation. The bird-like sound could then be filtered and speed/pitch shifted to bring it closer to the original bird sound. This proved extremely difficult to achieve in practice, and is used only twice in the piece, the transformation of a female human cry to birdsong (initiated by the syllable 'Li') in the section *Poet*, and a similar transformation into a screams texture heard in the *Universal Factory*.

A second approach involved producing a vocal performance quality with a view to a specific transformation. Thus the *Philosopher* has an extremely creaky voice, especially on the syllable 'Rea' of 'Reason', with a view to it being transformed into a creaking door-hinge later in the piece. The 'Lis' of *Lis → birdsong* (discussed previously) is another example. In another case, the initial transformation *whispered words → screams → gunfire* used a texture performed by several vocalists following a score. The written score involved the transition from words to syllables to clipped-consonants, and from whispering to voiced sounds to screams. The texture was created with a view to adding a studio-produced layer of clipped-voice-sounds moving to over-modulated, clipped voice sounds suggesting gunfire.

The most common approach, however, was to generate large quantities of vocal materials through improvised performance informed by written instructions. As many vocal parameters can (and do) vary continuously[24] over their range continuously through time, there is no systematic procedure for producing 'all' the possibilities. For non-verbal sounds (like screams), the performance text consisted of a short sequence of verbal instructions (e.g. Erotic → Terrified → ....). Screaming tends to be at its most authentic and inventive when uninhibited by complicated musical instructions.

For the verbal material, however, a much greater range of possibilities was explored. First of all the phrase 'Listen to Reason' and the word 'Reasonable' were dissected into constituent words, phonemes, vowels and consonants to produce the list in the *Vocal Sources Score* (see below). Next, with the aid of a rhyming dictionary (which lists all words end in '-ly' or '–ally', usually adverbs, together) a list of 105 qualities (or their combinations) applicable to speech expression was compiled, attempting to cover as wide a range of human expression as possible (see *Vocal Sources Score*). The performer was then asked to perform each phrase, each word, each phoneme etc. in each of these ways.

The recorded materials were then selected for their *perceived* (rather than their intended) qualities e.g. a sound produced 'Laughingly' might appear 'Terrified' when heard as an isolated recording, or take on an entirely different 'feel' when placed in a new context.

Finally, some of the material collected might be further altered by modifications in the studio. This might change the expressive quality of the material significantly e.g. changing 'Reasonable' to *pp crescendo* 'Reasona..' to *sffz* 'ble..' using gradual and then extreme level change, plus different reverberation and filtering on the two parts of the word makes it appear to 'explode' in a comical way.

VOCAL SOURCES SCORE

Speak the following list of words, phrases, phonemes and syllables in the ways indicated in the chart below.

1. **L**	2. **LI**	3. **LIS**	4. **I**
5. **LISTEN**	6. **STEN** as in listen.	7. **EN** as in listen.	8. **T**
9. **TO**	10. **R**	11. **REA**	12. **REA** as in reason.
13. **EA**	14. **REASON**	15. **SON** as in reason.	16. **LISTEN TO REASON**
17. **REASONABLE**	18. **NABLE** as in reasonable.	19. **BL** as in reasonable.	

a) Each to be treated as a separate entity. Do not string together in a sentence-like delivery.
b) If you cannot speak the item in the manner suggested, say it as best you can.
c) Types in brackets apply only to full words.
d) 'Long' variants do not apply to 'L' and 'Listen To Reason'.
e) CONSIDER THE EXPRESSION OF EACH SYLLABLE ON ITS OWN MERITS.
f) You may speak each syllable in all suggested manners, or every syllable in each manner, whichever order is easiest for you.

---

[24] i.e. not by step, but by gliding to anywhere within the range.

EXPRESSION	long	extra long		EXPRESSION	long	extra long		EXPRESSION	long	extra long
Flippant	X			Dsetermined	X			Squeaky	X	
Poignant	X			Fervent, Fanatical	X			Question (....?)	X	
Passionately	X			Triumphant	X			Answer (Yes) (....)	X	
Lovingly	X			Wicked, Demoniacal	X			2nd Question (....??!!)	X	
Drunkenly, Stupidly	X	X		Aggressive	X			2nd Answer (....!!)	X	
Sneeeringly imitating	X			Menacing	X			3rd Question (....???!!!)	X	
Annunciated	X	X		With Foreboding	X	X	X	3rd Answer (....!!!!!)	X	
Stressing the meaning	X			Insidiously	X			(Rhythmically)	X	
Incredulous	X			Frantically	X			(Rhythmically, different)	X	
Laughingly	X	X		Histrionic	X			(Rigid, Starchily)	X	
Weepily	X	X		Screechy	X	X		(Tersely)	X	
Resignedly	X			Sincere	X			(Jabber)	X	
Indignant	X			Sacred	X			(Very Rapid)	X	
Enraged	X	X		Concerned	X			(Woodenly, Whispered)	X	
Jolly, Bouncy	X			Beseeching	X			(Fitfully, Awkwardly)	X	
Delighted	X			Coaxing	X			(Encouraging, Friendly)	X	
Feebly, (Shakily)	X	X		Seductive, Enticing	X	X		(Authoritatively)	X	
Ponderous, Learned	X			Lewdly	X			THE FOLLOWING WHISPERED			
With Loathing	X	X		Cutely	X			Stupidly	X	
As if rejecting words from mouth like bad food	X	X		Coyly	X			Feebly (Shakily)	X	
Sceptically	X			Gruffly, Roughly	X			Ponderously	X	
Cynically	X			Grudgingly	X			As if announcing title of a play	X	
As if announcing the title of a play	X			Snappily	X			As if reading from a list of items	X	
As if reading from a list of items	X			Coldly	X			Nimbly, Delicately	X	
As if you might change your mind	X			Expansively	X			Sleepily	X	
Nimbly, Delicately	X			Giddily	X	X	X	Terrified	X	
Sleepily	X	X		Breathlessly	X			Histrionic	X	
Anxious	X			Hoarsely	X	X		Enraptured, Ecstatic	X	X	X
Terrified	X			Childishly	X	X		Menacing	X	X
Cheeky, Impertinent	X			Flowing	X			Aggressive	X	
Supercilious, Conceited	X			Florid, Extravagant	X			Seductive, Enticing	X	X
Fiery	X			Liquid	X			Snappily	X	
As if to contradict someone	X			Wailing	X	X	X	(Rhythmically)	X	
Enraptured, Ecstatic	X	X	X	Raucous	X			(Tersely)	X	
Amazed, Astounded	X			Explosive	X			(Jabber)	X	
								(Fitfully)	X	

Organising the Sound Materials

In order to access this bank of sounds, we must have some means of knowing, at least approximately, what each sound is like and where it is. Initially there were over 500 sources. As work proceeded and specific sources were transformed, combined or built into textures (and these textures themselves transformed, combined or built into further textures) the number of stored source sounds soon exceeded 2000.

The sounds themselves were stored on numbered tape-reels and, as all pieces of tape look the same, numbered on the leader-tape preceding each item, and named in an associated (paper) listing, also including details of tape-speed, channel-count and Dolby noise-reduction[25], with comments on the origin or potential use of the sound[26]. Sounds used within, or used to generate, other sounds for specific sections were stored and listed under the relevant sections, and given names related to their source, nature or use e.g.

Sources for multiple "Li⤸ "; prefiltering	Post-insectend sources
Frogs in drain	Machine-squeak bird 2
Multiple glasscrash	"T, T, T, T...." of Word-Machine
Ecstatic → wobblemix	Moan + pseudo-bark → semi-words
Laughing "Lis" x 4	Loving "Li" knot
Scream-loop 7	Bird-multichord, normal speed→ half speed
Tape-1 for following whispering mix	Starlingesque

The original source-material, having not yet been put through some process, could not be catalogued in this way so some other systematic way of storing and accessing them had to be used. For example, the bird sounds were assigned to 15 different categories.

1. SINGLE NOTES.
2. RAPID REPEATED NOTES.
3. RAPID REPEATED GROUPS OF NOTES.
4. SHORT MELODIC PHRASES.
5. SMALL 'UNPITCHED' MELODIC UNITS.
6. CHORDS, SLIDING CHORDS & 'KWARK' & CHORDAL 'YAP' TYPES.
7. 'YAP' NOTES, BARKING NOTES & GRATING SOUNDS.
8. REPEATED 'CHORTLE-NOTES', 'BUBBLING-GLISSANDI' & 'BUBLING-NOTES'.
9. SMALL UNITS BASED ON (AUDIBLE) SLIDING NOTES AND 'YAPS'.
10. SOUNDS WITH HIGH NOISE-TYPECONSTITUENTS.
11. ARTICULATE MELODIC BIRDSONG (with each song written out)
12. STRONGLY CHARACTERED, 'UNPITCHED' MELODIC PHRASES.
13. LONG CONTINUOUS ARTICULATE SONG.
...... and (eventually not used)......
14. TEXTURES OF SEVERAL BIRDS.
15. MASSED BIRDS.

---

[25] In contrast, computer storage of digital sound now forces sounds to be named and automatically links the name with the sound, through the soundfile name. In addition, properties of the soundfile, like the number of channels, are automatically stored in the file's header. Directory structures enable sounds to be grouped in a hierarchical fashion and thus easily retrieved (if stored rationally). However the habit of systematic and informative naming developed in the analogue studio proved a useful apprenticeship for the digital studio, as it is much easier to produce very large numbers of sounds while making a piece on a computer.

[26] As sources might be used at the original pitch, or transposed dramatically (over 1 or more octaves) where they had a completely different character, this change-of-character info was useful to have in the notes.

Each category was stored on a different reel of tape. Within each category there were some subdivisions, and materials were ordered in descending order of pitch, so that sounds with particular features could be found more quickly[27].

Postscript : Problems of texture generation in the analog studio

Red Bird uses multi-layered sequences of sound (*Universal Factory*) and sound textures (e.g. in the *Poet* section). In the digital studio these things are relatively easy to achieve for three reasons...

- Digital clocks are extremely accurate. Tracks laid against one another will reliably remain synchronised.
- Digital silence is silence; there is very little problem of unwanted noise.
- The sequencing of events can be automated (including the randomisation of time) or played directly from a sampling keyboard.
- Individual soundfiles have individual names.

Red Bird was made in a stereo analogue studio, and I was faced with four problems

- Analogue tape-recorders do not run absolutely in sync.
- All tape-recordings carry some analogue noise which accumulates as sounds are copied or layered on top of one another.
- The placement of sounds in time is determined by the physical position of items on a tape and these have to be cut together by hand.
- All pieces of recording tape look identical.

The problem of noise build-up was of particular concern because Red Bird involved transforming, then mixing (layering) sounds, then possibly re-transforming, remixing and so on. At each stage, more analogue noise is introduced, so every effort had to be made to keep the noise-level as low as possible.

Making a precise rhythmic sequence by mixing the separate layers from analogue tape-recorders meant making it in short sections, as the machines would not stay accurately in sync with one another over longer periods of time. In making the *Universal* Factory section, the *Body*-Machine and the *Word-Machine* streams were constructed separately, as each had edited interruptions independently of the other. Each stream had to be made in short segments as new layers (e.g. the 'machine squeaks') had to added *in time* with the basic materials, before the analogue machines got out of sync. The subdivisions were made at places where edits would not be heard when the sequence was eventually joined together i.e. at prominent attacks that would disguise any discontinuity in the cut sounds[28].

---

[27] Finding sounds on a tape-reel involved physically placing the correct reel on the tape-recorder and then winding through the tape from the beginning to the place you wanted. Having the sounds in pitch order made searching *by listening* much easier.

[28] Even with a multi-track machine, to get each layer to be rhythmically in sync with the already recorded tracks would have involved splicing the source tape, to place the sounds in the correct place, then refining the splicing.

Making textures of sounds was even more difficult. A texture might consist of many copies of the original sources, each randomly transposed to a new pitch within a specified range, each played at a different loudness level within a range of levels, then each of these copies placed in time with a certain time-density and a certain randomness of attack times, and these events distributed at random over the stereo space.

In the digital studio, each of these processes can be automated. To make such a texture in the analogue studio one began by making all the necessary transpositions of the original sound by varispeeding the original tape-recording, recording the result to a second tape. Every individual event had to be made in this way, even where some of these new events were identical, because each event was a separate piece of analogue tape. And to maintain good signal to noise ratios, all events were recorded at full level in mono.

These events then had to be edited out from extracted from the tape (removing any 'silence' from the start or end of the re-recordings), then positioned in time, by splicing them together, usually separated by short pieces of (plastic) leader-tape. Using leader-tape (rather than magnetic tape with no sound recorded on it) was not only essential to keep down analogue noise levels but also to enable one to know exactly where the sounds were (and in some cases, to individually identify them, by writing on the leader tape) - all recording tape looks identical. Where sounds needed to be time-adjusted the leader-tapes between the sounds could be cut shorter, or extended with extra bits of leader tape.

To generate a texture of sounds at different level, the sounds intended to be loudest were spliced together on one tape, those intended to be slightly less loud on another, and so on. In mixing the sounds, the sequences intended to be quieter were then turned down at the mixing desk; this reduces both signal and noise equivalently, reducing the analogue noise problem for the quiet sounds. Similar considerations applied to distributing sounds in space.

To make very dense textures, the process had to be repeated, superimposing layer upon layer, often with changes to the material (in the less dense layers, slight retiming of the events; in the denser layers, slight or evolving changes of pitch) either to avoid obvious echo-effects, or to achieve the pitch-wedges (the pitch-range expands gradually outwards from the original pitch) characteristic of the *Poet* section.

ANTICREDOS

ANTICREDOS

Anticredos is a piece for 6 amplified voices, using extended vocal techniques. It was written at a time when access to computer-music tools was severely limited (4 centres in the world had computer-facilities dedicated to music production, and only one of these, IRCAM, was in Europe). I submitted the idea for *Vox 5* as a project to IRCAM in 1979 but, with the project's future still uncertain, continued work on sound-transformation using the voice. Before the advent of powerful computer tools, the voice seemed the best medium for exploring the ideas of sound-transformation developed in the analogue studio with *Red Bird*. The human voice was the most malleable of musical "instruments", capable of generating a huge variety of spectra and of moving rapidly between these (as happens all the time in speech).

Origins of the Project

My interest in the voice was partly triggered by my work in the studio. With the technical limitations of the time, the flexibility of vocal sound-production was crucial in achieving whatever sound-morphs I could manage in the analogue studio. Contemporaneously Stockhausen's *Stimmung* was composed and the first recordings of Tuvan harmonic singing became available. I discovered I could perform these sounds myself, and began to explore the other sounds of my voice, keeping a systematic catalogue. Some time later, Warren Burt, then a member of one of the Californian extended vocal techniques groups, visited York and we exchanged information about what could be done with the voice. I continued with this exploration, bit I bit, while working on other projects, and by the time *Red Bird* was completed became more systematic. For example, if an articulation like vowel change could be applied to a voiced vocal sound, could it also be applied to an unvoiced rolled-rr sound; in what ways could different sounds (voiced, lip iteratives, tongue iteratives, noise bands) be combined; how could the air-stream generating the sounds be manually articulated. Eventually, by 1980, I had a semi-systematic map of the possibilities of human vocal production (described in *On Sonic Art* and since updated).

The idea behind Anticredos

Anticredos was a move from treating sound-morphs as transitions between recognisable sounds with metaphorical import (*Red Bird*) to the use of sound transformation as a general principle of organisation (*Tongues of Fire*). It began its life as a series of experiments in pure sonic transformation. However, to make a piece, a more defined structure was needed. Eventually I decided to take the word "Credos" as a starting point and to gradually deconstruct it through processes of sonic transformation. Apart from its meaning (and the meaning of deconstructing it), and the long history of its use in the musical tradition, the word itself employs many different sound-archetypes used in speech, the pluralising "s" being added to provide the noise-band archetype. Thus

- "K" : a noise transient. Extended in the pronunciation used in the piece to
- "X+": the arched-tongue noise consonant at the end of Scottish "loch"
- "R": an unvoiced iterative, and a non-laryngeal pitched sound.

- "E": a voiced pitched sound.
- "D": a (voiced) plosive.
- "S": a noise band.

Each of these sound elements can be used as the basis for elaboration and as the origin of an evolving sound-transformation stream.

Part of the task in composing *Anticredos* was to define potential transformations between vocal sound types. These fell into two classes.

- Continuous transformations, where a sustained sound begins with certain characteristics and ends with different characteristics. The sound itself could be generated by a single voice or by a group of voices (and the amplified sound-stream melded together by e.g. mixing to mono and then moving the stream around the performance space). In this example, voiced rolled "rrr" descends in pitch and morphs into lip–iteratives **(Sound Example 26)**.

- Textures of discrete sounds in which the constituents gradually change in quality, or where the balance of constituents of different quality gradually changes. In this example, within three sound-blocks separated by percussion attacks, the voices make transitions from one type of vocal "percussive" to another **(Sound Example 27)**. This type of transformation, already used in *Red Bird*, could be much more flexibly and powerfully controlled with computer texture-generation and the high density of events possible in the pure electro-acoustic domain.

The Form of the piece

The piece consists of 4 sections and a coda. The first 3 sections begin with the word (or the start of the word) "Credos" and then proceed to develop and evolve its sound constituents in different ways, often using continuous transformations, generating a whole gamut of possible vocal sounds. This leads to a section of seamless sound transformation and a coda in which the word "Credos" is recapitulated, but in a radically altered form.

The piece begins with a clear statement of the word "Credos", first voiced, then unvoiced, but even at the outset the sound begins to transform. The final "o" is sung with a slight detuning between the two voices **(Sound Example 28)**, and the "o" and "s" of the unvoiced rendition morph into one another **(Sound Example 29)**. In the next statement of "Credos" the entire (voiced) word becomes a continuously evolving, unsegmented stream **(Sound Example 30)**. At the end of section 1, the The opening "K" of "Credos" is smeared out to an extended X+ sound, the tessitura of the repetitions rising in one voice and falling in another, until they plosively reintroduce the "Credos" theme, now with "do" as a plosive textured element **(Sound Example 31)**.

Section 3 begins with an ululated version of the "E" of "KRE" (some vowel-renditions in the performance have unintentionally slipped from "e" to "ee") and in this stereo reduction of the live performance we can get some sense of the rapid rotation of this ululated material around the auditorium **(Sound Example 32)**. Spatialisation is used throughout the piece to define independent streams of sound material to which one or more voices may contribute. The spatial movement allows the vocal origin of the sounds and the perceived sound-streams to be separated from one another. In fact, performers are occasionally switched from one stream to another, to maintain continuity of the streams - for the performer this means an abrupt change to different material but for the listener the melded streams should remain coherent. And, of course, the performers remain in fixed positions on the stage whilst the sound-streams are free to moving (in sound-surround) as they please.

The separation of the theatre of the performers from the spatial theatre of the sound output raises interesting problems about staging this piece. Perhaps the most successful solution to date was the production devised by Lore Lichtenberg (CHECK) for students at the University of Durham in 2007. Here the performers vocalised behind a semi-transparent screen, backlit so that their moving shadows were visible to the audience. At the same time small video cameras, focused on the performers' mouths, sent their images to a set of video monitors around the auditorium. In this way the live-ness of the performance (and the efforts of the performers) could be conveyed to the audience, while allowing the evolving sound-streams to animate the space independently.

In the original performances, the sounds from the microphones were fed to two quadrapan joysticks. This required 3 performers at the mixing desk, one switching mike outputs into the appropriate quadrapan stream at the appropriate times, the other two operating the quadrapans according to the spatislisation instructions in the score. For *Vox 1*[29] this type of spatial control was computer controlled through a specially designed box built by David Malham of the York University Music Department, using ambisonic technology. Nowadays, many computer mixing environments permit this type of signal routing and spatial movement.

The third section of the piece arrives at a window of animal-like calls, the "garden" segment in the score, and reminiscent of the similar garden moment in "Red Bird". Following this, many types of vocal materials generated previously are juxtaposed in contrasting blocks until the energy of the section dissipates in a section of bird-like whistling.

This leads to the 4th section, where the various sounds morph into one another in a semi-continuous stream lasting for more than two minutes in which the segmented quality of language (and any sense of a fixed referent, or "Credo") has completely dissolved away **(Sound Example 33)**.

The end of section 4 segues into the coda, where a radically transformed version of the "credos" theme is presented , each element (K as X+ noise band, iterative (from "R"), pitch band (from "E") and plosive to noise (from "DOS") being completely recast **(Sound Example 34)**.

---

[29] See separate chapter.

Notation for Anticredos

Another major task in *Anticredos* was to devise a notation scheme that allowed sound itself, and sound transformation, to be written out in detail for the performers. The central idea in the scheme, the separation of the object notation – the notation of the sounds themselves - from the process notation – the notation of the processes of sound transformation, was first developed for the music-theatre piece *Tuba Mirum* commissioned by Melvyn Poore[30] in the late 70s. Part of the approach in this piece was to link the voice of the player with the voice of the instrument, both metaphorically – in the theatre scenario the player is a silenced political prisoner in (perhaps) a psychiatric hospital, and his instrument becomes his voice – and sonically – it is possible to use the Tuba as an acoustic amplifier for the voice, to play the instrument in the normal way and to do some of both at the same time. For example, at one point in the piece, normal high notes on the Tuba give way to laughter through the Tuba.

There are also visual transformations played out in the performance of *Tuba Mirum* – the Tuba's (absurdly large) mute, itself a visual metaphor for repression, becomes first a rattling affair (containing a hidden tambourine), then a black hood with red pom-poms disguising a device which explodes with smoke from the Tuba's bell, and finally a cornucopia of fruit itself hiding a loudspeaker enabling the Tuba to play in counterpoint with itself. The score for *Tuba Mirum* is large and elaborate, but for the actual performance a condensed version was provided (which would fit on the instrument's lyre) and this is reproduced below.

In *Anticredos* this transformation notation is elaborately developed, allowing both individual sounds to morph (e.g. the vowel shape of a sibilant)

e 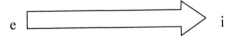 i

or the constituents of a texture to change...

s,ʃ,x,x+,{x+},|ʰₛ| {x+},{ts}

---

[30] With funds provided by the Arts Council of Great Britain.

The sound for each voice is notated in three layers.

- Upper layer: timing/rhythm plus any manual articulations of the sound such as cupped-hand filter-tremolo.

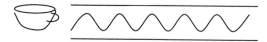

- Lower layer: contains the transformation arrow notation, and a specification of the sound constitutents in an expansion of the international phonetic alphabet with special modifiers (e.g. bold type for voiced, "!" for plosive attack, and so on).

- Middle layer: a graphic display of the sound as bands or discrete events, which rise and fall with pitch or tessitura required.

The middle layer divides sound production into

- Voiced pitches, indicated by a black band.

- Unvoiced sounds (noise), indicated by a white band with cross-hatching. The hatching changes as the noise-constituent transforms, and the details of the noise-type (e.g. s,f,h, or combinations and extensions of these types) are given in the lower layer.

- Complex sounds – a diverse collection of other sounds, such as ingressive multiphonics etc – indicated by a band with a chequerboard patter. This pattern also changes as the sound changes.

- Tongued iterates (various types of rolled-rr) are indicated by a wavy sinusoidal line.

- Lip iterates (flabbered lips) are indicated by a square-wave type line.

- Discrete sounds, like "p!" or "ts!" are indicated by hollow dots etc.

These various types can be combined, for example to indicate voiced rolled-rr.

TUBA MIRUM mnemonic score

Trevor Wishart

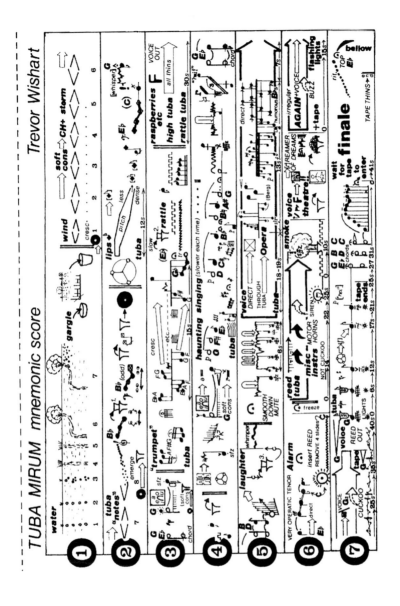

48

THE VOX CYCLE

THE VOX CYCLE[31]

In *Anticredos*[32] I attempted to write a piece of pure sonic transformation using the human voice as it is the most flexible of (non-electronic) sound-producers that we possess. Apart from the deconstruction of the word "Credos", its focus was almost entirely on the processes of sonic transformation themselves. Having completed the piece, however, I wanted to explore the many different aspects of human vocal production and, in a sense, through that to explore different aspects of our human 'being'. The *Vox Cycle* is thus a series of contrasting pieces concerned with different aspects of human experience, different music-structural ideas, different performance-techniques and different notation schemes, and most involve an accompanying sound-environment on tape[33]. The purely electro-acoustic *Vox 5* is described in the next chapter.

Poetics and Technics

Generally speaking I see no separation between the 'poetic' and the technical aspects of a piece of music[34] - musical forms themselves have idea-content. The motivation for *Vox* was both technical – to explore a wide range of human vocal techniques – and poetic – to explore the diversity of human experience. I'm concerned with myth, not in its everyday sense implying fabrication and falsehood, but in the sense of orientations or perspectives which underlie and inform our understanding of and conduct in the real world. 'Freedom' is a good example of a contemporary myth, an inspirational and liberating notion which, on close examination, is hard to define or pin down. Yet it is one of the most significant and normative ideas in our culture. This is what I mean by a myth. However, as I'm talking to composers, I'll focus here on the technical aspects of the composition of the *Vox Cycle*.

In music the formal ideas which really excite me are counterpoint (in its widest sense[35]), transformation and development (again in their widest sense[36]). I'm particularly concerned with formal clarity, particularly what can and can't be perceived in the musical experience (psycho-acoustics as opposed to dogma). Musical form has to be something that works *within musical experience* and not merely because it has all been explained to you in a lecture!

---

[31] This is a reconstituted and annotated version of a presentation at the University of York, UK, in November 1988.

[32] *Anticredos* (1980) for 6 amplified voices and minimal percussion, commissioned by *Singcircle* with funding from the Arts Council of Great Britain.

[33] The sound-environments for most of the *VOX Cycle* were made in the analogue studio, mainly at the4 University of York. *VOX 5* was made at IRCAM, Trevor Wishart's first piece of computer music. *VOX 6* used MIDI controlled black-box synthesizer modules to create the "instrumental" backing tracks.

[34] I no longer adhere entirely to this radical view and usually now (2011) describe the poetics and the technical aspects of my work separately. The poetic provides an over-arching motivation for the formal processes I will use, but the relationship between the two can be complicated.

[35] I later use the term counter-streaming, where different streams of sound interact with one another, as in the penultimate section of *Anticredos*.

[36] I characterise the panoply of sound-transformation techniques developed on the computer in the following decades as extensions of traditional notions of transformation and development into the domain of sound itself.

Internal and External Form

Here I'd like to make a distinction between internal and external musical form. External form is what we have dealt with in composing traditional instrumental music. Given sonic events are arranged in hierarchies, permutations, sequences and so on. And these formal approaches can be expressed and viewed in a musical text. Musical form-building is explicit and gains lots of brownie-points for the composer from the community of commentators and analysts. Internal form, in this context, is the internal structure of instrumental timbres to which, in the past, we had no access, or their articulation in performance-practice. Internal form is the acoustic structure of an event which enables us to recognise it for what it is.

Electro-acoustic composition can deal with this internal structure either through synthesis or (as in *Vox 5*) through analysis-resynthesis. And we can extend this notion to more complex sonic formations, anything from the timbre of a particular instrument or found sound to the internal structure of the sound of a crowd or a flock of birds. (In fact we can even extend the notion of internal form to entire musical structures if we deal with them as recognisable wholes e.g. in sound montage technique). But internal form-building is implicit. We hear the result, but do not see (in a score) the mechanics of how this is achieved. Success may in fact depend on inaudibility, the elegance of the transformation entirely disguising the mechanics of achieving it. But there are currently no brownie points for this kind of compositional finesse.

One other important distinction is that external form is usually discrete - discrete entities are explicitly organised – and notatability is dependent on this discreteness of the atoms of composition. But many aspects of internal form are seamless, or continuously flowing.

The Human Voice

The human voice lies somewhere between traditional instrumental sources and the electro-acoustic medium because it is such a rich and flexible sound-producer. It is capable not only of producing pitches to order, but can control the formants (vowel-production) of those pitches, modifying the sonority in a time-changing manner, and can also generate (formant-variable) noise sources, vocal grit and complex unstable streams of sound (via e.g. ingressive multiphonics), and morph seamlessly amongst many of these sound-types. Through my work on Extended Vocal Techniques I've developed a detailed notation for the sonic constituents of vocal sounds and means of notating seamless transformations between one state and another[37].

Furthermore, the voice is intrinsically multimedia. More than just a musical instrument, it can convey the age, sex and health-image of the utterer, the personality (or the pretended personality of the actor), the intent (friendly, malicious) and state of mind (angry, frightened), the basic emotions which we share with our primate cousins (laughter, screaming), or the meaning of a text and the speaker's attitude to that

---

[37] See the score if *Anticredos*.

meaning[38]. And all of these can be traced back to the acoustic properties of the vocal stream, whose mysteries we unravel through the complex hierarchy of perception.

We can't possibly deal with all of these perspectives in a piece - musical form-building demands focus. We articulate certain aspects of the sonic stream while ignoring, or holding relatively constant, others. To move all of them at once would destroy any clarity in the musical discourse[39]. *Vox* therefore adopts different techniques and different perceptual perspectives in its different movements.

The Text

Text is used in different ways in the different pieces of the *Vox cycle*. As a composer concerned primarily with pure musical organisation I have some difficulties with text and it's meaning, which can get in the way of the musical ordering of events (!).[40] Hence most of the text used in *Vox* is in invented imaginary language, designed to support the musical logic of the pieces. Nevertheless, the sounds of the worlds' languages have been an important source for my research into new vocal techniques.

Vox 1 begins with a single seamless sonic stream, mixed in mono, so that the individual performers cannot be distinguished, and this stream gradually segments into 2 streams then to 4, each stream now carrying a single performer's voice. As the piece proceeds the initially pause-free streams of utterance are articulated and segmented, eventually evolving into a kind of magical incantation in a language using imaginary vowels and consonants. (This is not a simple linear process of development).

The text of *Vox 2* is partly based on the sounds of the Japanese language (the flat vowels) and the exaggerated articulation used in Bunraku puppet theatre. But it is musically developed through the extension and inner articulation of sustained sibilants, rolled "rr" sounds and other sonic constituents of language, becoming more like the pure sonic substance of *Anticredos*.

In *Vox 3* there is a mediation between the instrument-like use of the voice, as in scat-singing, and a language-like approach in the spoken sections, where the dialogue is strictly meaningless, but the intentions of the speakers are indicated in the score so that meaning can be conveyed through tone-of-voice cues. As the speed of the rhythmic variations increases, it becomes impossible to use any articulations apart from the "tktk" and "dgdg" inflections of double and triple-tonguing, and hence, the language of the rhythmic games focuses increasingly onto these archetypes.

Vox 4 proceeds more like a piece of abstracted theatre interaction, in the manner of Ligeti's *Aventures*. The imaginary text comes in three varieties, polite, normal and expletive, characterised by changing the consonantal content of the texts from a focus

---

[38] And the text brings with it a potential baggage of history, poetry, dramatic convention or social context

[39] Typically, instrumental music keeps the total number of "voices" constant within musical sections, and layers musical ideas within timbre (and range) streams in which conventional, if elaborate, sets of articulations are applied by the performers. But these are no longer necessary, or even desirable, restraints in electro-acoustic music.

[40] See article in *Contemporary Music Review*.

on liquids and soft consonants (m,n) through a standard set of consonants, to the use of hard-edged consonants and consonant clusters (skr, sp). The text itself was generated by vocally improvising possible material, writing this out, deciding on which elements had which grammatical function (noun, verb, adjective, etc), then using a computer program to generate reams of similar utterances with different specified grammatical structures. Finally, the best of these were chosen as material. The computer was used here as a heuristic tool to extend the scope of my initial intuitions. This control of the syllabic content of the "text" enables me to organise the sound of a thick texture of speaking voices without the restraint of literal meanings. But sonic objects are constructed to appear like words and sentences, so you imagine real issues and concepts are being discussed in a language you don't understand.

The text materials are offered as lists of (specific) alternatives from which the performers chose the materials they will assign to each of their performance blocks in the piece.

Vox 6, which appears to have the most conventional use of word-setting, was in fact composed entirely as music before any text was written – so this is music-setting, rather than text-setting. The text was then constrained by tight rhyme schemes and rhythmic patterns, as well as the idea of the dance as a universal metaphor for human activity.

The tape part

The tape parts in *Vox* aim to cross-fertilise the notion of an orchestral accompaniment and an environmental context for the human utterances. The sonic landscapes of *Vox 1* (sounds suggested in creation myths from around the world – thunder, the parting of waters, the cracking of a giant egg, the rending of veils etc.) and *Vox 2* (sounds deriving from the natural world – wolves, whales, birds, insects, etc.) may appear naturalistic but are in fact highly contrived. In one sense they are shaped like an instrumental accompaniment would be, rhythmically, gesturally and harmonically interacting with the vocal parts at crucial junctures. In another sense they aim to provide a magical transformation of the performance space, the performers now placed in a mythic landscape somewhere beyond the concert hall. Similarly in *Vox 4* the developing 'dispute' amongst the performers tumbles out into the wider world as the intimidating voices on the tape gather into a sound-surround mob.

The use of computers

The composition of the *Vox cycle* spans the period when computers first became accessible for music composition. *Vox 5* was the first piece of computer sound-transformation I was able to make, developing the first sound-morphing programs based on Phase Vocoder analysis data. But computers were also used in simpler ways in some of the other pieces. The complex polyrhythms of *Vox 3* are made possible by the computer-synchronised but independent sync tracks fed to the four live performers. These were generated in Music 5 on a mini-computer (a very expensive 'miniaturised' version of the contemporary room-filling mainframes at IRCAM) at the University of York. The large-volume of text available for *Vox 4* was generated with computer assistance (see above). The backing tracks for *Vox 6* were created using MIDI controlled synthesis modules available at the time.

Notation

In *Anticredos* I had attempted to develop a universal sonic notation, and this is partly used in *Vox 2* with the addition of more detailed pitch-notation. However, the *VOX* project as a whole forced me to rethink my relationship to notation and the nature of musical form. Approaching the voice as an unlimited multimedia source, notation of all sonic details in all circumstances becomes unwieldy and impracticable. Instead, it became necessary to adopt, for each work, a *notational strategy* that reflected the focus of concerns in the piece. If one wants to focus on rhythm/pitch, as in *VOX 3*, standard staff notation is very efficient and efficacious, and one can use text as a shorthand for the sonic information. In *VOX 4*, an interaction of human personalities in theatrical scenarios, we're interested in those changes in a person's sonic vocabulary which indicate changes of attitude, psychological state and so on. This was best represented by characterisation/attitude notes written into the score alongside the blocks of (alternative) text materials, chosen for their sonic substance (see above). But we can also use the transformation notation developed for *Anticredos* to indicate gradual changes in the sonority, or the attitude of the characters on stage.

Musical Form

Vox 1

The poetic of *VOX 1* is the mergence of order from chaos. I wanted to trace the emergence of a segmented formal structure (in this case a kind of magical language) from an ever-changing continuum of sound. The piece was the most difficult to write and involved a lot of theorising about musical structure. It uses two approaches, sound transformation and gestural counterpoint.

The transformation proceeds from the seamlessly evolving mono stream of sound at the opening in which all four voices and the tape environment are as one, and differentiates into 2 bands – one high frequency, the other low – which then separate spatially (the sound pans from front mono to rear stereo, initially) before splitting, spatially and sonically, into 4 independent streams. Writing this section involved having a map of the sonic space of the voice, to understand how to move from one sound-type to another seamlessly. Each stream is gradually segmented (different types of material are juxtaposed) and then articulated by silent pauses, and by this stage we are becoming aware of four distinct personages, the 4 individual performers (an approach suggested by the physical division of the embryo as it develops).

The moment to moment organisation of the complex-sound groups in each stream is governed by ideas about gestural counterpoint[41] - notions of "To", "From", "Stable" and "Unstable" gestures – and the density of events. The complex materials in the sound-groups are gradually simplified, and slowed down, until they become text-like, and finally a unison textual incantation emerges, tuning to a major 9th (plus octaves) above the pedal pitch produced by filtering the final thunderclaps.[42] The progression towards the "text" is not a simple linear progression. The process of emergence back-tracks into the lip-flabber/sea section, and is then reinvigorated.

---

[41] Discussed in the book *On Sonic Art*.
[42] The sounds were played down a carpet tube and rerecorded, taking in the resonance of the tube, a technique I learnt from Andrew Bentley.

Vox 2

In *Vox 2* the poetic is one of an internal energy emerging from a meditative surface calm. The piece has a relatively simple, slow-moving external form, the melodic/harmonic frame of the piece, and a very active internal form, the inner elaboration of the note (syllable) events through pitch articulation, noise-band articulation and timbre articulation. I was particularly interested in how to handle the portamento articulation of a pitch-field **(Sound Example 35)**.

The piece begins with a solo suggested by the gestures of Bunraku puppet-theatre vocalisations, using controlled vibrato, pitch glides, subharmonics and cross-break attacks, all written out in the score. My perception was that musical cultures in which pitch-articulated ornamentation was prominent had a modal approach to pitch and that there were structural reasons for this (there needs to be a differentiation between pitch classes which are focal and others which are subsidiary, to give ornamentation and articulation its directedness). My pitch material uses a mode of limited transposition[43] so that, without changing the pitches used, we can apparently modulate to a new pitch-centre merely by taking the bass pitch down by a 3rd. The various sections of the piece are organised harmonically in this way (stepping down by a 3rd, without changing the pitch material), the final cadence of the piece stepping down by a tritone (the only other step available). And within the sections the basic pitches move very slowly.

Superimposed on this calm harmonic surface, the 'insides' of the notes (syllables) are increasingly elaborated until, in the midst of each modal section, the ornaments 'take-off' from the harmonic ground, becoming an intense interaction of sonic gestures, played off in counterpoint between the four voices.

In the central interlude of the whole piece a solo voice, doubled at the tritone by a harmoniser[44], is set against a canon of sibilant materials generated by 3 voices in concert. At the end of the piece, the ornaments break out of the containing form to produce a driving rhythmic texture which eventually subsides into the slow modal working before the final tritone 'modulation' step.

Throughout *Vox 2* there's a flow of relatedness between the sung material and the sounds on tape – for example, environmental pedals or harmonic fields reinforce the pseudo-modulations in the voices, vocal sibilants are counterpointed by (spatially) moving noise-bands, and the sounds of wolves, Great Northern Divers and other birdsong are echoed in the vocal line.

---

[43] See the works of Messiaen.
[44] An early type of pitch-shifter.

The most traditional of the *Vox* pieces, *Vox 3* has no tape-environment. The piece is concerned with intellectual pleasures or mathematical play. it is cast as a series of rhythmical 'games' amongst the four protagonists separated by spoken sections where they appear to discuss, respond to or dispute about the game playing. In the rhythmic sections a series of increasingly difficult polyrhythmic situations are presented. I'm here interested in *perceived* rhythmicity, not in some scheme which is complex on paper but heard as random or non-rhythmic in performance. Perceptual frames for the apprehension of multiple tempi must be established. Otherwise, when the rhythmic layers are combined, we simply lose our bearings and shift our attention to a broader, more general level - we hear density flow, but not a counterpoint of rhythms as such.

Even a simple rhythmic counterpoint which equates 2 equal beats in one line with 3 equal beats in another, can quickly become complicated if we group (accent) the 2 lines differently, e,g, the first in groups of 3 beats and the 2nd in groups of 5 beats. A long period passes before strong beats in the 2 lines coincide once again. If, we change the meter frequently in each line, introduce triplets into the faster line, and so on, an apparently simple juxtaposition of tempi becomes quite complicated. By chosing how and when to cause the lines to coincide (land on the same strong beat together) we can generate a rhythmic interaction *between* the lines, while making each line rhythmically interesting in its own right. However, to hold all this together a single conductor is insufficient, and each performer needs to follow a click-track (which is different to the click track of the other performers) which has been computer generated in order to coincide wit5h the other vlick-tracks at appropriate moments in the piece.

There are two types of polyrhythm, polymeter and polytempo. With polymeter, each line has the same basic pulse, but these pulses are grouped differently (in 2s, 3s, 5s etc.) **(Sound Example 36).** With polytempo the lines are in different but related tempi. **(Sound Example 37)**. As in the previous paragraph, we can have 2 beats of one tempo in the time of 3 beats of the other. In a mathematical sense polytempo is equivalent to polymeter as we can always divide the beats of the two tempi to find a common pulse (third-beats in the two-beat tempo correspond to half-beats in three-beat tempo), but once the pulse relationship becomes more irrational (e.g. 5 against 7) the common dividing pulse becomes too rapid for us to perceive it as a pulse in its own right. So perceptually polymeter and polytempo are distinct, except in the most trivial cases.

The first half of *Vox 3* is concerned with polymetric variations, starting with 2 counterposed lines, and leading up to 4 lines in 4 v 5 v 6 v 7 groupings **(Sound Example 38)**. The materials are counterpointed often by motifs being imitated, but recast in the different tempi of the lines. Towards the centre of the piece we have two very fast hockets (the voices alternate rapidly), the first with 2 lines **(Sound Example 39)**, and the 2nd with 4 lines at a breakneck speed. The second half of the piece develops mainly polytempic variations, and towards the end, the tempi become so fast, and the rhythmic relations so skewed that it is no longer possible for the listener to apprehend the polyrhythmicity – but the aim is to create the illusion that this perception is within our reach (the games have taken us down this path of increasing complexity, and we expect to be able to grasp the next rhythmic game!).

Vox 4

Vox 4 is a formalised theatrical scenario which explores the different modes of group cohesion and breakdown. The piece is organised as a sequence of theatrical voice-scenarios (often juxtaposed in short contrasting blocks), and the tone-of-voice/mode-of-delivery are the principle compositional tools, imposed on preformed "texts" of particular sound-quality selected by the performers from pre-ordained lists. There is an articulated process of development from the cohesive group breathing gradually breaking down at the start through the juxtaposed blocks of contrasting attitudinal postures to the hideous unison chant near the end.

Vox 6

Poetically *Vox* follows human activity through a cycle from the creation of order in *Vox 1* to the breakdown of social cohesion in *Vox 4*. The disembodied voice which erupts from the loudspeakers in *Vox 5* I've called the voice of Shiva, a voice from which the world emerges and into which it is consumed. Shiva is an archetypal representation of the cosmos and, in particular, of human endeavour, as simultaneously creative and destructive. Our own culture, ecstatic materialism, is at once exceedingly materially creative, apparently making everything available to us, while rapidly destroying the planet on which we depend. It seemed appropriate therefore to locate this mythology in our own culture, by casting the dance of Shiva Nataraja, the eternal dance of creation and destruction, in the established dance-form of the time[45] – disco.

This kind of ecstatic dance-music seemed to me to celebrate one aspect of what our culture is about, a kind of non-reflective hedonistic enjoyment. I wanted to retain this directness (i.e. you'd still enjoy the music in the same way) while at the same time reshaping it so that its meaning was double-edged. I didn't want to achieve this through the listeners' cerebral detachment from the music because that would completely destroy the experience I wanted to set up. Hence the formal structures of the music is retained but modified - there's no exact repetition in the structure, there are metric elisions, the rapping becomes polyrythmic and the tempo shifts up a gear two-thirds of the way through the piece.

---

[45] The 1980s.

VOX 5

VOX 5[46]

Vox 5 presents the image of a single (super-)human voice, front-stage, whose syllabic utterances are ejected into sound-surround space, metamorphosing into sounds from the real world - a crowds, a bell, a horse, bees, etc. - before returning to the mouth for the next syllable. It forms the 5th movement of a 6 movement work, the *Vox Cycle*, for 4 live amplified vocalists. Each piece in the cycle is concerned with different aspects of human experience, different music-structural ideas and different performance-techniques, and most involve an accompanying sound-environment. After the 'social breakdown' at the end of *Vox 4*, the voice of *Vox 5* emerges out of such an environment, like an apparition from another world. Musically speaking it has the form of an *Arioso*[47], forming a bridge to the final, dance-music-based movement for live performers.

Origins of the Project

Vox 5 grew out of my struggles to achieve sound metamorphosis in the analogue studio. Soon after completing Red Bird (1977), I conceived the idea of a piece for solo voice in which the syllables metamorphosed into recognisable real-world sounds. I was aware that it should be possible to achieve these transformations *elegantly* with advanced computer technology, but at the time had no access to those resources. So I devoted myself to exploring sonic transformation in live vocal performance, systematically classifying extended vocal techniques and developing a new notation for sound transformation, culminating in the work *Anticredos*[48].

In 1979 I decided to make a proposal to IRCAM in Paris, at that time the only facility for advanced computer-music in Europe, and as a result was invited onto their 6-week induction course in 1981. Whilst there I discovered some tools[49] which it might be possible to use and devised a few elementary software routines of my own. At the end of the course I was invited to make a second visit to realise my musical ideas. Unfortunately, before I could return, IRCAM decided to change computer hardware and it was not until 1986 that I was able to continue with the composition project. By that time I was already immersed in composing the *Vox cycle*. The metamorphic project became the 5th, purely electro-acoustic, movement of the *Vox cycle*[50].

In the meantime IRCAM's software environment had radically changed so it was necessary to start again, using the Phase Vocoder as my principal tool. The Phase

---

[46] A more complete description of the computer instruments used in making *VOX 5* can be found in the *Computer Music Journal* article, *The Composition of VOX 5 at IRCAM*. All these instruments are now part of the *Composers Desktop Project*.
[47] In eighteenth century opera and oratorio, recitative, rather like intoned speech performed at natural speech-speed, was used to carry information about the plot, without much attempt to build a formal musical structure. This contrasted with and linked together the *Arias*, which were melodic song in clear musical forms involving formal repetition of musical sections. *Arioso* was an intermediate form having the speech-continuity of recitative, but melodically and harmonically elaborated. A good example is *Ah Golgotha* in Bach's *St Matthew Passion*.
[48] *Anticredos* (1980) for 6 amplified voices and minimal percussion, commissioned by *Singcircle* with funding from the Arts Council of Great Britain.
[49] ...especially Linear Predictive Coding.
[50] The *VOX* cycle was written, piece by piece, between 1982 and 1988, commissioned by *Electric Phoenix* with funds from diverse funding bodies.

Vocoder program, from San Diego, was at that time new to IRCAM and noone was really familiar with its details. Only by 'breaking into' the binary files that it produced was I able to discover the structure of the analysis data, and hence work out how to modify it to make the sound-transformations that I was interested in.

The Source Material

Vox 5 uses recordings of my own voice uttering time-extended syllables, often employing extended vocal techniques (ingressive complex sounds, subharmonics, ululation, special consonantal production, etc.). Some of these are suitable for transformation into other sounds - the sound of bees can be matched to 'zzzz', the sounds of densely overlaid crowd recordings to 'shshsh', while the inharmonic spectra of bells can be approached by spectrally stretched vocal sounds of the correct morphology (see below). Other syllables are simply thrown out from front-stage to move around the space of the auditorium, e.g. the ululation soon after the piece begins (moving in 2 streams), or the ejected 'sss' sounds which race across the space.

The real-world sources came mostly from my collection of material accumulated in the analogue studio. The bees recording was a gift from my students at Sheffield Hallam University who worked with a beekeeper to contain the bees in a large glass container and record them on a professional analogue audio cassette.

Precomposition

Most of the pre-compositional work for *Vox 5* involved exploring the possibilities for morphing vocal sounds, and developing the software instruments to make these morphs. In addition I created a reverse wedge[51] from the crowd sounds, in the analogue studio, beginning with a dense (noise-like) overlay of several slightly different copies of crowd recordings out of which emerges a single layer[52].

Reverse Wedge

The noise band is transposed upwards at the start, falling quickly to its natural pitch before the real crowd can enter. The initial transposed noise-band can be more easily morphed out of a "kshshshsh" vocal event.

---

[51] The idea of the wedge had been developed in the analogue studio and used in the *Poet* section of *Red Bird*. See the *Red bird* chapter.

[52] I began with a time-reversed copy of the original source. Then slightly different copies were gradually faded in, slightly diverging in pitch as they did so. (Copies and time-synchronisation in the analogue studio are not precise, so there are no digital-delay-like artefacts). This initial wedge was then copied and the same process applied again and again until a 243-layered version was emerging from the initial sound. At this thickness, the spectrum is saturated with information and is effectively 'pure' noise. The sound was then time-reversed, restoring the original direction of time, so that the original source now emerges out of the noise-band.

Most of the events in *Vox 5* involve human vocal utterances transforming into other sounds, and then back to the voice source, for the next utterance. The vocal attacks are all 'mono' and located at front centre stage. These metamorphose into *stereo* events which may pass over the head of the listener, using the whole sound-surround space. The aesthetic aim is to make the sonic events plausibly vocal or naturalistic, even if startlingly unexpected in their evolving form. The transformation from mono into stereo enhances the sense that the events emerge *out of* the utterance.

The sound transformations in VOX 5 were largely achieved using the Phase Vocoder. This instrument analyses the input sound and generates its spectrum[53]. To keep track of
the changing nature of the sound, the process divides the input sound into a sequence of brief, overlapping time-windows (akin to the frames of a movie) and analyses the spectrum in each window. Each of these windows is itself split into a number of channels, dividing up the complete range of frequencies into equally spaced bands[54]. The output data for each band consists of the amplitude and frequency values for that band[55].

Frequency increasing ↓   Time advancing →

	Window 1	Window 2	Window 3	Window 4	Window 5	Etc →
Channel 1	AMP FRQ	AMP FRQ	AMP FRQ	AMP FRQ	AMP FRQ	
Channel 2	AMP FRQ	AMP FRQ	AMP FRQ	AMP FRQ	AMP FRQ	
Channel 3	AMP FRQ	AMP FRQ	AMP FRQ	AMP FRQ	AMP FRQ	
Channel 4	AMP FRQ	AMP FRQ	AMP FRQ	AMP FRQ	AMP FRQ	
Channel 5	AMP FRQ	AMP FRQ	AMP FRQ	AMP FRQ	AMP FRQ	
etc. ↓						

In simple cases, the individual partials of a sound will appear as prominently loud values in particular bands, while other bands carry low-level residual noise data. Regardless of the nature of the spectrum, the original sound can be synthesized anew from this analysis data.

---

[53] ..using the Fast Fourier Transform. For more technical details of sound analysis and transformation, see my book *Audible Design*.

[54] These bands are equally spaced in *frequency*, not in terms of pitch. In practice this means that there is too little analytical detail at very low frequencies, and too much at high frequencies. This imposes some practical limitations on resolving the spectra of low frequency sounds, especially if they are rapidly changing.

[55] Fourier Analysis generates amplitude and *phase* data. By equating frequency with rate of change of phase, and knowing the time-step between windows, the phase data is used to calculate the frequency.

This data itself can then be manipulated to alter the spectrum of the sound from moment to moment, and a resulting, transformed sound synthesized from the transformed data[56]. In all these changes, the time-frame (the total duration) of the source will not be altered. We can also use the analysis data to timestretch the sound, by generating new windows between the existing ones in various ways.

The first transformation procedure used in *Vox 5* involves *interpolating* between the spectra of two different sounds, creating a spectral morph. This can be heard in the sound *Voice→Bees* (**Sound Example 40**). To achieve this, the time-windows in the two sounds are paired with each other, moment by moment[57].

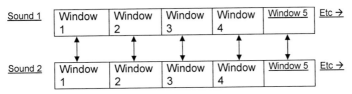

We then make a gradual interpolation, from the channel-values of the first sound to those of the second sound[58]. The two sounds themselves must be closely audibly related for the morph to succeed (this is intuitively obvious)[59].

---

[56] For example, if all the frequency information is multiplied by 2, the new sound generated will be an octave higher[56]. If we multiply the frequency data by a number that starts with value 1, then increments very gradually towards the value 2 as we pass from one window to the next, the new sound will gradually portamento up through one octave. (In reality, if we multiply all the frequency values by two most of the new frequencies will lay outside the appropriate range of their original channels, so we have to move the new frequency values into appropriate channels before making the resynthesis).

[57] The two sounds do not, of course, need to begin at the same time. We merely pair-off the windows over the time-period in each sound in which the morph is to take place.

[58] We create a new set of windows; the very first are taken directly from the windows of the first sound, and the very last from the windows of the second. In between these times, we take each corresponding pair of windows, then take the channel data from the first sound's window and move those values slightly towards the values in the corresponding channels of the second sound. Proceeding from window to window, we make the channel values move further from those of the first sound and approach closer and closer to those of the second sound.
Note especially that the values in each of the source sound will typically be *changing* from window to window. We are interpolating across the *difference* between the corresponding channel values in the two corresponding source windows.
Below is a *schematic* representation of interpolation for *just 1 channel* in successive windows of the two sounds (the interpolation would in reality extend over many more window, and apply to all channels; the frequency values are given as whole numbers simply to make the process clear)...

		Window 1	Window 2	Window 3	Window 4
Window 5					
Sound 1:	Channel N	Frq 200	Frq 230	Frq 210	Frq 190	Frq 220
Sound2 :	Channel N	Frq 180	Frq 170	Frq 200	Frq 210	Frq 200
New Sound:	Channel N	Frq 200	Frq 215	Frq 205	Frq 205	Frq 200
		= Sound 1	1/4 of way to Sound 2	1/2 way to Sound 2	3/4 way to Sound 2	= Sound2

Various perceptual issues also come into play. First of all our perception tends to be categoric, e.g. we hear sounds either as a voice or as the sound of bees. Hence there is a moment in the transformation, no matter how smooth, where aural recognition tends to suddenly switch from 'It's a voice' to 'No, it's bees!'. To undermine this perceptual switching, having made the smoothest morph I could manage, I re-engineered the sound at the point where my perceptual switch was taking place, sliding some non-prominent, high frequencies in the spectrum up then down in frequency. This seemed to distract my attention, in a subliminal way, from perceiving any sudden switch.

Secondly, making a convincing morph *from* the voice to some other sound proved easier to than making a convincing morph from some other sound *back to* the voice. This seems to be to do with our physical relation to our voices. Air is actively expelled from the mouth to bring a sound into being, and in each case in *Vox 5* there is a clear consonantal initiation of each vocal event. So uttering ('outering') some other sound does not seem completely psychologically improbable. However, having some other sound in the environment gradually become vocal seems much harder to accept. Hence, the transformations *from* the voice were always more satisfactory to my perception than the transformations back *to* the voice at the 'syllable' ends.

Thirdly, we need time to recognise both the initial sound and the final sound in a morph. This places limits on how fast a morph can take place. In the next example **(Sound Example 41)** we hear a much more rapid transformation (listen to the example now, before reading further!). I was very pleased with this morph, so I listened to it a second time – but this time I heard no morph. It seemed that once I knew what to expect from the sound, I no longer registered the (human voice) start of the sound, hearing only the (horse-neigh) conclusion. The morph seems to work better in the context of the piece where, by the time the sound arrives, we are primed to hearing human vocal sounds morph into other sounds.

In another case, the morphing task (from vocal "ksh" to the sound of a crowd) was made easier by first creating *a reverse wedge*, as described above, so that the crowd itself emerges from a noise-band. A second spectral process, spectral transposition[60] was then applied to the resulting sound, so it descends in tessitura to become a low, pitched drone[61] before rising back to its original register **(Sound Example 42)**.

Similarly, in the *Voice→Bees* morph the initial vocal sound is spectrally transposed. In this case, however, only a part of the spectrum is transposed[62]. The voice begins by singing a note with an added subharmonic one octave and 5th below the basic pitch. Spectral transposition is used to take just the subharmonic tone down a further octave, producing a sound that is hypothetically performable (the lowered note is still in the subharmonic series) but not possible to sing in practice.

---

[59] If the two sounds have no common prominent channels (channels in which the data is loud in *both* sounds), then the interpolation will merely cause the data in the prominent channels of the first sound to fade out, and the data in the prominent channels of the second sound to fade in, very close to the effect of a simple cross-fade. What we want is for the data in the prominent channels of sound 1 to *gradually and audibly change*, in the process becoming the prominent channels of sound 2.

[60] Multiplying all spectral frequencies in a window by the same number, and gradually changing the number from window to window, so the sound changes pitch or tessitura gradually.

[61] When transposed into the lowest register, all the partials are squeezed into the lowest channels and we have very little data left to represent the spectrum resulting in the sound briefly becoming a low, pitched drone.

[62] The option to transpose only a part of the spectrum is a feature of the resulting CDP software.

example of Harmonic Series			example of Subharmonic Series		
		C		C - - - - - - - -	*sung tone*
up octave		C	down octave	C	
up octave+5th		G	down octave+5th	F - - - -*sung subharmonic*	
up 2 octaves		C	down 2 octaves	C	
up 2 octaves+3rd		E	down 2 octaves+3rd	Ab	
up octaves+5th		G	down 2 octaves+5th	F - -*computer-transposed subharmonic*	

Then, as the sound glissandos upwards towards its final resting pitch, the spectral transposition is gradually removed.

The third spectral process used in *Vox 5* involves *spectral stretching*. In this case, the frequencies in the channels of the spectrum are moved, but each is moved *differently*[63]. As a result, the *relationships between* the partials in the sound are altered. If the original spectrum was harmonic it will, in general, become inharmonic[64], appearing to contain several pitches[65].

---

[63] As mentioned previously, multiplying all the channel frequencies by two will simply move the sound up by an octave. This is because this transformation preserves the *relationship between* the partials. E.g. in a sound having a single clear pitch 'A' and whose fundamental frequency is 110 Hz, we might expect to find prominent partials at 220 Hz, 330 Hz, 440 Hz etc. as these are simple integer multiples of the fundamental, known as *harmonics*. This set of simple relationships is what characterises a clearly pitched sound (as opposed to a noise band or an inharmonic sound) and the spectrum is said to be *harmonic* (not to be confused with the notion of *tonal harmony*; see *Audible Design*). If we multiply all these values by some number (say 1.5 or 2) they are all changed, but the *relationship between them* remains the same (they remain integral multiples of the lowest). So our new sounds, although transposed upwards, are still harmonic – they still have a single clear pitch.

original values	values X 1.5	values X 2
110	165	220
220	330	440
330	495	660
440	660	880
550	825	1100
660	990	1320
etc.	etc.	etc.
low 'A'	'E' one fifth higher	'A' an octave higher

If, however, we multiply the values in each channel by different numbers, this simple relationship will not be preserved. More detailed discussion of partials and harmonics can be found in *Audible Design*.
Note that we are simplifying matters for the sake of discussion. A naturally produced sound of pitch 'A' in this register will in reality fluctuate randomly over a tiny range, and the spectrum will not be completely steady (especially in the attack and decay portions of the sound).

[64] An *inharmonic* sound has a (roughly) steady spectrum with relatively stable partials, but these partials are not simple multiples of any fundamental. A fundamental need not be present even in a harmonic sound. See *Audible Design* for further details.

[65] In general, the pitches heard in an inharmonic spectrum do not bear a simple relationship to the partials (e.g. we are not simply hearing the 'pitch' of each partial). The human ear attempts to deduce pitches from any harmonic relations it thinks it can approximate from the relationships among the partials, and these are the pitches we hear.

In the next example (**Sound Example 43**)[66] we hear a vocal source being stretched more and more as we progress through the sequence. As a result, the initial vocal sound (ko→u) turns into a bell sound. The bell image is enhanced by gradually time-stretching the tail of the sounds by greater amounts as we go through the sequence[67].

For this morph to work, it was important for the original sound to have the *morphology* of a bell i.e. it starts with a sudden, brief attack ("k") which has a (noise-based) spectrum with energy across the entire frequency range. It then rapidly becomes a harmonic spectrum with a clear pitch ("o"). The spectrum is then gradually filtered by making the mouth cavity smaller ("o→u"), causing the higher frequencies to disappear from the spectrum while the lower frequencies are retained. This *morphology* directly parallels that of a real bell, which is initiated by a sudden, brief and bright attack (the 'clang') rapidly resolving into a clear pitch in which the high frequencies, being more easily damped by materials in the environment, die away more quickly than the low ones. If we had not started out with a vocal sound of this morphology we would not have succeeded in generating a bell-like result.

In *Vox 5* this sequence is not used directly. Instead, we begin with a sound where three vocal syllables with strong attacks are superimposed so that their attack points are precisely synchronous. With this precise, studio-contrived synchronisation, we momentarily mislead the brain into assuming there is just a single source (a bell-like source in this case) but almost immediately afterwards it realises that the source is vocal[68]. Hence we produce a dual-percept – *bell-voices*. In the sound example, the sound repeats, but with gradually increasing spectral-stretching through the sequence (as used in the previous example) so that the sounds become increasingly bell-like (**Sound Example 44**).

The *bell-voices* sound is used once again in the final section of the piece, behind the thunderstorm, but here extreme time-stretching is used both to change the attack-characteristics destroying its bell-like nature, while beautiful time-stretch artefacts ripple through the sound's tail (**Sound Example 45**). [1] As we can hear, simply time-

---

[66] The sequence in the sound example actually starts after the first small stretching, so the initial sound we hear is already slightly transformed.

[67] Note that the pitch appears to gradually rise (There is one place where the pitch steps down, caused by my slightly changing the stretch parameters at that point in the sequence, and another where it seems to drop by an octave, which is an artefact of the time-stretching process). This is interesting because the lowest partial (the fundamental) of the source is not being transposed. This illustrates how pitch is not simply equivalent to the frequency of the fundamental, but is a mental construction from the relationships between the partials in the sound. In a harmonic sound, this relationship is usually (but not always) consistent with the pitch being where the fundamental frequency is. In an inharmonic sound, the partials may *imply* a different pitch (or several different pitches). In our case, the majority of the partials are rising, but are still close to harmonic in their internal relationship. The implied pitch thus rises with them.

[68] Synchronicity of attack is one of the clues that the brain uses to decide that some group of partials it has extracted from the stream of sounds entering the ears is all emanating from the same source. In the real world it is not possible for three vocalists to synchronise their attacks in this precise way and so the brain is always able to resolve the sound they make into three separate sources, and we hear three singers singing a chord. In the studio however, we can fool our perception by using absolutely precise synchronisation, impossible in the real world.

stretching the very sharp attack of the bell sound destroys the character of this attack. We no longer hear a "bell" but more a sound that is coaxed into existence, like a brushed cymbal. This illustrates the importance of the attack of a sound in suggesting its cause – has the sound source been struck, stroked, shaken ? To preserve the sense of a bell-attack we would need to apply time-variable time-stretching, not time-stretching the attack itself, but only the tail of the sound (see discussion in the *Tongues of Fire* chapter).

....and finally

Vox 5 was made at IRCAM in 1986. I would like to acknowledge the insights gained from the 1981 psycho-acoustic lectures of Stephen McAdams, and the advice and assistance of Xavier Rodet, Yves Potard, Erik Viara, Dan Timis, Miller Puckette and others in helping to clarify aspects of the Phase Vocoder, ironing-out my C-programming techniques, and making helpful suggestions about avenues worth exploring.

TONGUES OF FIRE

TONGUES OF FIRE[69]

Tongues of Fire takes to a new level the idea of sound-metamorphosis, first explored in *Red Bird* and then, with more computer-controlled sophistication, in *Vox 5*. In the earlier pieces, metamorphosis has a more symbolic or dramatic role, relying more on clear recognition of (apparently) real-world sources. The dramatic/symbolic inplications of the materials in *Tongues of Fire* are largely (though not entirely) epiphenomena of the musical experience and the type of sound materials being used, rather than central to the organisation of the piece.

Origins of the Project

Tongues of Fire originated in a first attempt to run music signal-processing software on a PC. It was the first complete piece I composed on a desktop computer. The idea of doing serious signal processing on a PC originated with the *Composers' Desktop Project* (CDP) which developed out of a composers' discussion group in York, UK. The group began by porting public domain software, in use at IRCAM and Stanford, onto the Atari ST.[70]

However, the Atari was very slow, relative to IRCAM's mainframes - a process that took a few minutes at IRCAM might take a couple of days to rum on the Atari. The advantage of the CDP system was that you could run it at home, in your own time. Partly because my composition was then focused on live vocal and instrumental work, I did not use the Atari system for serious *sound*-composition. In the early 90s, however, processors had become very much faster, and when multitasking PCs became available we ported the entire system onto the PC.

Immediately after completing this task, in order to test the new system, I recorded a few improvised vocal sounds onto my computer and began using these to test the software. Very soon this testing task metamorphosed into real composing, and *Tongues of Fire* began to take shape.

---

[69] For a wider discussion of the conceptual and technical background to the musical approaches used in *Tongues of Fire*, see the article in *Computer Music Journal* Volume 24, No 2, Summer 2000, MIT Press, USA.

[70] In the late 70s our meetings had begun to focus on the possibilities of the new computer technology for transforming sound, but at that time there were no serious sound-transformation programs available on desktop computers. We knew that powerful public-domain software was running at IRCAM on mainframe computers, but current PCs were unable to handle the speed of data-transfer needed simply to play professional quality audio.
However, in the early 80s, the Mac and the Atari ST became widely available, and it became clear that we might be able to port those programs onto one of these machines. The MAC turned out to be too slow for professional audio so we opted for the Atari and, with the help of Martin Atkins of the York University computer-science department (who figured out how to stream sound *out* of the Atari's ROM port) and David Malham of the music department (who built a buffering box to stream the sound-data at a constant rate), we were able to set up the first, full sampling-rate music signal processing environment on a desktop computer.
Andrew Bentley, Richard Orton and myself set about porting Cmusic and the Phase Vocoder onto the Atari, and Archer Endrich took on the task of managing and documenting the project to make the software available to other composers. We also immediately began writing our own music signal processing software using the soundfiling system written by Martin Atkins. The CDP continued to develop as a composers' cooperative, and many composers and music programmers have contributed to the bank of processes that are now available.

The Source Material

The 'theme' of *Tongues of Fire* - selected and edited-together from those initial test-improvisations - is thus a rapid solo vocal utterance less than 2 seconds in length. This theme was constructed both for expressive reasons - it's recognisably human, but slightly grotesque, slightly comical and without any linguistic content in any existing human language - and for sonic-structural reasons - it is a sequence of several spectrally-complex and different sounds, hence making excellent raw material for many different kinds of sonic transformation.

Precomposition

All the sounds in *Tongues of Fire* are derived from the initial theme, and from closely related materials of a similar nature (all from my own vocal improvisation), by processes of sonic transformation.

Using different small elements of the theme and of the related vocal sound materials (with different sonic qualities e.g. noise content, plosiveness etc.), I made many different, small(ish), sound transformations.[71] I then had a node (the starting sound) and its branches (the new sounds generated). I then selected some of the new sounds (as new nodes) and made several transformations of them, and so on. In this way I ended up with a large tree of interconnected sounds. Along the way, the sounds I chose to transform further, or to use in the final piece, were selected on the basis of their intrinsic aesthetic quality[72] *and their audible relatedness to one another*[73]. Some sounds may be used purely because they form a perceptual bridge between two other more aesthetically striking sounds that I plan to use in the piece (analogous to passing notes in pitch-based musical organisation). In *Tongues of Fire* these connections are sometimes directly apparent (we hear one sound gradually changing into another)

---

[71] To be *musically* useful, a transformation must lead to a *perceptually similar* sound, otherwise the listener perceives no connection between the source and the resulting sound. See *Audible Design* for a full discussion of the importance of *audible* relations among sound materials.

[72] This process of variation and selection combines rational exploration with personal aesthetic choice. This balances two important aspects of composing for me, the things that we know that we know - explicit perceptual connections and rational processes of transformation - and things that we don't know that we know - cultural and personal implicit preferences which, in the long run, may turn out to be far more interesting to future listeners than all our intellectual ratiocinations, because they carry information about cultural context and our relationship to it that we have simply taken for granted.

[73] See Footnote 71. The signal-processing power of the computer means that, technically speaking, our starting sound is almost infinitely malleable. In these circumstances we need to make a distinction between what is *technically* a transformation, and what is *perceptually* a transformation. As an extreme example, any starting sound can be converted to noise by multiplying each successive sample by a different random number. Technically speaking this could be regarded as a transformation (the algorithm involved is quite straightforward), but perceptually there is no relationship between the starting sound and the resultant sound (and in fact the same, or very similar, perceived resultant could arise whatever starting sound we chose). Quite subtle changes in the nature of a sound (e.g. changes to the attack characteristics) can radically alter our source-attribution (what we imagine the source of the sound to be), so we must be quite circumspect if we wish to preserve some sense of connection between source and result. However, see my later comments on the *fireworks* transformation.

while elsewhere the various sound materials are used more freely to construct the music[74].

The genetic[75] process of forming a tree of related sounds was the groundwork for the next stage, in which sound materials were arranged in temporal sequence, or overlaid contrapuntally (strictly speaking, as counter-streams) to emphasise, mask or complicate their perceptual connectedness – forming an evolving structure in time[76]. In reality, there was not a simple dividing line between the two stages. Often, sets of transformed material were worked up into complete paragraphs at an early stage. Some continuous transformations called out to be treated as musical paragraphs in their own right, as they extended over a considerable time and provided a sense of musical motion (which I refer to as *sonic modulation*). Also, any concatenation of materials, at any stage of sequencing or overlayering, can itself become the subject of further transformation.

Many new (signal processing) instruments were developed for or during the composition of this piece, particularly *spectral tracing, waveset distortion, inbetweening, sound shredding* and *grain extraction and manipulation* (see below).

The Form of the piece

Tongues of Fire is concerned with continuous sonic development of its starting materials. These developments are set within a larger-scale form in which certain elements or sections are echoed at other points in the piece, which is analogous to formal constructions used in traditional instrumental music.

The piece begins by stating the theme, and then immediately repeating it. Structurally speaking the intention is to make apparent to the listener that this short (only 1.66 seconds), surprising and, on first hearing, apparently arbitrary event is significant for the piece – and in fact all the sound material in *Tongues of Fire* develops from this seed (The first two sounds of **Sound Example 46**)

Similarly, the initial 'paragraph' of the piece is followed (at c. 56 seconds) by an echoing paragraph, the (repeated) theme now developing differently.

On an even larger scale, the first major section ends at c. 10 minutes when the progressive granulation of the voice slows to a regular clock-like tick, leading to a pause. After the pause the (repeating) theme returns but is now followed by four cycles of a rhythmic variant of that theme which becomes crucial to the continuing evolution of the piece. This recurs at 11mins 50secs, 13mins 10secs, 16mins 5secs, and at 17mins (where it already takes on some of the pitchy character of the later development), and leads ultimately to the material at 18mins 20secs, where it forms

---

[74] In contrast, in *Imago*, the evolution of the materials is made clearly audible as part of the form of the piece.
[75] The approach used turns out to be quite similar to the computer graphics model of evolution proposed by Richard Dawkins in *The Blind Watchmaker*.
[76] It is primarily this temporal unfolding of the materials that I hope the listener will perceive and appreciate.

the rhythmic basis of an extended *pulsed-rhythmic climax* in which changing pitch-fields become important, and which forms the climactic conclusion of this part of the piece.

After the dying-away of activity (*the dissolution*) (20mins 40secs to c. 22mins 20secs) short segments from all over the piece are juxtaposed (amid silences) at the start of the *coda*, at the end of which the (repeated) theme is recapitulated in a truncated version of the opening. The piece concludes with a fragment of the theme as a cadential event.

Three other theme-variants play an important role in the piece.

The first (*voismetal*) is a transformation of the almost percussive vocal attack within the theme, in which the tail (only) of the sound is greatly stretched in time - the initial attack is not stretched, to preserve the sense of a vocal origin for the sound. With extensive stretching the noisy spectrum (rapidly varying in a brief space of time) becomes frozen (or, rather, slow-moving) in time and takes on a semi-metallic (inharmonic) quality. This tail glides slowly down in tessitura (the sound, and its derivation can be heard in **Sound Example 47**. This sound is the starting point (sonic node) for many sonic processes (see below).

The second theme-variant (which we'll call *gablcrowd*) is a texture of gabbling voices, extending the solo voice theme material into a disgruntled-crowd-like event (an example can be heard in **Sound Example 48**). This variant is also an important sonic node.

Last of all, the percussive vocal attack mentioned before is stacked (several sample-rate-change octave-transpositions superimposed) with attacks synchronised[77] and a kind of reverberant extension added to the higher (and therefore shorter) components. This brings out the pitch ('d') of this event (which otherwise is difficult to focus in the sonic context of the theme). This variant appears very close to the start of the piece, in the middle and, more emphatically, at the end of the first paragraph (at 19 seconds and 44 seconds respectively). And its pitchness[78] sets it apart in the largely non-pitchal[79] context. We will refer to it as *pichstak*. As one of the few steady-pitched sound-objects in the piece, it becomes an important marker, announcing the start of short or long phrases, sometimes transposed (variously), until it becomes the pedal-point of the harmonic sequence of the pulsed-rhythmic climax.

---

[77] The attack-points of various transpositions of a sound can be synchronised using the CDP process *(Modify) Radical : stack* .

[78] In a sonic context, some spectra have the quality of pitch e.g. a piano note or a bowed violin tone sliding rapidly, while others do not. This *spectral* quality of the sound needs to be differentiated from the concept of pitch-in-relation-to-harmony which we encounter in traditional western music. Traditional pitches are (usually) defined on the lattice of the tempered scale .. they are discrete and defined in relation to their tessitura, e.g. concert A at frequency 440 Hz. A sound has a pitch within the context of the chromatic scale. Thus the violin sliding tone (assuming it slides about rapidly over a wide range) has no pitch in the traditional sense, but has pitch-quality in the spectral sense. I describe such sounds as having *pitchness*, or as being *pitchal*. A more detailed discussion of these issues can be found in *Audible Design*.

[79] See footnote 78.

The Exposition

In *Tongues of Fire* sonic development starts from the very outset. The first paragraph can be heard in **Sound Example 49**. The vocal theme starts with a 'percussive' vocal attack and ends with a 'slurp' sound. These two elements are immediately developed. After the repeated statement of the theme a third statement begins with the percussive but is truncated directly to the slurp which is then repeated (semi-overlayed) at lower pitches/speeds leading to the *pichstak*, the strongly pitched version of the percussive. These two developments illustrate very different approaches to time-stretching. The simplest procedure for making a sound longer is to change its sampling rate[80] (equivalent to slowing the tape down in an analogue studio). This also results in a lowering of the pitch of the sound, but in some musical contexts (as here) this may be OK. The development of the 'slurp' element can be heard in **Sound example 50**.

The first occurrence of *pichstak* (immediately after the 'slurp' sequence) introduces a decelerating sequence of the original percussives (rhythmically prefiguring the *accelerating* 'bouncing' sounds to come). The deceleration is achieved with a non-standard time-stretching technique, giving stretched duration proportions 1:2:3:4:5:6:7.

The stretching process (*waveset distortion repeat*[81]) divides the original sound at every other zero-crossing, and treats the signal segments thus produced as individual wavesets. Time-stretching is achieved by the immediate (N-times) repetition of each waveset before proceeding to the next. Clearly, with a very simple waveform (such as a pure, fixed-frequency sinus tone), the waveset will correspond to a single cycle of the waveform, and this procedure will produce 'perfect' time-stretching of the original source. But applied to complex (or rapidly changing) signals strange artefacts are generated. In particular, if the original signal is relatively irregular (and therefore not very pitchal), once any waveset has been repeated about 4 times it will generate a unique pitch (and spectral quality) in its own right. Hence, as the number of waveform repetitions increases, the original signal gradually breaks down into an ultra-rapid stream of brief pitch-cells.[82] Towards the end of our sequence, therefore, this pitch-bubbling becomes apparent. **(Sound Example 51)**. This same type of pitch-bubbling can be heard more clearly at the end of the dissolution (see paragraph below) where a breathe-like sound is time-stretched in the same way **(Sound Example 52)**.

I refer to this kind of transformation as *constructive distortion* - completely new and surprising artefacts are generated out of the hidden details of our original source.

More typically, distortion techniques are *destructive* – they simply perceptually alter, or degrade, the original source. However the distinction is not so simple. In one phrase in paragraph 2 (1m 18 seconds into the piece), a small vocal element is

---

[80] We in fact resample the sound, as if it were at a different sampling rate, but represent the new sound in the original sampling rate – the sampling rate of the new soundfile is the same as the original.
[81] For further details of waveset distortion processes, see *Audible Design*. These processes are part of the CDP.
[82] It is possible to start with a complex signal and proceed, step by step, to e.g. a 256-times repetition of each component 'waveform', thus generating a arbitrary-rhythmed, arbitrarily-'timbred' melodic sequence. The pitchness only becomes apparent beyond about 4 waveform repetitions, aurally demonstrating the time-boundary at which perception of pitch becomes possible.

repeated while a cyclic loudness envelope is imposed on it. Initially the envelope is so brief in duration that it actually alters the *shape of the waveform* (and we here a vague extraneous pitch inside the sound, which falls as the envelope gets longer – the envelope itself is creating the pitch artefact), but as the envelope gets much longer it begins to shape the overall sound so that at the end of the sequence we hear just the original sound tremolo-shuddering. (The envelope repeat-time is not exactly regularly as the envelope durations are measured in complete wavesets encountered. In a complex signal the wavesets vary in duration from moment to moment, so the resulting time-sequence is irregular) **(Sound Example 53)**.

Continuing with the opening paragraph; before the 1:2:3:4:5:6:7 sequence can end, the percussive-vocal reappears, grouped into an accelerating and decrescendoing motif (suggesting a bouncing object). This motif is repeated with sonic variations. The wavesets (discussed previously) are altered to a different shape, one new shape for each bounce-sequence – perceptually we seem to hear bouncing on or in different physical materials e.g. sand[83] **(Sound Example 54)**.

The whole paragraph concludes with a repetition of the resonant D, sustained, with a slight tremolo as it decays to nothing.

The voismetal paragraph

After the 2 opening paragraphs, and a section of great activity, we arrive (2 minutes 40 seconds) at a new paragraph **(Sound Example 55)**. This begins with a D *pichstak* attack (which is anticipated by an E *pichstak* attack a few seconds before). This new paragraph is derived primarily from the *voismetal* sound The *voismetal* sound itself derives from the percussive attack in the theme by the process of *time-variable time-stretching*[84] **(Sound Example 47)**.

In the new paragraph, *voismetal* is heard immediately after the *pichstak* attack and is then developed. In particular, we produce a rather artificial tremolando in the tail by imposing a rapid sequence of brief, shallow loudness dips. The first of these is heard at the start of the paragraph. On each recurrence these loudness dips cut deeper into the sound and the tail begins to separate (perceptually) into a series of discrete 'struck-wood' events.[85] Using a grain-detection program[86] we can isolate these brief events and duplicate and/or transpose them[87], and this is used to produce a further variant that more strongly emphasises the perceptual distinctness of the 'struck-wood' events **(Sound example 56)**.

---

[83] For a more detailed discussion of *perceived physicality and causality* see *Audible Design*.

[84] As discussed in the *VOX* 5 chapter, time-stretching a very sharp attack can alter the causality of the source (we no longer perceive the imagined source as being struck, but perhaps stroked into existence like a brushed cymbal sound, see *Audible Design*). Hence, to preserve the vocal-percussive origin of the sound in *Tongues of Fire* we time-stretch only the tail.

[85] Descriptive adjectives like 'metallic', 'struck-wood' or 'cicada-noise' are meant to suggest the type of sound-event being referred to, rather than to give an accurate description of their physicality. I'm not suggesting that accurate representations are being created.

[86] The CDP *grain* program detects grains (defined by clear peaks separated by clear troughs) in a sound, and can divide the signal into the grains thus defined, and manipulate those grains (retime them, reverse the grain order *without* reversing the grains themselves etc.).

[87] The CDP *grain* process has options to duplicate, transpose and retime grains.

Using these transformations we have sonically 'modulated' from stretched-voice to a struck-wood-like motif. There are now more extreme variations of the tail, including large upward or downward glissandi, or vibrato to absurdly wide intervals, forming a bridge to a final strong statement of the 'struck-wood' motif where the separateness of the wood-events is emphasised further by the ritardando[88]. This is interrupted by a strongly pitched attack, a dramatic extension of the *voismetal* sound in which the resonance expands in tessitura and crescendos. We will meet this again as the penultimate sound of the whole piece.

The struck-wood motifs now accelerate and rise in pitch leading into a texture[89] of such higher pitched motifs over a small pitch range (vaguely like cicada-noise), an even more distant sonic modulation. (3mins 7secs to 3mins 17secs).

Below this we hear a slow percussive motif that accelerates into the same strong-pitched-attack (without the expanding resonance) followed by a further variant of the descending 'wood' motif. (This 3-part phrase is then echoed by a similar phrase). The accelerating motif is a spectral sequence[90] in which the wood-like events gradually transform into drum-like events. We begin with one of the 'struck-wood' events. This is then spectrally transformed by *waveset distortion replace*[91] (the individual wavesets of the sound – see above - are replaced by wavesets of a different shape). We can produce a series of sounds intermediate between the struck-wood sound and the drum-like sound by a process of *mix in-betweening*, akin to the process of creating the intermediate picture-frames in cinematographic animation[92]. Putting these mixed sounds together in a progressing sequence, moving from wood-like to drum-like, we produce a sense of sonic motion from 'struck-wood' to 'drum'. The sequence also accelerates (like the bouncing in the exposition) but also crescendos, suggesting, perhaps, intentional force, rather than the energy dissipation of free bouncing.
(Sound example 57).

The paragraph terminates (from c. 3mins 52secs) with yet another variant of *voismetal*. This applies the brassage technique (used in the 'harmoniser') that cuts up

---

[88] Deceleration.
[89] Texture: copies of the same sound (or group of sounds) are made within a specified range of transpositions, and mixed so they enter, timewise, in an irregular sequence. These are generated by the CDP *Texture* program. The program can also produce, regular (rhythmic) time-entries, or transpose materials onto specific pitches or harmonic fields (and vary these, and many other parameters, continuously over time). But the textures I use in this piece are either pitch-neutral (because the materials themselves do not have steady pitch, as here, or because the pitches are selected, completely at random – not over any specified scale or tuning system – within a given range) or with no change of the original pitch (as in the texture of *the dissolution*).
[90] These are discussed in more detail in the *Imago* chapter.
[91] The signal is divided into wavesets, and each waveset replaced by a waveset of a different shape, e.g. a sinusoid. The process is described in more detail in *Audible Design*, and is available on the CDP / Sound Loom as *Distort: replace*.
[92] Beginning with the struck-wood sound and the drum-like sound, we produce a sequence of intermediate mixes of the two sounds. In each successive mix, more and more of the new waveform is mixed in (and hence less and less of the original 'wood'). As the two waveforms have their zero-crossings in exactly the same place (by the nature of the waveset distortion process) we are effectively generating a set of transformations of the waveform itself (and hence of the sonority)....producing a set of spectral transformations through a time-domain process.

the sound into tiny segments then reassembles them in order[93]. This process can be varied in many ways. In particular we can adopt the following routine. Cut up the original sound as usual. Then for the first segment of the reconstructed sound choose the first segment of the original sound, but for the second segment of the reconstructed sound, choose the second *or the first* segment of the original sound. For the third segment of the reconstructed sound, choose the third *or the second, or the first* segment of the original sound ..... and so on. As a result of this selection procedure there is always a possibility that some of the early (percussive-attack) segments of the original sound will appear *anywhere* in the reconstructed sound. Hence, this attack quality gets distributed randomly over the time-stretched resultant sound, producing the 'gargling' quality that we hear **(Sound example 58)**.

Hence, by putting all these variants of our sound node (*voismetal*) together in an appropriate temporal sequence, we have constructed a complete paragraph based on the sonic development of the *voismetal* sound **(Sound example 47)**. This is an example of paragraph construction using (mainly) discrete sonic transformations. However, we can also generate entire paragraphs by the continuous or semi-continuous transformation of the starting sound.

Paragraphs derived from gablcrowd

In the paragraph that begins at 13m 20secs (lasting until 15mins 10secs), we generate the structure by the continuous transformation of the *gablcrowd* sound using the new technique of sound-shredding[94]. Any (complex) sound that is shredded, say, 1000 times will turn into low-grade noise, as all we are left with are the characteristics of the splices used to do the cutting. With less shreds, some sounds survive (remain recognisable) better than others. Of all our sound-sources, vocal sounds retain their recognisability even under extreme deformations. Thus, even after a hundred superimposed shreds, the shredded *gablcrowd* sound retains some vocal clues. However, there is eventually a point along this path of successive shreddings where the vocality of the source is lost, but not its sonic diversity. At this stage the sound becomes (to me) akin to the sound of water falling gently around stones in a mountain stream.

Our paragraph is constructed by splicing together successive (cumulative) shreds of *gablcrowd* so that the voices gradually dissolve into the water-like texture over the

---

[93] Standard harmoniser brassage chops up the starting sound into segments about 50 milliseconds in duration, sufficient to preserve the 'instantaneous' pitch of the event, but insufficient to give much of a clue to any *changes* in pitch that might be taking place. By splicing these segments back together again, in the same order, but with a greater or lesser degree of segment overlap, we can reproduce the original event with an altered duration, but with no shift in pitch. (In reality we have to slightly randomise the durations of the cut segments to avoid creating a spurious pitch from any regular sequence of splices used). Brassage, including the variant described in the text, was developed at the *GRM* in Paris.

[94] Sound shredding is a CDP process: (*Modify*) *radical: shred*. The shredding process takes a given duration of sound material and cuts it at a given number of randomly chosen positions e.g. 7 cuts divide the sound into 8 segments, each of random length (though the sum of these lengths equals the original duration). These segments are then shuffled into an arbitrary order, and rejoined to produce a new sound of *exactly* the same length as the original. This process is then repeated many times. In general, at each shred, the new cuts are unlikely to coincide with any existing cuts. So any preserved continuous stretch of the original sound will tend to be cut again into even smaller segments. So at each shred and shuffle the starting sound is increasingly fragmented and increasingly randomly shuffled.

duration of the paragraph. This basic structure is counterstreamed by other events – deep attacks initiating rising noise-bands derived from the shredded-voices.
(Sound example 59)

As you can hear, the paragraph continues, seamlessly, into a second continuous transformation process, evolving a pitched upward portamento out of the noise-texture to lead us into the pitch attacks of the next paragraph. The technique used here is end-synchronised delay. If several copies of a sound are made at very slightly different speeds (resampled at different sampling rates), and these copies are then superimposed so that they synchronise at their start, the resulting precise delays between the copies will be heard as a beat-frequencies creating a pitch portamento descending from 'infinitely' high at the outset (where the copies are all synchronous) through the audible pitch range (as the copies get out of sync, and the increasing delay gap generates a falling pitch) into the subaudio, resolving into a sequence of decelerating echoes. If instead we end-synchronise the copies we will begin by moving into accelerating echoes, leading into a rising pitch portamento. This is what we hear at our paragraph end. This effect occurs no matter what the nature of the original sound – it is a process-determined, rather than a source-determined, effect – so we can use it to move from non-pitchal sounds into pitchal sounds.

A second example of a paragraph based on the continuous transformation of *gablcrowd* starts at 17mins 7secs. The transformation begins by making the crowd texture increasingly dense, by superimposing randomly-delayed, inexact copies of the starting sound[95]. With complex material like this, at sufficient density, the spectrum 'whites out' i.e. the spectrum becomes saturated and we hear just a band of noise. At the same time this band is made to rise in tessitura. As the process (to be described further) continues, the original gabbling voices are made to re-emerge here and there, retaining the connection with the starting sound. The noise is next put through a filter-bank of increasing Q[96] *prior* to the application of portamento, so that it gradually becomes a set of parallel portamentoing pitches. The continuing portamentoing means that the 'chord' is never able to settle in any particular harmonic space.[97] The paragraph continues by reversing these processes, returning first to noiseband and then back to *gablcrowd*. A counter-stream of portamentoing parallel pitches splits away, during the course of the paragraph, and descends slowly in pitch in contrast to the up and down wave-like motion of the principle stream. This paragraph is thus based on a 'classical' arch form using continuous sonic transformations.
(Sound example 60).

---

[95] Using random delays and inexact copies avoids producing artificial-sounding (regular-pulsing or even pitched) delay effects between *identical* digital copies of the sound. This was less of a problem in the analogue studio, where no two copies were *exactly* alike in the digital sense.

[96] The Q of a filter is a measure of the narrowness of the filter band. Filtering broadband noise with a filter at, say, 2000 Hz and a low Q will produce noise of higher frequency (centred on 2000 Hz). If the filter Q is high, only noise close to 2000 Hz will emerge and if the Q is high enough this will appear as a single tone of frequency 2000 Hz.

[97] Technically speaking therefore it is not a chord in any traditional sense.

An arch form might be regarded as a sequence of events or sounds followed by its retrograde. The idea of a retrograde, however, is not as straightforward as it seems. In traditional notated music, a retrograde of a sequence of musical events usually means that we play the original events in reverse order. We are retrograding the *start-times*, only, of the events. We do not reverse the time-flow *inside* the events themselves. In the previous example, however, we were dealing with an *absolute* retrograde – in the second half of the white-out paragraph, the events of the first part of the paragraph are themselves reversed in time, as if time were flowing backwards. This works OK where the sounds have no clear attacks (as with the stream of noise or filtered tones), or are sufficiently dense for us not to notice the reversal (the *gablcrowd* texture), and where the transformations are continuous (smooth).

However, in general, if we reverse the flow of time itself (by running a tape backwards, or reading a soundfile in reverse order of samples) the result is often surprising to us. Very many natural sounds are initiated by some sudden action (hitting, plucking), bringing an object into a sudden state of vibration, and those vibrations then die away gradually (an attack-resonance event). The sound typically has a loud attack followed by a gradual decay to nothing. When we reverse such a sound we hear an event that emerges from nowhere and rises gradually to a sudden loud moment. As a result, the perceived *causality* of the sound (how we imagine the sound to have been brought into being) is changed. And the reversed sound seems, intuitively, quite unrelated to the source[98].

Hence if we want to produce a *clearly perceptible* retrograde with a paragraph containing attack-resonance sounds we must reverse the *order* of the events, rather than the events themselves.

There are two related paragraphs in *Tongues of Fire* using sounds derived through *spectral tracing*. The 2nd is a varied retrograde of the first.

Spectral tracing involves throwing away the *least* significant data in the spectrum of the sound *on a window by window basis[99]*. In some simple situations this can be used for noise-reduction (low level noise features of the signal are discarded). However, with a complex signal, if we choose to retain only the 16 loudest spectral components out of (say) 512 in each spectral window, those 16 loudest will not be the same 16 in each window. So when we resynthesize the sound from the spectrally traced windows, components will suddenly drop out and (more significantly for our perception) suddenly enter. In the following example, in which the number of retained partials used in resynthesis is gradually reduced as we go from one sound to the next, the source has been time-stretched, before tracing, so that prominent partials persist for longer within the traced spectrum **(Sound Example 61)**.

The first of the two paragraphs (7mins 40secs to 8mins 30secs) begins with a particularly plosive version of *gablcrowd*, which becomes very dense, then rises gradually to a higher pitch where it begins to be spectrally traced – the sound becomes more pitchal (less noisy) and then the texture thins leaving wildly fluctuating pitch-lines. We then hear a trombone-like sound beneath it, leading to a 'metallic clang'

---

[98] For a more detailed discussion, see *Audible Design*.
[99] For more details, see *Audible Design*.

event. This is derived from the spectrally traced material by giving that an attack-resonance loudness-envelope and stacking transposed, attack-synchronised copies **(Sound Example 62)**. This phrase ushers in the granulated voice that gradually slows and transforms to the clock-like tick which ends the first part of the piece.

This material is recapitulated in the later paragraph, but in retrograde form (10mins 50secs to 11mins 40secs). In this case it is important that we recognise the connection, as the recapitulation is only one layer of the texture. In the foreground, after the initial attack, a 'puffing' sound accelerates into a rapid series of click-like attacks, which begin to 'tick' like a more active variant of the clock-like tick mentioned above. Behind this, very quietly, we hear the wildly fluctuating pitchlines that gradually transform into the upward-transposed *gablcrowd* texture, which then falls in pitch to reveal the original *gablcrowd* source. This is a true *time-reversal* of the original material. The metallic attacks, however, appear here *not* time-reversed, so that we clearly recognise them **(Sound Example 63)**.

The climax and dissolution

The climactic section of *Tongues of Fire* (at 18mins 20secs) is generated from one of the rhythmic variants of the theme, used as a repeating rhythmic cell. Banks of tuned filters (where the lowest frequency is always the same) are applied to these cells (the filter-bank changing from cell to cell) with the Q gradually increasing as the sequence progresses. As a result of the increasing Q, the material becomes more and more pitchal through the sequence[100] **(Sound Example 64)**.

This type of filter sequence occurs three times, while free-rhythmed gestural sounds are superimposed to impel the music forward.

The music finally 'explodes' into the *fireworks*' transformation. This is perhaps the most extreme transformation used in *Tongues of Fire*. The immediate starting sound (or sonic node) is the sound *voismetal* having a percussive vocal attack leading to an extended 'metallic' inharmonic tail whose tessitura descends slowly. The *fireworks* transformations use waveset averaging[101] (the duration and shape of the source sound wave between each pair of zero-crossings is averaged over time[102]), which, on such a complex source sound, produces a host of unpredictable noisy artefacts. **(Sound Example 65)**.

The only perceptibly retained feature of the starting sound is the descent in tessitura. Although on the edge of perceptual justifiability, I felt that this extreme transformation fitted well at this particularly dramatic moment in the piece, where the energy of the preceding pulsed rhythmic material 'boils off'. Here in fact the piece has reached its transformational outer limits and is about to tie up ends in a 'traditional' coda, using mainly recapitulated (rather than further transformed) materials from all over the piece.

---

[100] Working on this sequence led me to develop the filters in the CDP leading eventually to the time-variable-Q, time-variable-(multi)-pitch, multi-harmonics filters of *Filter varibank* completed while composing *Fabulous Paris* and used towards the end of that piece.

[101] One of the group of *waveset distortion* programs I had developed, and now available on the CDP.

[102] A full desciption of *waveset distortion* techniques can be found in *Audible Design*.

The momentum of the music is then dissolved by using the same rhythmic cell source filtered with a variety of filter banks but blurred together by 'mixing' them all into a texture[103] (the common pitches reinforce one another) with no sense of pulse, and giving the whole sound a slowly fading attack-resonance loudness-envelope. **(Sound Example 66)**.

....and finally

I hope I have given sufficient insight into the musical processes at work in *Tongues of Fire*. I have concentrated on the use of sonic transformation in phrase building, and have said little about criteria for counter-streaming or for the more general sequencing of events.[104] These are of equivalent importance in putting together the piece, but are probably easier to relate to traditional musical form-building techniques.

Tongues of Fire was realised almost entirely on a low cost home computer, using software developed by myself and other participants in the Composers' Desktop Project with the support of public domain software (Barry Vercoe's *Csound* and Mark Dolson's *Phase Vocoder*).

The final mixdown was planned at the GMEB studio in Bourges, but realised in the CDP system on a desktop computer. The final planning was made possible by a commission from the GMEB studio and the assistance of the British Council. The premiere took place at the 1994 *Synthese* Festival in Bourges.

---

[103] See note 22.
[104] Nor have I discussed issues of sonic landscape (which in *Tongues of Fire* are dealt with in a more tangential manner than in either *Red Bird* or *Fabulous Paris*).

FABULOUS PARIS

FABULOUS PARIS

Introduction

In contrast to *Tongues of Fire*, which starts with a very small number of vocal utterances, developing these by processes of sound-transformation, *Fabulous Paris* was created from a very large number of sources, and a new approach and new software instruments had to be developed. The piece started life as a standalone composition, but later two other movements were added to create the 3-movement work, *Fabulous Paris : a virtual oratorio*, with the original piece becoming the final movement. In this chapter I will discuss only this single movement.

Origins of the Project: The Source Material

The origins of *Fabulous Paris* lie in the early 1980s when I had residencies at the analogue studios at the University of Texas at Austin and at San Jose State, California, working on *Anna's Magic Garden*. In between studio sessions I became fascinated by the outpourings of US television stations and collected lots of recordings of and game shows, news programs, commercial breaks, cartoon voices and canned laughter onto audio-cassette tape. I also explored the various second-hand record stores in San Jose and Berkeley, looking for news reportage on vinyl, Kennedy's speech about going to the moon, the assassination of Lee Harvey Oswald, the Appolo 11 transmissions from the moon (all of which would appear in the final composition). I had a vague notion that it might be interesting to make a piece with these materials but, as is often the case, the sounds languished in my cupboards for many years.

On a later visit to California I was struck by the elaborate vocabulary of traffic announcements on the many small radio stations that came into focus as we travelled down the freeway, and asked my friend, the sound-poet Larry Wendt, if he could record some of these for me. At the time Larry made the recordings there was unseasonal flooding in the state leading to many accidents on the freeway and many warnings on the radio. In addition I had recordings (many on minidisk) made in cities that I had visited to present concerts or to work - the traffic tunnels of Stockholm, the cornering screeches of the Paris metro, an amusement park in Kobe.

Eventually, having moved onto computers and completed *Tongues of Fire*, my interest in these old materials was revived by reading a report about increasing migration to cities in the developing world. It was estimated that, by the year 2010, more than 50% of the world's population would live in major cities (and in reality this milestone was passed even earlier, in 2007). I decided to attempt to capture something of the exciting yet frightening flood of information and experience provided by the modern mega-city, and dug out these old materials together with a mono vinyl recording of Hitler speeches, transferring as many as I could from the original analogue sources to DAT tape, the favoured digital medium at the time.

Developing new instruments

The main expressive problem to solve was how to create a sense of an overwhelming amount of information without simply overwhelming the listener with an impenetrable mass of sound. The principle approach adopted was the use of filters to help articulate the dense soundscapes. In particular I developed a method to harmonically-colour the massed materials by using a bank of filters tuned to specific harmonic fields (Harmonic Field filters). By (gradually) varying the tightness (Q) of the filter, these massed sounds could be strongly or subtly harmonically coloured (or not) as the music progressed. Initially I extended the core band pass filter in the CDP software to produce a bank of such filters tuned to pitches specified in a controlling textfile. As work on the piece progressed I developed this design to allow me to filter at the harmonics of the specified pitches, in a controllable way. This filter-instrument proved to be very useful in future pieces - applied to a broad noise band it could be used to create, depending on the Q setting, choric or string-like tuned masses or melodic lines (used to mirror some of the pitch-lines of the speech in *Angel*) or (once pitch-variation of the filter had been added) to filter speech at its own tracked pitch, varying the weighting of harmonics used, gradually exposing the bare melody of the speech (used in *Encounters in the Republic of Heaven*).

The Form of the piece

Formally, the piece falls into three long sections, the last being a telescoped recapitulation of the opening. The piece starts with a layering of the traffic-announcements from the California freeways. Here filter-layering is used to differentiate the many superimposed voices. As in popular-music production, where careful filter focusing is used to place each percussion instrument in the most telling frequency-band, the various voices are filtered into different bands (low-pass, mid-low, centre, high etc.) , then spread across the stereo space, so that they 'tell' against one another in the mix. The voice materials are joined by doppler-shift panned car-horns, and the whole section sits on a pedal which accumulates into a chord for the crash-sound, triggering multiple panned motor-cycles and (what appear to be) Doppler-panned traffic sirens **(Sound Example 67)**.

In the ensuing mass, the vocal materials are used as they are, in bands of time-contracted (speeded-up) texture, time-stretched, spectrally blurred, irregularly echoed over the stereo stage and in many other transformed formats, contributing to the welter of information thrown out by the City. The tuning capabilities of the filter-bank described combine with tuned material derived from some of the intrinsically pitched sources (e.g. the screeching-metro) to provide harmonic foci as the music proceeds. For example, the phrase "Fabulous Paris" (the top prize in a game show) first occurs in this section, and is then extended by time-stretching **(Sound Example 68)**. As the time-stretched version is repeated, its intrinsic pitches are underlined by the harmonies of the stacked filtered materials and the pitches chosen for the metro-screeches **(Sound Example 69)**. At the end of the first section of music, as the sirens reappear, the filter-bank is used to cadence the cityscape on a G (the chattering voices can be heard inside the final tuned event) **(Sound Example 70)**.

The central section begins with new, more rhythmic, material. Here cartoon voices and effects, canned laughter and creaking sources recorded for the making of VOX 1 and recovered from the analogue tapes, supplement the welter of vocal transformations, and the "Fabulous Paris" motif recurs, here animated by a deep-cut tremolo and panning, and passed through a sequence of different harmonic-field filters **(Sound Example 71)**. (The need for several harmonic filters here encouraged me to develop the time-variance of the harmonic fields in this instrument). This eventually leads to one of the principal transformations in the piece. The traffic-sirens we heard near the opening of the piece (in Sound Example 67) are revealed as the ranting of a demagogue - the voice of Hitler **(Sound Example 72)**.

This central section ends with the interplay of various types of pitch-materials, including the use of tuned stacks of pitched events. For example, the final bright attack has several transposed copies of a source, stacked together so that they synchronise near the end of the sounds. In this way, higher transpositions enter at later times, and the final chord appears to well upwards from its base. As this final event dies away, the bass of the harmonic field shifts downwards, preparing us to modulate to the pedal of the opening, for the recapitulation **(Sound Example 73)**.

In the final section of the piece, the massed voices of the opening now slowly transform into the voices of frogs and insects as the other sounds of the city float off into the aether – Ur dissolving into dust, poetically speaking.

.. and finally

Fabulous Paris was commissioned by Swedish Radio, Malmö, and by the Birmingham Rumours Festival. Apart from the final post-production mix (Birmingham University Studio), the piece was made entirely at home on an IBM PC using the Composers' Desktop Project software.

THE DIVISION OF LABOUR

THE DIVISION OF LABOUR

Introduction

The Division of Labour is the first movement of *Fabulous Paris : a virtual oratorio*. The three pieces *The Division of Labour, Globalalia* and *Encounters in the Republic of Heaven*[105] display contrasting approaches to the use of spoken language as sound material for composition. *Globalalia* takes as its source-material the syllabic elements of words collected from many different languages and many different speakers. The piece exploits the sonic properties of particular syllables, or vocal features (vocal grit), to create a series of sound variations each based on just one or two sound archetypes (e.g. "ma" with Dutch and Arabic "rrr"). In this situation the narrative content, and the sense of any personal voice is discarded. At the other extreme *Encounters* takes whole phrases and works with the musical characteristics of these larger elements of natural speech, the melody and rhythm of the phrase, as well as the sonority of individual speakers. In this situation the narrative, and the sense of the personal voice are retained. (This approach was first explored in *Angel*, the central movement of *Fabulous Paris : a virtual oratorio*).

In contrast *The Division of Labour* focuses on the text spoken. It treats Adam Smith's famous text about the division of labour in a Pin Factory, a sacred text of our times, and musically examines its meaning by creating a series of sonic variations on the text itself. For much of the piece, the text is delivered in its original order - it is not totally discarded as in *Globalalia*. However, the original rhythm of the text may be radically altered, there may be phrase or word or syllable repetition, or extreme transformations (retaining the pitch-line only), so the narrative-line and the phrase-characteristics of the original speaker are not preserved as in *Encounters*. And in fact, part of the poetic of *The Division of Labour* concerns the gradual deconstruction of the text as a meaningful entity.

Origins of the Project: The Source Material

Since the late sixties I had wanted to make a piece around the wonderfully productive but potentially alienating notion of the division of labour. This I originally imagined as a humorous music-theatre piece in which 4 people, in a single 4-person suit, attempted to perform texts by increasingly sharing out the words, or syllables. This sound-process was, however, used by Berio in *Arroné*, so the idea sat on the shelf. After completing *Tongues of Fire* I found myself in many friendly arguments about wealth distribution and how markets do or don't work in economic theory, with my friend, Alex Gordon, an economics lecturer. Alex comes from Glasgow, where Adam Smith studied, and has a characteristic Glaswegian accent, so I asked if he would mind my recording his voice, speaking the famous text (shortened slightly for musical use),

---

[105] Details of the composition of *Encounters in the Republic of Heaven* can be found in the booklet accompanying the Stereo Remix CD of this piece.

"A workman not educated to the business could scarce make one pin a day. But one man draws out the wire, another straightens it, a third cuts it, a fourth points it, a fifth grinds it at the top. The head requires three distinct operations. To put it on is a peculiar business, to whiten the pins another. In this manner, making a pin is divided into eighteen distinct operations, and those persons can make forty-eight thousand pins a day." [106]

I then began working on this sound material, 'dividing the labour', so to speak, in numerous ingenious ways, in line with Adam Smith's dictum....

Preparing the materials

The source voice was initially divided up into its constituent syllables, to make detailed treatment of the text possible. Most of the work involved either exploring these materials with existing sound-transformation programs or developing those or new processes to make new sound variants [107]. In particular, the extraction of pitch from speech was importantly improved [108]. I also created a synthesized version of the spoken recording, developing a new process to combine the extracted pitch-line with data, in a text file, describing the evolution of the vowels [109]. When describing the characteristic formants of English vowels, textbooks tend to assume that everyone speaks 'standard English'. Glaswegian vowels are markedly different from 'standard English' (as are my own). So I had to do some experimentation to define the appropriate filter characteristics.

The Form of the piece

The piece is a set of 14 variations on the Adam Smith text recording. These occur in sequence in the final piece, so the reader should refer to the piece itself to understand the following comments.

Statement

The text is heard in its originally recorded version against some 'metallic' sounds derived from later in the piece (see *Hubbub/Toll* below).

Imitation

The text vowels are re-synthesized (see above) and combined with resonated versions of the original consonants. This material is presented in canon, initially in 2 parts, then 4, then (at the end) very many.

---

[106] Adam Smith : *The Wealth of Nations*
[107] All these processes are now available in the *Composers Desktop Project* software.
[108] Extracted pitch-lines were still 'tweaked' by hand, for which I developed a graphic pitch-line editor.
[109] This resynthesis approach was partly motivated by the difficulties I encountered in developing a means to remove the sibilants from the speech line. I finally found a (relatively straightforward) way to do this after completing the piece, using it in the the *Ts_canon* section of *Globalalia*. See the *Globalalia* chapter.

Song without words

The pitch contour of the speech-line plays as a sliding triad, with attack points from the original consonants, and ornamentation from traffic sirens, kookaburras and starlings (the only sounds in the piece not derived from the original voice recordings).

Inflation

Speech syllables are extended in time, through different types of time-stretching, 'bouncing' transformations, imitation or rhythmic repetition.

Hocket

The syllables of the text are individually time-squeezed, making them extremely brief, and played in very strict pulsed time. 8 versions of this material are hocketed against one another, distributed in the stereo space, gradually filling all divisions of the pulse. At this point the sound is filtered through a bank of filters centred at the most prominent pitches of the voice material. The hocket layers are then peeled away from each other to reveal the original solo line, a sort of retrograde of the opening process.

Chorus

The choral sonorities are derived from instantaneous harmonies cut from *Word Dance 1* (see below). For each original source, a dense texture (at the original pitches) was made (in essence an infinite-reverberation procedure) and then played through filter banks of time-varying sharpness (Q) tuned to the internal harmonies of the material[110]. Against these 'choric' sonorities, vastly time-stretched syllables can be heard, decorated through pulsation and panning.

Flecks

Isolated slices of the text, often derived from sharp cuts into the trailing edges of syllables, are revealed.

Word dance 1

Irregular loops of speech material, and 'bouncing' syllables develop in an agitated rhythmic frame.

Compression

The text, at an ultra-fast pace, pans around the space, sometimes emerging from a (spectrally blurred[111] and time-stretched) noisy transformation.

---

[110] CDP's varibank filter, a bank of filters focused at particular pitches (which, in this application of the program, remain fixed over time) defined in a text file list, plus the (specified) harmonics of those pitches.

[111] The phase Vocoder represents a sound as a series of windows, like the frames of a film, each window describing the instantaneous spectrum of the sound at that time. *Spectral blurring* blurs the spectral detail of a sound by discarding a specified proportion of these spectral windows, replacing them with data interpolated between the remaining windows. Compare *Spectral Tracing*.

Word dance 2

Syllables are looped at a regular speed, with simple polyrhythmic and imitative devices, underlining the harmonic qualities of the various speech-segments.

Perturbations

Zig-zagged readings of successive text elements[112], and rapidly panned individual syllables, sometimes evolving in colour, pitch or articulation, form an evolving panorama.

Misstatement

So far we have produced various surprising new materials by 'dividing the labour' - reconstructing the original text. Here, however, the original text appears to be recapitulated in its original setting but, despite the plausible tone-of-voice delivery, the original phrases have their syllables rearranged. The meaning of the text is pointedly destroyed.

Liquidation/Toll

A dense mass of syllables from the text 'breathes' through two alternating tuned filters. Beneath this, the words of the text are spectrally traced[113], and their most prominent partials bubble through the texture. In the *Toll,* a sequence of syllables in descending pitch order is chosen from the text. As the falling sequence repeats, the pitches are focused through filters tuned to each particular word, which becomes more invasive on each repetition. A second filter is tuned to *all* these text pitches. The words eventually dissolve, generating the metallic 'grand bells'.

Hubbub

Toll continues over layers of *Imitation* & *Song without Words*, decorated by extracts from *Word Dance II* and *Chorus* (plus other variations).

Trace

A trace of the pitch and vowel colour of the text remains, with a faint echo of the changing rhythm of the speech in the tremulations of the sound. The human voice has finally disappeared from view

.. and finally

Work on this piece was made possible through an AHRB Creative Arts Fellowship, and a residency at the University of Birmingham electro-acoustic music studio, director Jonty Harrison. It was made entirely on a PC, using the CDP software.

---

[112] i.e. the soundfile is read first forward to some point, then in reverse from that point to an earlier time, then from that time forward again to another later time and so on.

[113] *Spectral Tracing* discards a specified number of the (least loud) channels of spectral information *within every window* of the phase Vocoder representation. Discarding almost all the channels leaves a thin trace of the most prominent partials of a sound as it fluctuates from moment to moment.

TWO WOMEN

&

AMERICAN TRIPTYCH

TWO WOMEN & AMERICAN TRIPTYCH

Introduction

Two Women and *American Tripytch* marked a new departure in sound composition for voices. Rather than working solely with sound transformation, or with a mythically constructed world, I decided to attempt to treat the voices of well-known public figures in the manner of personal portraits or political cartoons. I called these new works *Voiceprints*, after the voice recordings used by the police to trace suspects or missing persons.

For this to work successfully for a worldwide audience I needed to find voices which would be recognised on the world stage, rather than just in the UK. At this time (the 1990s), the most well-known British voices in the wider world were those of two women, Margaret Thatcher and Princess Diana, and not the voices of any male politicians or dignitaries, a significant fact in itself. My aim was to work with the grain of the recorded voices to comment on the personalities or stances of the speakers.

In the longer term, however, these pieces would have to stand in their own right, once the persons involved were no longer household names (and I have already played the piece to young people who have no idea who either Princess Diana or Margaret Thatcher are). So they would need to be satisfying musical experiences even when the voices of the subjects were no longer recognised.

Two Women

Two Women uses the voices of Princess Diana and Margaret Thatcher. It was important to work not only with the voices of recognisable people, but to develop the distinctive characteristics of their voices in some appropriate way.

Margaret Thatcher is said to have had her voice coached to lower the pitch and to project a more dominant personal style. The particular pronouncement here from St Francis of Assisi - *"Where there is discord, may we bring harmony"* - completely contradicts her political style, as testified by members of her own cabinet. Her rise to power coincided with the end of a long libertarian era in British life, and this speech heralded the market astringencies to come.

The piece opens with railway station announcements, but the implied journey becomes increasingly unreal as the voices of the Apollo 11 astronauts float by, and the sound of a wailing siren adds a sense of foreboding. The siren is in fact derived from Margaret Thatcher's voice, but as we don't at first hear this connection, it appears to be simply a siren. The voice is revealed as the music unfolds.

The sound is generated by vastly time-stretching the initial syllable of the vocal phrase, pitch-shifting it (without vowel change) to two other pitches, mixing these in parallel and sliding the pitch slowly up and down (sample-rate variation). Eventually the time-stretched syllable leads into the complete spoken phrase, but retaining the parallel pitches of the siren. The word "harmony" is repeated, and on its final appearance its last syllable is greatly extended while the parallel pitch-lines slide together into a jarring cluster and the sound is distorted by phasing artefacts (from the time-stretching). This leads us into the cutup voice of a sheep salesman at Malton market. The clattering bells which accompany him are the clattering of the metal-grill doors of sheep pens (passed through pitch-sliding filter banks) as the sheep are delivered for sale **(Sound Example 74)**.

In contrast, Diana's voice seems to suggest a fragile personality, and my aim in working with this material was to emphasize this fragility. In movement two, I use a process of waveset repetition, and this is one of the few of my pieces where I focus on a single transformation process. This process divides the sound-signal into chunks called wavesets, measured out by counting zero-crossings, and these chunks are then repeated. As this method of chopping up the signal is somewhat irrational, the process can throw up musically interesting transformations. It can also produce unwanted artefacts, so it is a matter of experimentation to discover appropriate settings - the number of wavesets to grab as repeatable blocks - that give musically useful results with the sound being processed. Also, it's necessary to choose enough wavesets to capture features of the existing signal if these are to be preserved – too few and the source is simply grittily distorted, too many and one produces a simple montage with odd glitches.

The algorithm works interestingly with speech because the voiced and unvoiced parts of the speech-stream are transformed quite differently. The voiced elements of speech have significant-sized wavesets, related to the pitch of the voice at that moment so that repeating a small group of wavesets effectively echoes the pitch-content of the voice. The unvoiced elements, however, consist of noise signals, which have very many random zero-crossings, and hence many tiny wavesets, within the same time-span as a single waveset of the voiced material. Although these tiny wavesets are of random duration and shape, once any one (or small set) is repeated a sufficient number of times it becomes a tiny oscillator producing a brief high pitch, and the sequence of these arbitrary pitches and colours appears like strange electronic birdsong. Using this algorithm progressively, the fragile voice is increasingly fragmented.

The phrase used (about professional photographers) is *"There was a relationship which worked before, but now I can't tolerate it because it's become abusive, and it's harassment"*. Each section of the movement has several layers of the waveset-treated phrase, each with a different number of waveset-repetitions, positioned differently in the stereo space. This produces a delayed echo between the layers with the delay-time increasing but in a random way depending on the durations of the individual waveset-blocks captured.

As we progress from one section to another the number of wavesets in all streams increases so that the twittering and other artefacts become more prominent and the voice gradually begins to dissolve in these artefacts. As it does so, certain pitches emerge and these are emphasized through selective reverberation **(Sound Example 75)**. Towards the end of the movement we hear the soft sound of breaking glass and the soundscape shudders before the opening material re-emerges.

Movement three takes a sermon of Ian Paisley, a fiery preacher and politician from Northern Ireland, condemning Margaret Thatcher to the wrath of God for her role in the developing political process. *"O God, defeat all our enemies ... we hand this woman, Margaret Thatcher, over to the devil, that she might learn not to blaspheme. And O God in wrath, take vengeance upon this wicked, treacherous, lying woman ... Take vengeance upon her O Lord!"*. This material is already melodramatic, and the melodrama is parodied in various ways.

Words are extended by first converting them to a time series of spectral windows (with the Phase Vocoder). Two identical copies are then stretched by freezing the sound at a specific (but different) time-window in each copy. The two copies are then precisely synchronised.

Original pitchline

At A and B below, 2 signals identical, so combination indistinguishable from original

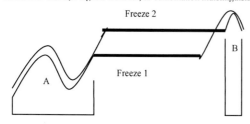

Freeze 2

Freeze 1

A

B

Canonic repetition of speech phrases (*"Defeat all our enemies"* etc) at rising pitches using a process which does not preserve the original speech vowels makes the voice increasingly comic as it ascends. Metallic-sounding long-timestretching of transient-consonants create a percussive vocal weaponry, reminiscent of similar procedures in *Red Bird*, and the whole scene is animated by miscellaneous thunderclaps, rentings, tearings, growlings, and randomly cutup line-dance music.

Movement four plays with very-long time-stretches of the voice source, and harmonic materials derived from these. For example the pedal points of the opening derive from huge time-stretches of pitches of the phrase *"a fairy story"*. The phrase itself is then introduced at normal speed, repeated, emerging gradually from a spectrally blurred version, and then subsiding back into it **(Sound Example 76)**. The phrase *"It's been worthwhile, yes it has"*, is textured, becoming very dense, then filter focused to a pitch as it rises to eventually tune onto an octave of one of the pedals **(Sound Example 77)**.

Later on the phrase *"60 to 90 photographers"* is time-variably timestretched in an elaborate way, the sibilants in particular being extremely extended, and the similarly extended final "rapher" articulated by steeply falling repeated envelopes which pluck the sound, their fluctuating durations determined by waveset counting. These various noiseband and plucked variants pan around the stereo space **(Sound Example 78)**.

The four movements are tied together by the station announcements and the sounds of trains from York station which open the piece and the journey, and into which the final movement merges at its close. The sounds of the train-wheel screeches have been made more melodious by passing them through filter-banks tuned close to their original pitches.

Two Women comes with specific suggestions for diffusion (see the last chapter of this book). The 2nd movement should be quiet, and intimate (using small loudspeakers close to the audience). This can be developed to fill the acoustic space, as suggested in the final chapter. The 3rd movement, God's wrath, requires exaggerated spatial projection, using the full range of the space in which the piece is played, the voice coming from many different directions at different moments. This was first diffused in the Parochialkirke in Berlin, a church in the form of an equal-armed cross, with loudspeakers placed deep within each arm, as well as at standard positions in front and around the audience seating in the centre of the cross. The voice could be made to emerge (and rush between) the four distant locations, or to fill the whole space.

American Triptych

Having worked successfully on the four short portraits of *Two Women*, and in response to a commission from the G.R.M. in Paris I decided to try the same approach in a more through-composed piece, with three icons of the American dream, Martin Luther King, Elvis Presley and Neil Armstrong, the first man on the moon.

In addition to who and what they represented, these voices were chosen for their contrasting characteristics, each offering different musical possibilities. Martin Luther King's voice has the feeling of heightened, floating song; Elvis' is full of exaggerated rhythmic articulation; Neil Armstrong's, although much more ordinary in most respects, has been captured through the distorting prism of transmission from space over a narrow-bandwidth communication channel, and it was this aspect of the voice source I would work with. These voices, and some bleeps and distortion noises from the space-transmission, form the substance of the entire piece, and I'll point to just some of the ways in which these materials are developed.

The song-like projection of Luther King's voice is captured simply by extremely long time-stretching of individual syllables, using a combination of spectral domain stretching (with the Phase Vocoder) and time-domain stretching (with Brassage). The fluidness of vocal pitch and spectrum within tiny syllables and the artefacts of the various time-stretching processes extends these tiny syllables into grand lines with unusual cadences **(Sound Example 79)**. At the end of the piece, repetition of a motto

"Let" is eventually released into the full phrase "*Let it ring*", where "ring" is time-extended in the same way but steep descending envelopes are gradually added to the sustained sound, timed (semi-irregularly) by counting wavesets, producing bell-like sequences. These occur simultaneously in different streams of rising and falling pitch (sample-rate variation) alongside other related materials **(Sound Example 80)**.

Various "boo-bop" syllables from Presley's voice are assembled into a stereo texture, which increases in density and is later transformed in various ways (waveset enveloping with very very short envelopes, giving the sound a gritty quality). These are animated by foregrounded individually attacked syllables **(Sound Example 81)**. In the third section of the piece this strand returns, using its unattacked pitch material against the consonant attacks **(Sound Example 82)**, and using a "bounced" editing-together of one-syllable as a response to the Martin Luther King material **(Sound Example 83)** and in various other guises. Also, more sibilant-based attacks are used which, towards the very end of section one, are spectrally blurred, losing their rhythmic edge. At the section end, these combine with the rhythmicised attack syllables, now clipped (edited very short) **(Sound Example 84)**.

In contrasting sections using Armstrong's voice, I decided to expand the low-quality aspects of the transmission, using the communication bleep and fragments of the transmission noise as sources. The voice itself is treated in ways which distort it further, many different types of waveset distortion being applied (e.g. waveset averaging, waveset omission). At the start of section two the voice is shredded (this involves cutting the source into random segments, reassembling these in random order, then repeating this process on the output as many times as desired). This material is followed by an area of more radical fragmentation using waveset-block-repetition (see above), with layers of the resulting material transposed to different registers **(Sound Example 85)**. During the section, such textured distorted materials are intercut with clear vocal phrases ("*Tranquility base here*").

Later these three approaches to the voices (long extended syllables, rhythmic pulsing, heavy distortion) are combined over all three voices **(Sound Example 86)**.

.. and finally

Two Women was commissioned by the DAAD, and received its first performance in the 50th Anniversary of Musique Concrete concert at the Parochialkirke in Berlin in September, 1998, using the diffusion system of the Berlin Technical University. *American Triptych* was commissioned by the French Government for performance at the G.R.M.'s January, 2000 *Cycle Acousmatique* at Radio France in Paris.

IMAGO

IMAGO

(Sound examples are on disc 2).

Origins of the Project: The Source Material

In 2002 I was asked to make a one minute piece for Jonty Harrison's surprise 50th birthday concert, using sound sources from his work. The piece was to be just 1 minute long, part of a collection of 50 pieces by various composers and students. I used two brief sources for that piece, but one of them, the single clink of 2 whisky-glasses from '*et ainsi de suite*', proved to be much more interesting. This superficially 'simple' pitched sound contained a surprising richness of possibilities which I only touched upon in making the 1 minute piece, so I began to explore it further.

At about the same time I was challenged by a composer friend[114], a sophisticated listener to instrumental music, who claimed he found it impossible to follow the logic of sound compositions, i.e. compositions not involving live performers. I have subsequently heard related comments from other traditional instrumental/vocal composers e.g. that all electro-acoustic music appears to them to be monophonic (i.e. having just one musical line, as opposed to polyphonic, carrying several musical lines simultaneously). *Imago* was partly a musical riposte to this challenge – to make an electro-acoustic piece whose musical logic is extremely clear (just as, say, the unfolding of a Fugue is very clear) but without sacrificing the sensuous excitement of the sounds and their transformations.

Precomposition

As with *Tongues of Fire* I began by systematically exploring the source. In this case the sound is less than $1/10^{th}$ of a second in duration **(Sound Example 1)**. The most obvious initial approaches were to time-stretch the sound in various ways (discussed below), and to develop these time-stretched variants. Time-stretching might involve preserving the attack, so the tail of the sound gets longer. We still associate the new sound with the original, as the most characteristic feature of the original sound (in fact almost its only obvious feature) is the attack. For example, as the loudness of the tail is rapidly decreasing and its spectrum rapidly changing, if we read rapidly back and forth at random along this tail[115] the sound level and spectral-brightness rise and fall with the back and forth reading, making the sound 'flutter' in quality and level. Such sounds can be heard in paragraph 2 of *Imago* (see below). Or the whole sound, including the attack, might be stretched. In this case, with a sufficiently long stretch, the attack-characteristic of the sound, its most defining feature, dissolves away and we generate spectrally fluid coloured-noise sounds. In this case we have to be sure to link the listener's perception to the original source if we wish to preserve the notion that noise-like sounds are *musically* derived from the attack-resonance source. More elaborate developments of the source are described in more detail below.

I also decided to use a very simple motif, the original sound rapidly repeated, rising in pitch **(Sound Example 2)**. This simple motif can itself be varied in several obvious ways. It can e.g.

---

[114] Jolyon Laycock.
[115] The CDP program *zigzag* allows random (or user-specified) back and forth reading of a soundfile.

- rise by portamento (each item glides up to the next) or by step (the items do not glide, but the pitch steps up from one item to the next);
- rise-then-fall, or fall-then-rise;
- accelerate, or decelerate, or accelerate-decelerate etc;
- run faster, either by placing events closer together, or by contracting the events themselves;
- become extremely regular, like a rhythmic pulse;
- move in space;

and so on. The various sound elements generated in this way were then used to create musical phrases which then combine to create the entire form of the piece.

The Form of the piece

The essential feature of the piece is the gradual metamorphosis of one sound or soundscape into another. The piece moves from the initial bald statement of the 'theme' (the single 'clink') and the related motif (see above) to generate more and more sonic materials by (I hope) clearly audible processes of sonic transformation. These eventually lead to a number of surprising 'meta-events', sounds suggesting ocean waves, the human voice and the music of a 'scrapyard gamelan'. The larger scale form also involves some (obvious) 'repetitions' (usually in contracted or extended form) of materials heard earlier in the piece, acting as large-scale structural markers, as with a traditional piece of instrumental music (e.g. the section of very slow, soft vibraphone-like 'bells' starting at c. 7mins 13 seconds into the piece, and 'repeated' at c. 16 minutes 25 seconds).

The piece clearly falls into a number of distinct sections or 'paragraphs' (not necessarily with complete breaks between them). I will begin by discussing the first 2 paragraphs in detail, which will illustrate some of the principle features of *Imago* and then go on to describe the emergence of larger scale features in the rest of the piece. I won't attempt to discuss every facet of the work here.

Paragraph 1
(Sound Example 3)
In this paragraph, the whole agenda of the piece is laid out, the ideas of motivic and, most importantly, spectral development. We can divide the paragraph into 6 distinct phrases (although the 5th, the *'spectral cauldron'* is more like several phrases rolled into one).

Paragraph 1: Phrase 1

(Sound Example 4)
The first phrase presents us with the source material of the piece. We hear the single source-sound, then we hear it repeated, to emphasize its importance. Then we hear it repeated as a (portamento) rising motif. One important aspect of this phrase is that it is relatively uninteresting. Just a few notes, all the same spectrum, no movement or reverberation to give it any sense of space - a 'flat' image. But as the piece unfolds we will develop some truly surprising sound-landscapes from this apparently unpromising material. The later sense of 'magic' is thus underlined by the apparent lack of excitement of this opening.

As described previously, the source of the entire piece lies in the very first event, the single clink of two whisky-glasses. Although we will also develop the simple motivic idea, most of the sound material of the piece evolves out of this single clink. Superficially the sound appears very simple, and clearly pitched. However it is quite a complex sound, with a rich inharmonic[116] attack, leading to a more pitch-focused ending, but all going past in the twinkling of an ear (within $1/10^{th}$ of a second). We can't focus on these details unless we time-stretch the sound.

Sound Example 5 progressively time-stretches this sound to reveal the inharmonic attack spectrum. We now hear the initial *inharmonicity* of the sound - but stretching this attack has also generated an altogether *different* type of sound. It no longer appears to be struck - The percept "struck-resonate" disappears - a significant transformation has been made. To generate sound-types more closely related to the original we must use types of time-stretching which *preserve the attack of the sound*. We can create a great variety of bell-like sounds with different, but related, spectra by freezing the spectrum[117] of the sound at different points. For a more inharmonic result we freeze the spectrum near the start of the sound; for a more pitched result, we freeze it near the sound's end.

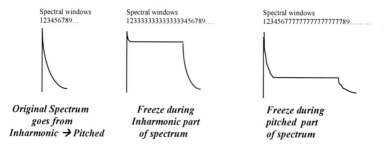

Spectral windows
123456789....

Spectral windows
123333333333333333456789....

Spectral windows
12345677777777777777777789.........

Original Spectrum
goes from
Inharmonic → Pitched

Freeze during
Inharmonic part
of spectrum

Freeze during
pitched part
of spectrum

(The representation of the sequence of *spectral windows* here is only schematic;
there are hundreds of spectral windows in the spectral analysis file of our source sound).

Because the attack part of the spectrum is relatively unstable (changing all the time), by choosing slightly different times near the start of the spectrum we can generate different inharmonic spectra.

---

[116] Sounds with a single clear pitch (known as harmonic sounds) have a spectrum in which the frequencies of the individual partials are integral multiples of the frequency of their lowest partial. In an inharmonic spectrum, this simple numerical relationship between the partials does not hold. Even sounds which appear clearly pitch can however have inharmonic components in their attack portion, as here.

[117] A spectral analysis of the sound is made, consisting of a time-sequence of spectral windows. The sound can be resynthesized from these windows taken one at a time in sequential order. We then specify a specific window (or the time of the window) and a duration, Resynthesis then proceeds normally, from each window in sequence, up until the specified window; then the next part of the sound is synthesized entirely from the selected window, for the duration specified; then we continue synthesizing from the succeeding windows in the normal way.

We must also re-envelope the loudness contour of the time-frozen sound, to retain the attack-resonance morphology (a sudden attack dying gradually to zero).

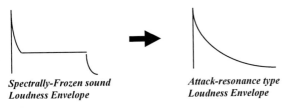

Spectrally-Frozen sound
Loudness Envelope

Attack-resonance type
Loudness Envelope

We may also transpose (change the sample-rate[118]) of the sound to change its pitch (the attack is so abrupt on the source sound that it is not significantly perceptually altered by such transpositions) and we can stack transposed copies on top of one another so that their attacks are *absolutely in synchronisation*[119]. In this way, the resulting sound appears as a *single percept*; we hear a single sound source with a harmony resonance, not a chord of several sources (psycho-acoustic merging of sources[120]). A variety of bell-like sounds can be generated in this way **(Sound example 6)**. The last bell in the sound example is stereo, with slightly different spectral characteristics on each channel, and a semi-irregular tremolando has been added to give the long sound some 'life'. These bell-like sounds are heard together at the culmination of a paragraph 1 phrase **(Sound example 7)**.

Paragraph 1: Phrase 2

In the 2nd phrase of the 1st paragraph **(Sound example 8)** we introduce a simple variation of the motif. . Here the variations of the motif already begin …

- It is longer and slower. The events rise and then fall in pitch.
- Each note is stable in pitch (the notes originally slid upwards), a subtle spectral variation.
- Most importantly, the motif *moves* (circles) in the stereo space.

This introduces the idea of spatial articulation, which is very important in the piece. Spatial motion helps to characterise individual musical streams in counterstreamed[121] sections. The continuous motion (or lack of motion) of a stream of events helps to make it cohere, and differentiates it from other lines which move differently (or fail to move). Unlike instrumental lines in traditional music, individual sonic streams may undergo sound metamorphosis as they unfold, so spatial coherence becomes a more important clue in differentiating the different streams.

---

[118] We in fact resample the sound, as if it were at a different sampling rate, but represent the new sound in the original sampling rate – the sampling rate of the new soundfile is the same as the original.
[119] Stacking transposed copies of a single source on top of one another, and synchronising the attack time of the various copies, can be achieved in the CDP *Radical: Stack* program.
[120] See my book *Audible Design* for further discussion of such psycho-acoustic phenomena.
[121] By analogy with 'counterpoint' in traditional scored music. In counterpoint, two (or more) independent melodic lines are composed to be performed at the same time, but in such a way that the harmonic progression produced makes sense within the harmonic tradition of the musical language. Counterstreaming implies the superimposition of sound-streams, each if which may be developing or metaporphosing in its own right, but in such a way that the streams interact (rhythmically or 'gesturally') in a way which is meaningful in a larger musical scale logic.

Paragraph 1: Phrase 3

Phrase 3 is suddenly more interesting **(Sound example 9)**. Here, the final rising figure, *motivically*, is just a rapid accelerando, a variant of the original motif. But the acceleration is so rapid that it actually generates a *rising pitch*[122]. So we've converted motivic variation into spectral variation. This first piece of 'magical' transformation is emphasized by adding reverberation to the end of the sound, and it leads without a pause into the next phrase (phrase 4) which starts with the rising motif (rather than the single attack which starts the first 3 phrases), enhanced by adding a rapid upward portamento to the resonance of the last note, giving the music (so far quite static) more sense of forward momentum.

Paragraph 1: Phrase 4

And in this next phrase, the music begins to take off **(Sound example 10)**. The simple sequence of 3 events, heard in phrases 1 and 2, is now dissolving. We can think of this new phrase in 2 parts. In the first part, we begin with the motif (rather than the single attack) and the 3rd item (which was the motif in the 2 previous phrases) is greatly expanded into a rapidly repeating note which gradually spreads its pitch-range, and its range across the stereo space.

The part two, which follows on without a break, **(Sound Example 11)** also starts with the motif, now on a fixed pitch, much longer, and circling in space, echoing the tempo of the immediately previous version material. The 2nd event of this second part is attackless (for the first time) and crescendos to the position of the 3rd event where the motif is reintroduced as anacrusis to phrase 5. By the end of this phrase, the simple 3-event structure of the opening phrases has dissolved away.

More importantly we now begin to develop sounds with completely new spectra. In the first sound of part two, we move from a single pitch to a harmony, not via any chord progression but simply by a transformation of the spectrum itself. This is the first example of a *spectral sequence,* and much of the spectral development of the piece depends on these. A spectral sequence is a succession of events in which the spectrum, or quality, of the sound used gradually changes. In this way we can 'modulate' from one kind of sound material to another, analogous to the idea of modulation between keys in traditional tonal music. In *Imago* these new sounds become material for further sound transformations and for musical phrase-building.

This transition from a single pitch to a harmony is made by...

- making a harmonic stack from (precisely synchronised) transposed copies of the original sound;
- making a series of sounds intermediate between the original (singly pitched) sound and the harmonic sound, by a process of inbetweening (essentially a set of weighed mixes)[123].

---

[122] The same effect is generated if two heavy bottomed glasses and lifted out of a washing-up bowl. The 2 glasses bounce off each other in a rapidly accelerating sequence, and we hear a rising sliding pitched sound.

[123] *Mix inbetween* in the CDP allows a sequence of weighted mixes between two sounds to be made. E.g. specifying 3 intermediate mixes of sounds A and B will produce 3 mixes in the (loudness) ratios 1:3, 2:2 (= 1:1) and 3:1. Non-linear sequences can be generated. The *Sound Loom* includes an *Interpolation Workshop* where the sequence of mixes can be adjusted (e.g. interpolations between

The precise attack-synchronisation prevents us from 'reading' the combined sounds as a chord of separate events. The harmonic content appears to gradually emerge *within* the sound itself.

Inbetweening works best with sounds derived from one another by *waveset distortion*[124] in which the zero crossings in the source remain synchronised with those in the transformed sound. Mixing between sounds generated in this way is in fact a spectral transformation as we are merely altering the waveshape of the sounds. But waveset distortion is a physically irrational process leading to curious (and musically interesting) artefacts which radically alter the spectrum of the original sound. Using waveset distortion and inbetweening to create spectral sequences we can make sounds with completely new spectral characteristics emerge from our original source.

Many of these sequences are used in the next phrase, the *'spectral cauldron'*. Here is an example where the bell-like original becomes more like a 'drum' or 'thump'.
(Sound Example 12)
Or, we can make a spectral sequence, then accelerate the sequence so that the elements and effectively fuse together **(Sound Example 13)**[125]. And finally we can make this event portamento slide in pitch[126] **(Sound Example 14).**

Returning to the second sound in this second part of phrase 4, after the bright bell-like attacks we hear a sustained sound which crescendos, then fades (before more 'bells' enter). This is the first attackless event we have heard. **(Sound Example 15)** and in the context of all the brightly attacked events around it, it appears *un*impressive. But it will become very significant later.

It is an example of a *Fugu* sound, and it is made from our original attack-resonance source. The natural characteristics of an attack-resonance sound are that it begins very brightly and then its high frequencies fade away more quickly than its low frequencies while the level dies away to nothing. We make the Fugu sound by first making a time-reversed copy of the sound, then splicing this copy onto the start of the original.

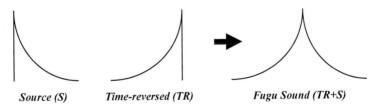

Source (S)   *Time-reversed (TR)*   *Fugu Sound (TR+S)*

With the fugu sound, the sound emerges very quietly with low frequencies only and, as it gets louder, it becomes brighter as the higher frequencies in the spectrum enter. It then reaches a peak of maximum loudness and brightness before dying away, with the high frequencies disappearing first. This is exactly what happens when we hear a

---

already interpolated sounds can be made, or individual interpolated items deleted) until an audibly satisfactory sequence of interpolations is produced.
[124] See *Audible Design*.
[125] Note how the rapid double-pan is used to spatially characterise this event.
[126] By progressive sample-rate change.

sound moving towards then away from us. So these spatial implications of the fugu sound can be very useful.

We can make a whole sequence of fugu sounds from the same source, by fading in towards the peak, but reversing (into the fading out portion) *before* the true peak is reached. In this way we produce a sequence of fugu sounds which approach closer and closer to the loud, bright peak before receding.[127]

The sounds can also be varied by transposition, and subsequent stacking **(Sound Example 16)**. In this case, as our Fugu examples are symmetrical (the 2nd half is the mirror of the 1st) we can simply mix transposed copies of the sound, synchronising them at the centre points of the sound[128], this becomes a very significant transformation later in the piece.

Paragraph 1: Phrase 5: 'spectral cauldron'

The next phrase is where different kind of attack-resonance spectra are generated from the original source, using the *spectral sequence* idea, rapidly expanding the sound-palette of the piece. For this reason I call this section the '*spectral cauldron*' **(Sound example 17)**.

A particularly significant phrase is the 'dipper', using the transformation towards a 'drum-like' sound (heard in Sound Example 12) and back again. This is used as an anacrusis[129] event throughout the piece. We hear it here for the first time, twice, in the spectral cauldron **(Sound example 18).**

Paragraph 1: Phrase 6

We now come to the final phrase of paragraph 1. Here the tail of our source gets a *pitch-slide* (and no other spectral change), and then the starting pitches of the motif move about. Once the attack-resonance sound glides, it suggests an elasticity or fluidity in the physical nature of the source which we unconsciously associate with vocal production (rather than with rigid objects, like whisky-glasses or bells). This is the first of several *sonic allusions* to natural-world sounds in the piece. This one

---

[127] This explains my use of the term 'Fugu'. The Fugu fish is a Japanese delicacy. The fish has a poisonous liver, but tastes best close to the liver. Cutting pieces closer and closer to the liver is more and more tasty, and more and more dangerous. The idea for making Fugu sequences of sounds came from Denis Smalley.

[128] Centre-point synchronisation of mix data is an option in the CDP.

[129] Anacrusis: a musical event that leads into, and announces the arrival of, another, more significant, event.

suggests birdsong: it clearly is not birdsong but makes a sonic allusion to it, lying ambiguously between an attack-resonance event and a vocally-produced event. **(Sound example 19)**.

This bird allusion is reinforced by flocking these sounds into a texture[130] (birds in flocks typically produce the same song, varied over a narrow range of pitches, in a time-random way, e.g. herring gulls or starlings). But the texture soon becomes so dense that the original characteristics of the sources are smeared out; the spectral range is filled. This smeared out texture slides in pitch, then undergoes a final transformation. The texture fills the stereo space, but the illusion of stereo is created by just two signals in the two loudspeakers. By applying slightly different, steeply falling waveset-based[131] envelopes to these two channels the mass of sound resolves into two musical streams of noise impulses. As this sequence of impulses is made to decelerate, it is gradually filtered[132] with Q[133] sufficient to make the filter pitches 'ring'. The resulting sounds appear 'plucked', leading us back to the attack-resonance character of the source.**(Sound example 20)**. Thus the whole *spectral metamorphosis agenda* of the piece is set out in this first paragraph, it's an exposition of this idea of continual spectral development.

Paragraph 2

We'll now pick up one or two threads from Paragraph 2 **(Sound example 21)** to help us in tracing the larger-scale developments in the piece. This paragraph generates many other new sound types from the source, particularly extensions of the tail of the sound whose spectra 'flutter' or have irregular tremolo or vibrato effects. One of these circles around the stereo space like a glass marble rolling around a dish[134] **(Sound example 22)**. Also important are regular pulse variants of the motif.

---

[130] In a 'texture' (as used here) many sounds are overlaid in a time-irregular way. If these are copies of the same sound, these will usually vary, at least slightly, in pitch and amplitude.

[131] The envelopes are generated at times defined by counting zero-crossings in the signals. In a complex source such as this, counting a fixed number of zero-crossings leads to a semi-random (naturalistic) time-sequence of envelope attacks.

[132] Using the CDP *varibank* filters.

[133] The Q of a filter is a measure of the narrowness of the filter band. Filtering broadband noise with a filter at, say, 2000 Hz and a low Q will produce most of higher frequency (centred on 2000 Hz). If the Q is high enough this will appear as a single tone of frequency 2000 Hz. If the filter Q is not quite so high, noise strongly coloured with the 2000 Hz pitch will be produced.

[134] The spatial circulation is created by left→right→left→etc panning, slowing at the edges of the space, and an increase in level moving to the centre in one direction, but a decrease (plus some filtering out of high frequencies) when moving in the opposite direction, creating a sense of front and rear for the rotation. The level changes rotate slightly ahead of the spatial panning (so the sound is at its loudest just after leaving the loudspeaker, as it moves 'towards' us, rather than when it reaches the centre of the space) giving a more psychologically convincing illusion of rotation. Also, as no doppler shift is used, the illusion is that of observing rotation in a *magnified small space* rather than rotation around a large spatial arena.

1: The Gamelan

To follow the emergence of larger-scale events later in the piece, we begin by tracing the development of the click-like pattern which appears in paragraph 2. At the very start of that paragraph, we hear this click-sound emerging from the source (via waveset distortion) in a spectral sequence, ad on its next occurence this sound is 'looped', or rather it moves back and forth between the source and the click-like variant with a crescendo-decrescendo while moving around in space. **(Sound example 23)**

Eventually it evolves into a repeated rhythmic cell, forming an introductory phrase to a rather ungainly melody on a clunky-gamelan-like sound. This concludes with a machine-like riff derived from the click-sound and a decelerating tail **(Sound example 24)**. Later in the piece, these 3 types of material, click-looping, funny gamelan and machine-riff, recur with the machine-riff heard first **(Sound example 25.)**

There are also soft echoes of this 'gamelan' and also of the 'dipper' spectral sequence (see earlier), at certain points in the piece, to give both a memory-trace of past events and a sense of expectation. These traces are softened by *smudging* the spectrum (like smudging an image drawn with a very soft pencil), using *spectral blurring*[135]. The blurring averages the spectrum over a given number of time-snapshots (spectral windows), and we can increase or decrease the amount of smudging, depending on the situation. Here we can hear the original source of the dipper, followed by the same sound extended and smudged in **Sound example 26**.

The dipper is used as an anacrusial event in the piece, announcing the arrival of other sound events. In the middle of the piece both the dipper and the funny gamelan, both in smudged form, appear behind the foreground sounds. The first occurrence of the dipper here (overlaying the second entry of the softened gamelan) is an almost continuous line of soft 'noise' (rather than a sequence of discrete attacks) as it is very strongly blurred. As the dipper recurs, it comes increasingly into focus (less blurring) until eventually precipitating another occurrence of the machine-like riff heard in sound-example 24 **(Sound example 27)**.

Eventually the slightly comic 'funny gamelan' material emerges as a magnificent large-scale event **(Sound example 28)**, like the swan from the 'Ugly Duckling' in Hans Christian Andersen's tale. The gamelan instruments are constructed from spectral objects derived from the original source, especially by octave-stacking copies to make (apparently) larger and larger 'gongs' **(Sound example 29)**. The slightly clunky quality of the instruments is produced partly by using two copies of any

---

[135] Spectral blurring is a CDP process I wrote many years ago, but first used significantly in *Imago*. The sound is analysed into a time-sequence of spectral windows, using the Phase Vocoder. Then a certain portion ($> \frac{1}{2}$) of the windows are replaced by new windows which are simply interpolations of the values in the remaining original windows. Thus, the time-detail of the spectrum is lost. For example, speech treated in this way appears increasingly 'drunk' as the blurring becomes more intense (a higher proportion of windows are replaced).

particular 'gong', separated in space, with a slight time-delay between them. This is an 'urban gamelan' of car hub-caps and the like, rather than of traditional gongs. The melodic material employs an oddly tuned scale, not a standard tempered scale, nor a scale of equal intervals (as used for some traditional gamelan tunings) but a mixture of both **(Sound example 30)**. The gamelan music is constructed in the traditional way, using rhythmic layers which have tempi in multiples of 2. The material in each rhythmic layer is very similar but not completely identical, and there are several other elements in the 'orchestrated' mix, especially when the whole gamelan phrase is repeated.

2: The Oracle

We can now trace a 2nd feature which emerges in paragraph 2. We have already noted that time-stretching the attack of our source by a large amount destroys the attack-resonance sound-image. The attack moment is smeared away, and we are left with spectrally-coloured noise. This noise-like quality can be enhanced by mixing many (transposed) versions of the time-stretched sound in a texture. This begins to happen to the source in paragraph 2. In our sound example we hear the rising motif being repeated, but as it repeats the attacks of the sound events are gradually smeared away **(Sound example 31)**. Putting this into context, we now hear these events interrupted by a foreground of attack-resonance sounds but, at the very end, our noise background *shudders*[136].
(Sound example 32).

This eventually leads to the 2nd magical transformation in the piece. Here the noise-texture gradually emerges in the pauses between the dramatic foreground events (various waveset distortion transformations of the source), then grows much louder after a deep bell sound, until eventually (triggered by the rising motif from the opening of the piece) it shudders and begins to disappear into a reverberant abyss. Finally, triggered by another deep 'bell' sound, a completely surprising transformation occurs **(Sound example 33)**. This voice-like metamorphosis is produced by using time-varying filters (on the spectrum of the shuddered noise) which mimic the behaviour of vowels. Here I devised an instrument where one specifies the required vowel (as a text) and the time at which it occurs. If the vowel at the next specified time is different, the filter will interpolate from the first vowel to the second, as in the natural flow of human speech (our mouth moves in a continuous fashion from one vowel to the next; it naturally morphs from one vowel shape to another). In the piece, there is a different vowel-articulation on each of the left and right channels. Here's an example from one of the mono sources **(Sound example 34)**.

The characteristics of the vowel filters were derived partly from the published literature and partly from experimenting (especially with placement of the third formant[137]). The standard literature tends to assume that we all speak with a standard

---

[136] Shudder: a time-randomised tremolo which is randomly spread over the stereo space. Now an algorithm in the CDP.
[137] Formant: roughly speaking, a peak in the spectrum of a sound. Vowel sounds are characterised by such peaks in the spectrum, so that we can hear the same vowel, *even if the pitch of the underlying sound changes*, because the spectral peaks can remain *at the same (central) frequencies* even when the

accent. In the piece *The Division of Labour* I had to model the Glaswegian accent of my source speaker, which is not at all close to 'standard English' pronunciation. This led me to try to model formants for myself.

3: Fugu and The Sea

In many of the previous examples we began by time-stretching the source, but we can also use time-contraction. This works best on the motivic *sequence* of events. Pushing the events very close together can lead to a 'gritty' or 'scratchy' result[138] **(Sound example 35)**.

Here is a section where this time-contraction is used. The falling pitch sequence is repeated with the sound events closer and closer together, and eventually they almost merge into a continuous sound. The spectrally rich tail of the resulting sound is extended, made to glide down in pitch, and subtle irregular vibrato adde. **(Sound example 36)**. After the 2nd group of these events we can hear the *Fugu* sound once again, now much extended in time, and with more harmonic content (produced by filtering, then stacking transpositions) **(Sound example 37)**.

In the next examples, over the pitched bubbling, we hear our motif both time-contracted and time-expanded. The time-contractions become very gritty in quality as the attacks become extremely close together. The time-stretched sequences have their attacks smeared out, becoming more like coloured noise **(Sound example 38)**. More and more events, some pitch-sliding, are added to the texture, the gritty events in particular racing around the stereo-space, creating a hyperactive texture **(Sound example 39)**

Finally, the texture becomes very dense, and the gritty mass metamorphoses into an allusion to waves breaking in the sea. This is achieved partly by changes in loudness, pitch[139] and filtering (selectively de-emphasizing the higher frequencies). Once again the sound is an allusion to the sea, not a representation of it: we can still hear the gritty source within the large gestures.

Counter-streamed with this is the apotheosis of the Fugu sound, massively extended in time, and in harmonic depth[140]. In addition, at the point of maximum

---

pitch of the sound changes. At least three such peaks are usually needed to define the particular character of a vowel sound.

[138] We can time-contract an event by using standard time-stretching with a stretch value of less than 1. This contracts the events themselves. If we have a sequence of events created in a mix (where the start-time of each event is specified) we can make the events occur closer together *without contracting the events themselves* by simply contracting the distance between event entries. Mix contractions like this can be achieved on the CDP mix pages, or in the *Table Editor*. It is also possible to use the CDP *Grain* algorithms to separate the attacks in a premixed sequence and then move the attacks closer together, though this involves losing decay details of the sounds, as the original sound is cut and respliced to make the resulting time-contracted version.

[139] ...or, rather, tessitura. This noise-based texture has no audible pitch, but we can move it up or down the pitch-range by (progressively) changing the sampling-rate.

[140] Many transposed copies are superimposed so that they synchronise at the midpoint of the mix (where all the sounds reach their brightest). Sounds of higher pitch enter (each imperceptibly) later in time, so that the whole event builds not only in loudness and brightness, but in high-pitch content.

loudness/brightness the sound is momentarily time-stretched, but slightly differently on each channel. The effect of this is to cause what was a mono sound to change into a stereo sound at the peak of the event. As the event also suggests motion towards (then away from) us (see earlier discussion of Fugu sounds) there is an illusion that the sound soars over our heads, like a wave. So, here, an allusion to the actual sound of ocean waves is combined with a metaphor of a wave (**Sound example 40**).

Towards the end of *Imago* various references to earlier events in the piece are heard (like a Coda[141]). In particular, after some references to the *Spectral Cauldron*, the grand Fugu event is recapitulated (at approximately 22 minutes 50 seconds). However, in this case, at the peak of the Fugu sound, the noise-texture drops away, and the Fugu sound, gliding slightly up then down in pitch, drops rapidly in level, becomes tremulous and transforms into pure noise, rising in tessitura and circling around the stereo space. For me, the psychological effect is that the sound disappears *upwards* into the heavens (**Sound example 41**).

This leads directly into a varied recapitulation of the original phrase of the piece, and the final cadencing materials.

... and finally

Work on *Imago* was made possible through an AHRB Creative Arts Fellowship.

---

[141] End section of a piece, after the main structure has concluded.

112

GLOBALALIA

GLOBALALIA

(Sound examples are on disc 2).

In contrast to *Imago* which uses a single source sound, *Globalalia* uses a multitude of sources. The piece is organised as a suite of small pieces, or 'narratives', exploring the qualities of the sounds of language itself.

Origins of the Project: The Source Material

On my travels I'd noticed that national and local radio-stations in many countries had popular music programs where records were introduced by DJs with a special kind of patter. It was possible to recognise this patter by its tone of voice, attitude, use of sound-effects etc. regardless of which language was being spoken. I wrote to several friends and colleagues asking them to collect such voices from their local radio stations. However, they interpreted my request in many different ways, and I ended up with a very large collection of speech material of different kinds, in many languages.

At this point I changed the goal of the project. I became more interested in the qualities of speech sounds themselves. I bought a new book "The Sounds of the World's Languages" and looked in detail at what sounds humans used, and the subtle distinctions that occur in sound usage in different languages. However my interest lay more in what was common to human speech practice. I wanted to explore the similarities of human speech expression between different cultures, to focus on what we hold in common as human beings. I increased my stock of source sounds by recording speaking voices from digital television stations from around the world and, in the end, had assembled sounds from 134 voices in 26 different languages.

Selection and Preparation of the Sources

I began by editing all these texts into their constituent syllables, and syllable-pairs.

This editing process had its own technical problems. Voices from far-away media stations are often distorted or made noisy in the transmission process, speaking voices may not be recorded in ideal circumstances (ambient noise, microphone noise or distortion, room acoustic etc.). More significantly, it is very hard to clearly separate individual syllables within the flow of speech without clipping the preceding or following syllable, as spoken syllables flow seamlessly into one another. I eventually developed a special editor that took account of syllable overlap when chopping out the syllables. Nevertheless, most of this work was 'by hand' (looking at the waveshape while listening, and deciding where to cut) and took 3 months to complete, The initially edited syllables were only cleaned-up and normalised later, when they were selected for possible use in the piece.

Syllable-pairs retained more feel of the original language source, but in the final piece I used the pairs very little e.g. the section "*Tristan*" (see below) focuses on the spoken pitch of individual syllables. It begins using the syllable-pairs in a texture[142] of voices,

---

[142] In a 'texture' (as used here) many sounds are overlaid in a time-irregular way. If these are copies of the same sound, these will usually vary, at least slightly, in pitch and amplitude.

choosing these so that only the first item of the pair is guaranteed to be at the chosen pitch. I can then gradually pass to using only the initial syllables of the pairs (these being definitely at the chosen pitches), so that the pitch focus of the mass sharpens, without any obvious treatment of the materials.

Organising the Sources

I needed some way to deal, in a musically useful way, with the 8300+ syllables thus garnered. I therefore created a database program within my composing environment (the CDP running on the *Sound Loom*)[143] that allowed me to list the properties of each source. The database allows arbitrary (composer-defined) properties and values to be created, but demands that every source is assigned the same set of properties (with an option to mean 'not known' or 'not defined' for any particular property).

The properties I decided were most useful to know about for this material were ...

- Which individual speaker's voice was used.
- The language spoken.
- The sex/age of the speaker.
- The initial consonant group (if any) of the syllable.
- The vowel (including vowel glides) of the syllable. (The final event in the 'Scheherezade' theme uses elements with vowel glides: end of **Sound Example 42**).
- The final consonant group (if any) of the syllable.
- The pitch of the syllable.
- The pitch glide (if any) of the syllable, and its direction/size (e.g. one of the injected textures in the 'Tristan' section uses organized pitch-glides: **Sound Example 99**).

..... and various other qualities (brassy, breathy, rasping, shouting, vocal brightness).

Syllables could then be chosen according to specific criteria, e.g.

- those beginning with "m", vowel "a", no end consonant, and spoken by male voices;
- those with large rising or falling pitch glides;
- those whose initial consonant group contained the 's' sound;
- those whose initial consonant group was 'sp', 'sc', or 'st';
- brightly voiced syllables using the start consonant 'rr', in Arabic, French, or Dutch;

and so on....

---

[143] Now installed as *Properties Files* on the *Music Testbed* of the Sound Loom Workspace.

The Form of the piece

In composing *Globalalia* I explored the sound-world of particular groups of vocal sounds, selected using the database, creating a suite of short connected pieces or 'narratives' which try not to stray too far from the qualities of the speech materials themselves.

The piece has strong speech-related qualities. The 'words' and 'phrases' constructed by joining individual syllables have the quality of normal human speech, but the events usually juxtapose syllables taken from different voices, from different cultures, and mixing both male and female speakers. This creates a curious hybrid, a language-like medium spoken by everyperson **(Sound Example 80).**

To provide a coherent shape I adopted the literary convention of the *frame tale*. This is a device where one story (the frame) is used as a device to tell other stories. The most famous example is the tale of Scheherezade, or the Arabian Nights. Scheherezade, after a night of passion, is meant to be executed by her husband but each day she distracts him by telling a story, and thus prolongs her own life.

The first phrase we hear in *'Globalalia'* is the frame, which I'll call the 'Scheherezade' theme **(Sound Examples 42)**. One problem, in a piece based on a great diversity of speech material, is to clearly differentiate the Scheherezade theme from the other 'narratives'. This is done in 4 ways.

- It contains widely diverse materials, which are not individally extended (through repetition or other musical patterning). In contrast the 'narratives' contained within the frame use consistent sonic materials, and/or musical devices (repetition, rhythmic placement of events etc.) that give them a more clearly *sonic* sense of coherence.

- The materials are expressively contrasted (they hang together in the manner of a disjointed spoken narrative): this sounds more like a 'recitative'[144] than an 'aria'[145].

- It begins with a striking 'cry' which is immediately recognisable (loud, high, shouted) which is a clear marker that the frame has returned. It is also used within other narratives (sometimes in a time-extended, gliding-upwards variation) to link these to the frame e.g. **Sound Example 92**.

- The theme ends with a few undemonstrative syllables, a kind of 'throw-away' speech cadence.

---

[144] Form of vocal delivery in opera, normally at the speed of normal speech with few changes in pitch except perhaps at the end of a sentence. The idea is to convey the story clearly via the words.
[145] Form of vocal delivery in opera, like normal singing, where the shape of the vocal line is governed by musical rules of melody, harmony and rhythm and musical tempo, rather than the typical tempo, rhythm or pitch-changes of speech.

The Scheherezade theme recurs, in varied forms, on 5 more occasions. The variations are quite simple as it is important that the listener recognises the frame's return.

- No 2 uses *sustains* (which slowly transform) **(Sound Examples 43)**.
- No 3 is greatly time-contracted **(Sound Examples 44)**.
- No 4 uses time-extension (of various kinds) initially, then changes to a regular rhythm using echoes. **(Sound Examples 45)**.
- No 5 is also more regular in rhythm and is loosely canonic[146] **(Sound Examples 46)**.

In the 6th and last variation, at the very end of the piece, each element is extended or elaborated in its own way, with long pauses and recollections from the piece interjected **(Sound Example 47)**. At the very end of this variation, the rather unpromising final utterance is developed and extended using a procedure used widely in the piece, filter focusing where a filter tracks the pitch and pitch-motion of the syllables. The filter is tuned to the fundamental[147], *and to the harmonics[148]*, of the pitch it follows. By gradually increasing the filter Q[149], the speech-like characteristics of the source are slowly suppressed so that an almost instrumental version of the speech's pitch-line emerges.

There are other variation factors at work here. The last element in the theme has low-octave doubling **(Sound Example 48)**, then waveset-distortion[150], and spectral time-stretching[151] are applied and a stack of filters tuned to the harmonic series of the dominant pitches[152] of the syllables and used to filter the reverberant decay of this variant **(Sound Example 49)**. This kind of detailed working is applied throughout the piece, and it is not possible to describe every procedure used.

This distinction between the frame and the other narratives is not absolute; the idea is to abstract the notion of a frame tail and create a musical equivalent to it. And, in fact, in order to achieve purely musical coherence, *the frame itself is made up of sounds that will be developed in more detail in the contained narratives.*

---

[146] Canon: musical form in which an original musical line is copied by another player/singer, but at a later time, while the original line continues. The 2 parts are intended to fit together rhythmically/harmonically. There can be more than one copy, to make a 3-part canon, a 4-part canon, and so on.

[147] Lowest frequency in the spectrum of a 'harmonic' sound i.e. a sound having one distinct pitch (not to be confused with idea of 'harmony' used to organise pitches in a musical score). Not all sounds have a distinct pitch. More confusingly, some sounds having a distinct pitch do not have a fundamental in this sense!

[148] These are the other frequencies (other than the fundamental) found in the spectrum of a 'harmonic' sound (a sound having one distinct pitch). They are integral multiples of the frequency of the fundamental.

[149] The Q of a filter is a measure of the narrowness of the filter band. Filtering broadband noise with a filter at, say, 2000 Hz and a low Q will produce noise of higher frequency (centred on 2000 Hz). If the filter Q is high, only noise close to 2000 Hz will emerge and if the Q is high enough this will appear as a single tone of frequency 2000 Hz.

[150] *Waveset Distortion* is described in my book '*Audible Design*'.

[151] Time-stretching using the Phase Vocoder (time-windowed Fourier Analysis) to extract the (time-changing) spectrum of the sound, followed by resynthesis of the sound over a larger (or smaller) time-frame. See '*Audible Design*'.

[152] *Filter Varibank* in the CDP.

The Narratives, in order of appearance

Commotion

Voices selected are loud, often shouted, often bright or brassy. The main texture creates the sound image of a heated argument, and this is interrupted by a variety of processed variants of these voices (waveset-interpolation distortion[153], time-contraction[154], waveset-enveloping[155], rhythmic sequencing[156], spatial redistribution, reverb etc.). The 'cry' from the Scheherezade theme is also prominent, morphing in various simple ways, from pitch glides to the fanfare-like ending.

Ma-rrr

This narrative contrasts two very different syllables. "Ma" is soft edged and can be time-stretched[157] considerably without losing the form of the syllable 'm' (many consonants are destroyed by simple time-stretching as they are intrinsically short change-of-state events). The time-stretched events can have a slightly pleading or pathetic quality, as the mouth appears to open more slowly to form the 'ma' sound **(Sound Example 50)**.

In contrast the single "rrr" sound used is 'matter-of-fact', emotionally detached in comparison. It too is time-stretched, but in a very different way. The iterative character of the 'rrr' is merely extended ... it does not have the same expressive connotations (of slowed delivery) and the fact that a single item is being repeated adds to its deadpan quality. A special process (Grain Extension) was developed to do this time-stretching. Normal time-stretching would destroy the character of the individual tongue-flaps, while any attempt to loop the material produces a very implausible result (it sounds like a studio artefact, not a natural extension of a human vocal sound). This is because there is no exact repetition in the natural sound – each tongue flap has a lightly different level, duration and quality. In order to preserve this unpredictability, the new algorithm searches for the individual tongue-flaps of the (iterative) 'rrr' sound, cuts them out at zero-crossings (so no splices need to be used in the process) then regenerates a longer sequence by reusing these same tongue-flaps in randomly permuted sequences (iterative extension)[158] **(Sound Example 51)**. By using random pitch (and amplitude) variation (over an increasing range)[159] the voice material can take on a watery quality **(Sound Example 52)**.

In the first 'ma' variations, waveset counted enveloping[160] (with a steeply falling contour) is applied to the texture of 'ma' sounds, which thus parallel the gritty quality of the 'rrr' material **(Sound Example 53)**. The final very long time-stretch version of

---

153 See footnote 150.
154 Using the Phase Vocoder: See footnote 151.
155 See footnote 150.
156 Using the CDP sequencer, but any sequencer would do.
157 Usually, here, Phase Vocoder time-stretching. See footnote 151.
158 Algorithm now incorporated in the CDP.
159 Now part of the CDP algorithm.
160 See footnote 150. In a complex sound, setting the duration of the falling envelopes by counting a fixed number of wavesets (or zero crossings) will produce a variable length for each enveloped attack.

the 'ma' texture is spectrally traced[161] in its higher register to extract the higher partials of the voices, which have a pure bell-like quality, and these are superimposed on the original. There are two overlaid variants of this material here, and you can also hear some time-varying tremolando **(Sound Example 54)**.

Maccordion

This narrative, and *Mamumi Hocket* below, use a set of female voice syllables, "mi", "me, "mo", "mu", "ma" in a regular rhythmic sequence which circles rapidly in space. We're not really aware of the circulation, but perceive that the individual syllables have moved to different places and are not easily localisable **(Sound Example 55)**. In fact each constituent goes through a number of forms, for example some distorted, some reverberated **(Sound Example 56)**. In "*maccordion*" this sequence is gradually filter focused on the pitches of the syllables. For Example, one of the filterings might produce the line in **Sound Example 57**. When all these filtered versions are overlayed, the narrative takes on the character of an "accordion" or "concertina" **(Sound Example 58)**.

Blcl

The *Maccordion* and *Mamumi Hocket* rhythmic narratives are separated by a short humorous section using start-syllables containing "l" proceeded by a more plosive consonant (e.g. "bl", "cl"). These sounds have morphological similarities to the sound of large water drops falling into water, so the rather serious tone of voice of the opening is undermined by this watery association **(Sound Example 59)**. The narrative proceeds to a combination of rhythmically regular, diatonically[162] tuned syllables, and a more random, less-tuned texture **(Sound Example 60)**.

Mamumi Hocket

The "*mamumi hocket*" uses the same material as *Maccordion*, adding a lower octave layer, and gradually applies waveset-omission distortion[163], so the sound becomes de-pitched and filled with grainy noise **(Sound Example 61)**. This resulting noise-stream rises (in pitch) out of the texture, and is filter-focused into a strong pitch-band above the rhythmic material and as it disperses it reveals a hocketed[164] version of the original material **(Sound Example 62)**. The narrative finally fades out on a tremolando running at the same speed as the pulse of the material **(Sound Example 63)**.

The 2nd version of the Scheherezade theme occurs here.

---

[161] *Only* the most prominent partials in the spectrum are retained, *on a window-by-window basis.* See '*Audible Design*' for more details.

[162] Diatonic scale. The normal scale used in Western musics.

[163] See footnote 150.

[164] Musical device: alternate notes (or groups), usually over a regular pulse, are sung by different voices.

This narrative, in ternary form[165], uses two types of the syllable "rrr". The outer sections focus on the "rr" rolled at the front of the tongue, as found e.g. in Glasgow-pronounced English[166]. The middle section focuses on the "rr" rolled on the arch of the tongue or in the back of the throat, as found in Dutch, Arabic and many other languages. Both "rrr" sounds can be extended by the iterative extension technique described previously. The front-rolled "rr" of the outer sections is less gritty, more regular, and often clearly pitched. Its pitch can be more easily changed in the mouth by simply increasing tongue pressure on the roof of the mouth. It is therefore plausible to glide the pitch of these sources (by sampling rate variation[167]). But we don't need to stay in the plausible range, we can make this material move and spin in space **(Sound Example 64)**.

This is counterstreamed[168] with speech-like lines of syllables based on the same sound, or syllables distributed in the stereo space **(Sound Example 65)**. At the first section end, these two streams can be heard working together. The continuous rolled "rrr" is reinforced by the lower octave at its end. Note how the speech stream tails away to indistinct grittiness. The sound is being processed by waveset-omission distortion[169], which simply replaces more and more wavesets by silence. The sound becomes increasingly indistinct and granular, but the transformation closely matches the granular quality of the rolled "rrr" itself **(Sound Example 66)**.

In the middle section, using the arch-rolled "rrr", we have two streams of transformation, articulated by short speechlike phrases. In the first, the three rising events, taken from Arabic male voices, are gradually transformed until they become trumpet-like. In this case the pitch was tracked exactly from the sources[170] and then used to synthesize a trumpet-like spectrum[171]. Then an in-betweening process[172] (a gradual mixing of the pitch-parallel sources) was applied to achieve the morph between the two **(Sound Example 67)**.

---

[165] Sequence of 3 musical sections in the pattern ABA. In most cases, the 2nd 'A' is a variant of the first.
[166] Strongly rolling with the tip of the tongue against the soft palette.
[167] We in fact resample the sound, as if it were at a different sampling rate, but represent the new sound in the original sampling rate – the sampling rate of the new soundfile is the same as the original.
[168] By analogy with 'counterpoint' in traditional scored music. In counterpoint, two (or more) independent melodic lines are composed to be performed at the same time, but in such a way that the harmonic progression produced makes sense within the harmonic tradition of the musical language. Counterstreaming implies the superimposition of sound-streams, each if which may be developing or metaporphosing in its own right, but in such a way that the streams interact (rhythmically or 'gesturally') in a way which is meaningful in a larger musical scale logic.
[169] See footnote 150.
[170] The pitch-tracking algorithm is part of the CDP.
[171] Spectra can be synthesized from a pitch line (with a pitch moving through the continuum of values, not just on a tuned scale) and a spectral description, in the CDP.
[172] *Mix inbetween* in the CDP allows a sequence of weighted mixes between two sounds to be made. E.g. specifying 3 intermediate mixes of sounds A and B will produce 3 mixes in the (loudness) ratios 1:3, 2:2 (= 1:1) and 3:1. Non-linear sequences can be generated. The *Sound Loom* includes an *Interpolation Workshop* where the sequence of mixes can be adjusted (e.g. interpolations between already interpolated sounds can be made, or individual interpolated items deleted) until an audibly satisfactory sequence of interpolations is produced.

In the 2nd transformation stream, a repeated speech-like phrase of Dutch female "rrr" sounds circulates in space **(Sound Example 68)**. This becomes separated into two different sub-streams. A first process extracts the gritty noise-like constituents of the sound, and applies a strongly pitched filter bank. The material comes to resemble the sound of a wire scraping a large metal plate. It is the high frequency band in **Sound Example 69**.

The second process focuses on the pitches of the individual syllables, filtering out the high frequencies, and increasing the filter Q so that the gritty constituents gradually disappear, leaving a stream of pitch only. If we listen carefully we can hear the muffled pitch-only stream cycling in the background in the same example **(Sound Example 69)**. This becomes denser, and begins to resemble rapidly articulated mellow brass instruments (French Horns?), in the background here **(Sound Example 70)**.

These transforming streams are articulated by small speech-like phrases, using the same "rrr" consonants, but taken from different languages - here we have Italian and Turkish respectively **(Sound Example 71)** - and a " rrr" cry in Japanese, articulated by spatial movement and changing reverberation **(Sound Example 72)**. When the initial section recurrs, it is brought to an end by grouping the syllables in rhythmic motifs e.g. **(Sound Example 73)** and the resulting phrases filtered on the harmonic series of the pitches of the source syllables, with tighter and tighter Q-values, **(Sound Example 74)**, cadencing the entire section **(Sound Example 75)**.

So_Saiso

This narrative is an animated conversation piece around the sibilant[173] "sss".
(Sound Example 76).

The very rapid sections are made by overlapping the syllables (rather than by time-contracting them) and as a result the "sss" sounds elide into one another.
(Sound Example 77)

Near the end, the sibilants detach themselves momentarily from the speech stream (they are sustained by texturing and the extended versions then made to emerge out of their sources by cross-fading, so that the sibilants appear sustain while the remainder of the syllables do not) **(Sound Example 78)**. This process of separating sibilants from vowels is used more elaborately in the narrative "*stscsp*" (see below).

---

[173] Sibilant. Noise-based consonants e.g. s, sh, ch.

Morphing Hocket

The morphing hocket was the first narrative of the piece to be made. It consists of 4 lines chasing each other around the space, each based on a different vowel (at the start we hear "va", "mi", "mai" and "cu"). The "va" "mi" and "mai" lines morph their consonants, e.g. "va" becomes "ma" becomes "ra" etc. These morphs proved extremely difficult to achieve; the consonants pass through intermediate less-definite states that are not clearly vocal, but retain the pitch and formant[174] of the line. The lines are also animated from time to time by sustained tones, and by time-changing echoes.

The "o" line alternates between "ro", "co", "to", "vo", "mo" etc. and, on the "co", uses a bouncing motif which sometimes passes to the other lines where they have the "c" consonant. All the lines dissolve into pitch-free sibilants (or fade out) at the end. **(Sound Example 79)**

The 3rd version of the Scheherezade theme occurs here.

Pipapobo

The "p" and "b" consonants in this narrative have a strong percussive characteristic[175]. The piece starts out as a conversation exchange between male and female voices **(Sound Example 80)** but soon becomes rhythmic in character **(Sound Example 81)** and then pulsed (all the syllables are now very short) **(Sound Example 82)**.

Towards the end, some of the percussive elements have their decay[176] time-stretched (but *not* their percussive attacks). Speech sounds do not (in general) have *steady* pitch, but go past too fast for us to notice this. Once we time-stretch the decay-part of the sound, we hear the glides in pitch clearly, producing a comical sound like strange plucked gongs **(Sound Example 83)**.

Stscsp

This narrative deals with plosive consonants which follow a sibilant, "sc", "st" and "sp". These events can be expanded in time both backwards (the sibilant will time-stretch convincingly) and forwards (the final vowel can also be extended) and hence both ends of the syllable can be elaborated by pitch-glide, tremolo, spatial movement etc. The central attack consonant cannot be time-stretched (while preserving its recognisability) in the same way, but we can develop it by stacking it (superimposing

---

[174] Formants: roughly speaking, peaks in the spectrum of a sound. Vowel sounds are characterised by such peaks in the spectrum, so that we can hear the same vowel, *even if the pitch of the underlying sound changes*, because the spectral peaks can remain *at the same (central) frequencies* even when the pitch of the sound changes. At least three such peaks are usually needed to define the particular character of a vowel sound.

[175] Like percussion instruments, they have a strong, brief attack, like something that is struck. In fact these are small explosive releases of air caused by an aperture (e.g. the lips, or the tongue+soft-palette) suddenly opening to release the air trapped behind.

[176] The end part of the sound which falls away to zero level, after the initial attack.

e.g. lower octaves, but synchronised precisely on the attack, so we hear a single bigger event rather than a chord[177]), giving it its own reverberation, or developing it as a texture. Here is an example of elaborating all 3 elements (extend,stack,extend), **(Sound Example 84)**, two examples of developing the attack as a texture **(Sound Example 85)**, and a more complex elaboration, using the sound as a 'hard object', skimming, bouncing or rolling around the space **(Sound Example 86)**. In a further example, the sibilant sound becomes detached from its following attack consonant, it continues as a stream in its own right. Then the final attack triggers two streams of extended-vowel elaboration **(Sound Example 87)**.

As the narrative progresses, the sibilants and vowels develop in different directions. We begin with the two in their normal relationship, except that the sibilants have been reinforced. (A copy is made with the vowels silenced, and this copy then mixed synchronously into the original source) **(Sound Example 88)**. The pitch of the vocal line (and its vowel structure) are extracted and resynthyesized[178] without the sibilants, and then filter reinforced **(Sound Example 89)** and the sibilants take off on their own **(Sound Example 90)**.

En Masse

A piece of "choral speech". Syllables have been chosen purely for their pitch, though, because speech syllables almost always glide in pitch, the pitch bands are richly thickened by the speech articulation, and there is lower octave reinforcement. The massed sound occasionally trembles[179] **(Sound Example 91)**.

The texture dissolves through spectral blurring[180], and the fade-out is produced through time-stretching (used frequently to end narratives in the piece) with the tail being filtered by a filter bank tuned to the harmonic series of specified pitches. The "cry" from the Scheherezade theme also rises over the end **(Sound Example 92)**, and links this narrative back to ….

The 4th version of the Scheherezade frame-theme occurs here.

---

[177] See *Audible Design* for further discussion of psycho-acoustic phenomena resulting from procedures like attack-synchronisation.
[178] See footnotes 170 and 171.
[179] Using the *tremolo* or *shudder* program in the CDP.
[180] A proportion of the spectral windows, extracted from the *Phase Vocoder* analysis of the sound, are omitted and replaced by (the same number of) windows which merely interpolate between the values in the surviving original windows. For more details, see *Audible Design*.

Rasp

Spoken syllables often descend into a vocal rasps, and this narrative plays with this rasping quality. The rasping is extended by a similar process as the one used to expand "rrr" sounds (iterative extension) but over a much longer time. In the examples, the first sound of each sequence is the original, and the following sounds are naturalistic extensions using the iterative extension process **(Sound Example 93)**. Once this plausible extension has been created the resonant pitches of the individual grains of the rasp are picked out and emphasized by filters[181], and these pitch-coloured streams circle around the space. The streams are also made to decelerate (the grains themselves preserve their original durations; they are not time-stretched) and as they slow down, the grains are gradually positioned on a regular pre-specified time-grid. Because of the way the extended grain-streams are made (using zero-length splices) we know exactly how long each grain is and hence the exact time at which each starts. Using an algorithm we can interpolate between this original 'natural' timing sequence and a strictly regular timing sequence. Then, using the same kind of timing control we can make the different *regular* streams merge (synchronises) in time[182] **(Sound Example 94)**.

At the end of the narrative, waveset-omission distortion[183] is used, as in *"ra trumpets"*, to dissolve the sound substance to a gritty trace, as heard in the stream of repeating-voices in the example **(Sound Example 95)**.

Tristan

This narrative uses the gradual tuning of a texture of syllables chosen for their pitches. The pitches chosen relate to the 'Tristan' chord[184]. Initially the texture is made from syllable-pairs, only the first syllable of each pair being chosen for its pitch. This is one of the source layers, using several pitches **(Sound example 96)**. As the texture develops, the 2nd ("out of tune" syllable) is omitted. On subsequent repetitions, each syllable is treated by a filter centred on the harmonic series of its principle pitch, with the filter Q gradually increasing, and the low notes becoming more prominent **(Sound Example 97)**. In the final recurrence, the texture is 'plucked', independently on the two channels of the stereo, by a rapidly falling loudness envelope produced by waveset enveloping[185] **(Sound Example 98)**.

The interruptions in this narrative illustrate two other approaches to organising syllables. In the first, the voice of a single speaker generates a rapid stream of plausible speech. The syllables are patterned so that certain items recur regularly while most do not recur at all. This gives the speech a strange insistent intensity **(Sound Example 99)**.

---

[181] CDP *Filter varibank* allowing pitches (and harmonics of pitches) to define filters, in a time-varying way, with time-variable Q.
[182] Algorithms for such interpolations are part of the *Sound Loom's* 'Table Editor'.
[183] See footnote 150.
[184] Famous harmonically ambiguous, unstable chord used by Wagner in the Opera 'Tristan and Isolde'.
[185] See footnote 150.

The other interruption uses syllables which have a large internal pitch glide. These are organised to follow each other up, then down, the tessitura of the voice, forming a rising and falling arch of pitch **(Sound Example 100)**.

Ts (chochiche)_canon

This narrative has three layers. In the first layer, a sequence of "ts" sibilants is presented, followed by the sibilants separated from their ensuing vowels, followed by the vowels separated from their preceding sibilants. The original, and then the separated consonants and vosels in context, can be heard in **Sound Example 101**. The sibilants and vowels are then reassembled but with different treatments (percussiveness, resonance, reverb etc).

In the second layer, syllables with pitch-glides are each repeated in such a way that syllable duration grows with each repetition **(Sound Example 102)**, while in the 3rd layer the sibilant content of a vocal stream is etched away (filtering etc.) to leave a bare pitch stream **(Sound Example 103)**.

At the end of this narrative we hear all 3 layers used together **(Sound Example 104)**.

Funk

This narrative begins with a strongly pulsed stream of syllables but without syllable repetition, to preserve the speech-like quality of the material. This gradually metamorphoses into imaginary percussion instruments, with the Scheherezade "cry" floating over the top **(Sound Example 105)**. This began as a regular sequence of syllables selected for their specific pitches **(Sound Example 106)**.

A cyclic "plucking" envelope, at the same tempo as the syllables, was then gradually imposed on this, to produce a strongly rhythmic sequence[186]. (As the perceived attack of vocal syllables is not always at the start of the sound, the syllables themselves had to be individually timed so that the perceived attacks fell under the exactly timed envelopes. An attack detection algorithm was used to help with this[187]). The natural variation in loudness and brightness of the syllables produces the irregular sequence of accents.
(Sound Example 107)

The same envelope was then applied to various 8va transpositions of the vocal material, for example **Sound Example 108**, and these gradually combine to create the percussive stream.

The 5th version of the Scheherezade theme follows.

---

[186] Cyclic envelopes can be generated in the CDP.
[187] Attack detection was done with a CDP algorithm.

Chunchincha

This narrative deals with the sibilants "ch" and "zz", and their release from the syllables that contain them. There are three sounds in the example. In the first, the relative level of the voiced material and the "zz" sibilants gradually changes, the sibilants begin to move in space and finally the synchronisation between the two is broken and the sibilants are released. In the 2nd we hear a sequence of "ch"-initiated syllables, while in the 3rd these become desynchronised and treated in different ways, the sibilants getting a strong regular tremolo **(Sound Example 109)**.

Ceracu

This narrative, based on the consonant "c", begins conversationally, but then leads into a strongly rhythmic section. We begin with conversational gestures **(Sound Example 110)**. When they pause, they reveal a texture of free "c" consonants, and this texture gets gradually denser[188] **(Sound Example 111)** until, in the rhythmic section, it begins to circle around the space.

Certain elements in the speech stream are emphasized by repetition, and then form the basis of the ensuing rhythmic section.
This has 5 elements. ...

- 2 repeating phrases on "ceracucu". These are at the same tempo, but in the *exact* duration proportion 14:15 with one appearing to the left and the other to the right. (There is no time-stretching of the materials. The events are simply placed more closely in time in the 15-cycle). The cycle begins with both sequences in synchronisation, making the sound effectively mono (as left and right cannot be distinguished) with the sound image at the centre of the stereo stage. Then, immediately, as the 2 phrases begin to be out of phase, the image first becomes 'reverberant' in the stereo space then echoes itself from left to right, returning through 'reverberance' to re-synchronise at the end of the cycle, when "ceracucu" suddenly appears at stage centre again **(Sound Example 112)**.
- A bass voice with an extended final note ("corucu-cecucu-coi") gives impulse to each phrase, and some high repeated phrases syllables help define the fundamental tempo **(Sound Example 113)**.
- A pulsating bass note, deriving its pitch from the bass-voice, pulses at odds with the fundamental tempo (a 3 v 2 relationship).
- The texture of "c", getting increasingly dense, begins to circle slowly, then faster. It shudders[189] in loudness as it circles, and this shuddering itself accelerates. It is also gradually high pass filtered so it moves higher in pitch **(Sound Example 114)**.

---

[188] The gradually changing texture is generated using the CDP *Texture* program.
[189] Using CDP *Tremolo* program.

This whole rhythmic structure is given impetus by moments of spectral blurring[190]. When the entire sound-world is spectrally blurred over many windows, not only is the spectral detail warped, but the rhythmic structure of the music is momentarily lost. Then, as the blurring factor is rapidly decreased to zero (vibrato-ing the signal as it does so), the rhythmic energy of the music is released. Where this coincides with the rotating "c" texture, this appears to be thrown out of the spectral blur into the space. **(Sound Example 115)**

Rocrio

This narrative resembles "*en masse*" and "*tristan*". Again, speech elements are chosen for their pitches, and these pitches are gradually brought into focus with filters over the harmonic series of those pitches. Filters with very sharp Q produce the semi-metallic sounds. As the speech dissolves into abstract pitches, it leads into the final "scheherezade" variation, through a harmonic modulation[191] **(Sound Example 116)**.

At the end of the final Scheherezade frame-theme variation, we hear the beginning of the theme again, very distantly. A frame-tail can, of course, go on indefinitely ... there's no end to the number of stories we can tell .... so our storytelling simply disappears from 'view' without a sense of permanent closure.

.. and finally

Globalalia was made entirely on desktop PCs, using the CDP / *Sound Loom* software. It was commissioned privately by Folkmar Hein for his 60th birthday and premiered at the *Inventionen Festival, Berlin* in the Summer of 2004. Special thanks are due to Natasha Barrett, Andrew Bentley, Warren Burt, Jane Kasam, Patrick Kosk and Kouhei who all responded to my request to collect speaking voices from the airwaves. Composing time for the piece was partly financed by a DAAD Fellowship, supporting my residency as *Edgard Varése Visiting Professor* at TU, Berlin, during the Spring of 2004.

---

[190] See footnote 180.
[191] i.e. an apparent change of key, in the traditional sense.

ENCOUNTERS
IN THE REPUBLIC
OF HEAVEN

ENCOUNTERS IN THE REPUBLIC OF HEAVEN

Encounters is an exploration of the music inherent in everyday speech. Unlike *Globalalia*, however, the aim of this project was to capture the musical features of speech at the level of the spoken phrase, its melody and rhythm, and the sonority of individual speaking voices, that indefinable yet recognisable something that enables us to distinguish one person from another. I especially wanted to capture both the diversity of human expression, and the sense of an entire community of speakers, a poetic snapshot of the diversity of human life.

As the piece would attempt to encapsulate this community of speech, I decided to work in 8-channel sound-surround, so that the audience would be embraced within this community. I had worked in 4-channel sound-surround in the past (*Anticredos* and *Vox*), but when the 4-channel analogue tape-format died in the late 1980s I found it increasingly difficult to perform any of my 4-channel analogue works, and became cautious about embracing multichannel formats. Hence my works over the previous 20 years had been in stereo format, which could be expanded in performance by appropriate diffusion over multi-loudspeaker systems (see the chapter on *Diffusion*).

For *Encounters* I both modified my compositional tools to operate in (any) multichannel format, and developed new tools specifically for this work e.g. multichannel sound-spatialisation software. Also, the award of the *Giga-Herz Grand Prize* in 2008 enabled me to re-equip my studio to work in 8-channel sound, so I was able to experience directly the sound-surround output of the piece. This was essential to composing the work, as electro-acoustic composition relies crucially on the direct feedback of listening to the created sound output.

Origins of the Project: The Source Material

The composition of *Encounters* posed quite different problems from *Globalalia*. To capture a diversity of human speech across an entire community I would need to ..

- find people who would agree to have their voice recorded.
- make many recordings, to capture a wide range of vocal styles and colours.
- capture natural speech (i.e. not the voices of actors, media presenters, or interviewees).

The original idea was to make the piece around my home county of Yorkshire, in the North of England, where I might at least be accepted as a (possibly slightly eccentric) local. But even here, it's not possible to simply wander up to someone in a pub and, out of the blue, ask to record their voice. And to get a representative cross-section of vocal 'colours', you would need to make many more recordings than would finally be used, involving lots of recording time and the logistics and expense of recording equipment, materials and travel, all of which required funding of some kind. I couldn't see any practical way to proceed, so I demoted the project to my wish-list.

Then, in 2006, the 3-year post of Composer-in-Residence based at the University of Durham was announced. Funded partly by the University and partly by the Arts Council, this job involved obligations both to teach students and to work within the local community, but its primary purpose was to provide the opportunity for a composer to pursue musical composition. For very particular reasons the Durham department was also keen to appoint an electro-acoustic musician. This seemed the ideal opportunity to realise my project in the North, particularly as work in the local community would be an essential part of it. So I applied and was fortunately appointed to the post.

The first few months work involved making contacts with local community and arts organisations through which I might meet people willing to take part in the project. As human voices alter significantly with age (particularly during childhood, but also in later life), I aimed to record a cross-section of voices, both male and female, across the widest range of ages. Schools and drop-in centres for the elderly were obvious places to investigate - recording working-age adults was more of a problem. Initially unsure of how the speech sounds would eventually be organised, I also recorded speech in the street and in markets and the crowd at the Newcastle football stadium, together with the voices of amateur choirs to whom I provided a skeletal structure for improvising with different speech colours. As the project developed, however, I decided to generate the massed voice from the voices of the individual I had recorded.

To capture 'natural' speech patterns I wanted to avoid recording in a staged situation - a recording studio or an interview. Instead I went to people in schools, meeting centres, homes, pubs and clubs and encouraged them to talk freely with almost no intervention from me. Often it was only some way into the session that speakers began to relax into a more freely flowing style. In schools I quickly discovered that children had much more to say when talking amongst themselves in a group, so I usually recorded with 2 or 3 kids together in a small room. I also recorded types of everyday speech 'performance', in particular the sales patter of a travelling Butcher selling meat from a lorry in Chester-le-Street market.

Selection and Preparation of the Sources

Having gathered a large volume of recordings I now needed to select what I needed for the piece. There were five preparatory tasks

- Deciding how to put together these more clearly recognisable materials as music
- Selecting appropriate voices
- Selecting appropriate narratives of a suitable duration to use
- Cleaning the sources
- Extracting the musical information needed to make the piece.

By extracting the syllabic content of speech in *Globalalia* I had removed both the narrative content and the sense of individual personalities delivering the words. In the new piece, using entire spoken phrases, the subject matter being talked about could no longer be ignored - I would need to run with the narrative threads. More importantly, in *Encounters* the individual speakers were immediately apparent. The sound material could no longer be treated simply as a set of 'musical instruments' - the personal embodiment of the speaker had to be respected. This meant that the type of sound-transformation techniques employed would need to be restricted so as not to 'do violence' to the materials. I decided therefore to make a sequence of individual sound-portraits (or portraits of groups of children), preserving a narrative in most of them. These would be set amongst two other types of materials, the first using voices organised en masse in various ways, and the second using sounds abstracted from the speaking voices and deployed more like musical instruments.

From the many recordings made, I selected a set of voices with contrasting colours and styles of delivery. There needed to be a balance of male and female, and of ages (the very young, teenagers, adults, elderly people) but, most of all, voices with their own special features, so that sound-portraits with distinctive musical and sonic characteristics could be devised. Speaking voices can often be typed almost like singing voices - James Bell (*The Soldier's* Tale) was a bass and Alan Sambrook (*The Bellydancer*) a tenor (a fact which later becomes apparent when his voice is made to 'sing' at the end of the piece). Sometimes the use of the vocal range is important - Joyce Dent's voice (*The Dancer's Tale*) plays across a wide range of pitches, which had strong harmonic implications. Other voices have noticeable sound markers, Kathleen Teward's (*The Farmer's Tale*) a distinctive cross-break leap (often by the interval of a 5th), Edna Gallagher's (*The Budgie*) a sub-audio rasp.

Next, particular materials had to be chosen from each speaker. For a narrative we usually want to elaborate the story and fill it with descriptive detail. From a musical perspective, however, a limited set of sound-material (which can then be further developed, as sound) is usually preferable. Taking into account the total scale of the work, this suggested that each portrait should be around 2 or 3 minutes in length, and should perhaps focus on key phrases or sounds within the narrative. I had up to 2 hours of recordings from each speaker, and the large amount of material collected made the task of selecting a short, interesting narrative easier. Some materials could be excluded for technical reasons (e.g. too noisy, too quiet, too many people talking at once), some for lack of 'naturalness' (e.g. too stilted, too unnaturally hesitant in front of the mike), some for reasons of narrative content (e.g. too repetitive, too predictable), and some for musical reasons (e.g. too similar in sound to already selected materials).

The final stage of this preliminary selection used standard sound-editing procedures for narrative or documentary, removing hesitations, repetitions and vocal glossalalia ('um', coughs, breath sounds etc.) then condensing narratives to their sparest form (removing narrative repetition, and so on). This material was then separated into short vocal phrases, the musical 'units' of the piece. When the portraits were later assembled, these narratives would be slightly rearranged from a musical/poetic perspective, for example repeating key phrases or interjections ('uh, huh'); smaller or greater adjustments towards a more metronomic pulse (done largely by adjusting the time-gaps between successive phrases, rather than by altering the phrases themselves); gathering together hesitations, repetitions and glossalalia for their expressive content (*The Dancer's Tale*), and so on.

Next began the processes of cleaning and cataloguing these materials. The decision to record in relaxed settings, like the home or pub, or in small groups (the children), in order to obtain 'natural' speech, created its own technical challenges. These materials had now to be cleaned up. To achieve this I gathered together existing CDP tools for editing, filtering, masking with silence, and spectral subtraction (of the noise floor) into an integrated package (the *Cleaning Kit*) and developed new tools, in particular a means to remove one of two pitches, when two voices are speaking (vowels) at the same time. Using these tools I painstakingly went through all selected materials, systematically eliminating blemishes, wherever possible.

Organising the Sources

To enable me to organise these source phrases I greatly expanded the *Properties File* tool developed for *Globalalia*. Clicking on the name of a property file now displayed it as a graphic table from which the listed sounds could be played. In addition there were graphical means to enter rhythmic patterns and motivic shapes, a mechanism to hear pitch motif and harmonic field properties and, most importantly, means to compare the property values and to extract statistics about them.

I used a large set of properties, not knowing initially what might be most important.

(1) Information about the origin and type of the speech material

- src   source recording from which the phrase was taken
- who   the individual recorded
- sex   gender of the person
- age   child, teen, adult, elderly

(2) Information about the musical content of the speech

- motif   the sequence of pitches defined by the speech line (if any)
- HF   the Harmonic Field defined by the pitches of the speech line
- tonic   any implied tonic of the pitch line
- rhythm   the rhythmic pattern of the speech e.g. "5:4", "fast6:8"
- MM   the tempo of the speech, as a metronome mark
- rcode   the rhythmic pattern of the speech, graphically encoded
- quality   The quality of the voice - bright, light, soft, laughed, hoarse etc

(3) Information about the narrative content

- text   the words spoken in the phrase
- keywords words emphasized by stress, or repetition within or between speakers e.g. 'never-ever', 'remember' etc.
- markers   verbal markers e.g. 'you know', 'of course', 'aye'.
- hes-rep   hesitations and repetitions e.g. 'but-uh', 'uh-aye', 'uh-uh'

(4) And

- ideas   ideas about how to use the particular phrase.

Classifying the pitch properties of speech was not as straightforward as this might suggest. A speech phrase doesn't initially appear to have a melodic shape, partly because our attention is focused on the meaning of the speech and this is conveyed mainly by changes in the spectrum (the change from vowel to consonant to vowel) rather than by the pitch. Also the pitch is neither steady (it slides about) nor focused on any familiar scale. However, if we play a recording of a spoken phrase repetitively we usually hear a melody emerge - repetition reinforces our perception of the limited set of pitches which the speech-line uses, its harmonic field. We also tend to unconsciously approximate these pitches to the familiar tones and intervals of musical scales we know. For the "Speech Harmony" section I wanted to work with many speech phrases at the same time, so I needed their harmonic fields to fall on the same tuned scale system. I therefore approximated the pitches of the speech to the nearest tones of the tempered-scale when creating the "motif" and "HF" properties[192].

Speech has distinctive event-groupings and accents (the metrical feet of poetry) similar to musical groupings, and speech tempo is consistent within a small range but rather fluid, unlike the regularity of dance music. 'Rhythm' and 'rcode' captured the rhythmic pattern of the spoken phrase as closely as possible, and 'MM' recorded its tempo.

More important were the Statistical Tools which helped me to determine which Harmonic Fields, which Tempi, or which words (word-starts etc) were most common amongst my collected materials. For example, although it's clear that speech tempo falls within a fairly narrow range, I expected different tempi to lie smoothly across this range, perhaps like this.

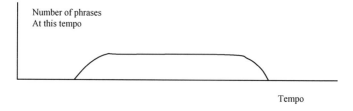

When I plotted the tempi of my collection of phrases, however, I came up with a tempo plot like this ..

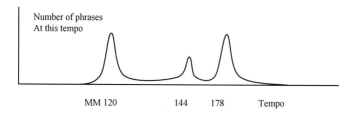

MM 178 is close enough to MM 180 to be one and a half times MM 120, the ratio of, say, quavers to triplet quavers, and this immediately suggested a way to organise the rhythm of the speech material (used in the central interlude of Act 1).[193]

Statistical analysis of the text (set to search for sub-phrases, common words, word-starts, rhymes and assonance) uncovered common words and syllables (like 'remember', 'different' and 'li') used in constructing the 'Clouds of Speech' central interlude of Act 2.

Later, in order to organise the speech-phrases in terms of their implied harmonies (central interlude of Act 3), I needed to find appropriate vocal phrases. As much speech falls in a narrow range, many phrases generate a chromatic cluster of small intervals as their harmonic field. I didn't feel that these clusters would produce a sufficiently interesting musical result so, using the search tools, I looked for phrases which had larger intervals (a minor 3rd or greater) in their harmonic fields, ascertained which of these (with specific pitches) were the most common and, given these, decided which might be combined to produce interesting chord formations.

This is one example of how the process of cataloguing materials, particularly in its early stages, constantly threw up new ideas or insights about how to organise the piece, on the small or large scale. Hence the "ideas" property was added to the table to enable me to keep track of these thoughts, and cross-reference between the ideas themselves and their associated sounds.

After the first year of establishing contacts and making recordings, this cleaning and cataloguing stage of the work occupied me for the following 18 months.

The Form of the piece

The final form of the piece gradually crystallised around the extracted narratives in the 2nd year. I envisaged the piece falling into four separate Acts, each presenting four sound-portraits projected in front of the audience in wide stereo.

These would be embedded in an 8-channel sound-surround sea of vocal or voice-derived materials. Acts 1 and 3 (the start and mid-point of the work) would start with introductions using the "Voicewind" sound generated from a very dense mass of speaking voices, and the entire work would end with the voices dissolving back into this sound.

The first 3 acts would also contain a central interlude using all the voices in sound-surround, each organised using a different common property of the speech

- for Act 1 the rhythm of the spoken phrases.
- for Act 2 the sonority of words or syllables.
- for Act 3 the harmonic fields of the spoken phrases.

---

[193] It's interesting that MM 120 corresponds roughly to double a fast walking pace, and is the tempo of much late C20, early C21 dance-music, while MM 144 is a typical Allegro in Western classical music.

The finales of the first 3 acts would seek to draw out key musical elements from the voice-portraits within the act, and develop them into a more abstract, purely musical world. This helped to determine the final order of the portraits (which also took into account the balance of vocal quality, gender, age, musical treatment and narrative content) as the sound materials from the portraits within an act would determine the musical nature of these finales.

Act 4, starting as Act 2 with 2 portraits, would merge together the interlude and finale, drawing on and developing 8-channel materials from the earlier acts, and leading to the final transformation of the spoken voices into song, before the voices remerged into the Voicewind.

The portraits themselves were each to be approached differently, depending on the sonic character of the vocal material. The technical "abstraction" of vocal-character (one of the technical goals of the piece) proved elusive, too complex a web of favoured rhythms, pitch-contours, accentuation-tics, glossalalia, verbal-markers and so on to be extractable using computer algorithms, and I had to fall back on musical intuition. The final form of the piece looks like this.

ACT 1
Introduction: Voicewind
Portraits: The fisherman's tale
                     Children's stories I (mainly boys)
Interlude: Speech waltzing
Portraits: The budgie
                     The bellydancer
Act 1 Finale: (to Voicewind)

ACT 2
Portraits: Teens gossip
                     The dancer's tale
Interlude: Clouds of speech
Portraits: Travelling butcher
                     Children's stories II (mainly girls)
Act 2 Finale:

ACT 3
Introduction: Voicewind
Portraits: The farmer's tale
                     Heathcliffe, come here!
Interlude: Speech harmony
Portraits: The stories I hear
                     The soldier's tale
Act 3 Finale:

ACT 4
Portraits: The poet's tale
                     The best thing that ever happened to me
Interlude/Finale: leading to Speech Singing
                     (to Voicewind)

137

A Sound-Surround Working Environment

For Encounters, a new environment had to be built for mixing sounds with more than 2 channels. I had developed a way to specify the signal routing from an input sound (with any number of channels) to an output space (of any number of channels), and a mixing process allowing multichannel files to be mixed together in an entirely flexible manner. To avoid having to write out the complicated-looking text-files controlling this process, I developed a high-level tool which would alter lines of the mix text at the click of a button e.g. to change the output level on all channels at once, or copy the signal routing of some channels to others, or from one file to a file with a different number of input channels. I also added a means to alternate easily between building musical phrases in the mix environment and building sounds themselves.

Algorithms to generate convincing rotation around or panning across the ring of loudspeakers were developed. Panning the signal rapidly across a changing (random) permutation of all the speakers produced a strange sense of everywhereness which can be heard with some of the "It's a bloke" transformations in the Finale of Act 1. Once a multichannel sound-image has been made it is possible to put the entire frame in motion e.g. spinning the whole 8-channel image clockwise, a procedure I'd speculated about in a chapter in "On Sonic Art" in the 1980s. And I added wrap-panning, taking a stereo image, itself already in motion across the stereo panorama, and moving it through the 8-channel space, e.g. out of a mono-condensate to a stereo display at the front, wrapping it around the listener to a stereo-display and thence a mono merge at the rear. In addition, processes such as texture-generation and brassage, which originally took mono input sounds and generated stereo output, were extended to generate output in a multichannel space.

Adding reverberation to signals in a multichannel space also raised new issues. In stereo, reverberation is produced by very many echoes of a sound returning from different locations in the stereo space, creating the sense of sound being reflected around a room. With a multichannel space one could either create these reflections around all the channels, so the sound appears to resonate around the entire surround space, or e.g. make 8 signals in the 8-different channels reverberate from a restricted (e.g. stereo-width) space around their current location retaining a strong sense of the original spatial layout (channel-centred reverberation).

The musical sections

It's not possible to describe in detail every compositional process used in *Encounters*. I will outline some key features in each section. As a general observation, each process applied would typically vary over time. And several such processes were often progressively overlaid. For example we might begin by applying a time-varying time-stretch to our source; we then apply a low pass filter to the resulting output, increasing the filtering progressively; we then gradually shift the pitch of the end of the sound, upwards; we then introduce slightly randomised tremolo to the end of the sound, gradually increasing the tremolo depth from zero, and progressively changing the tremolo frequency; we then dovetail the end of the sound (its level falls away to zero), and so on.

Introductions, Interludes & Coda

Introductions Acts 1 and 3: Coda Act 4: Voicewind

(All examples from 8-channel sections are stereo reductions from the 8-channel originals, so cannot always convey the exact musical output composed).

If many different vocal phrases are overlaid in a texture, the sound space becomes increasingly crowded - we hear human voices, but not individual speech. When the density approaches a thousand vocal phrases per second the sense of human voices is almost completely lost, and by ten thousand voices per second we hear only a wall of noise, the average colour of all the voices, spread around the 8 outputs. A stereo sound which presents such a space-filling image can be made to shudder across the stereo space[194]. Treating each adjacent pair of the 8 output channels as 8 stereo pairs, independent shudders were applied to each pair. The resulting sound appears like the noise of a gale force wind blowing around our ears in a storm. At a lower density, where human voices can still be heard, the shuddering effect is not apparent (we seem to hear only random fluctuations of loudness of individual voices in a very dense mix), so we can make a transition from a mass of speaking voices to shuddering wind by gradually increasing the density.

Interlude Act 1: Speech Waltzing

Collecting together spoken phrases at MM 120 and synchronising their attacks as closely as possible produced only a sense of a crowd of speakers – the underlying rhythm of the phrases wasn't apparent. The phrases were therefore subtly retimed[195] so that attacks were precisely synchronised, whereupon the many voices locked into a clearly pulsed rhythm. This approach was also applied to the MM 178 materials.

The opening uses such rhythmically retimed phrases with each word in each phrase sent to the next loudspeaker in the ring, the phrase thus stepping rapidly around the ring (stepped-rotation) **(Sound Example 117)**. Soon, whole vocal phrases from different voices enter on successive loudspeakers around the ring, but the phrases themselves do not move. As the phrases had different pitch-ranges, lengths, qualities, and emphases, each had to be carefully chosen to tell effectively against the previous and following overlapping phrases. In the overall form of the interlude, sections in 2-time (MM 120) and 3-time (MM 178) alternate. The rhythm is pushed forward by tutti moments (voices synchronised on all loudspeakers) emphasizing the rhythmic pulse **(Sound Example 118)**. Canon and echoes (synchronised to the pulse) are also used at some points. Occasional bursts of double-speed material, some randomly panned, animate the mix. Laughter and time-stretched exclamatory words in continuous-rotation (rather than stepping from channel to channel) - lubricate the flow. Towards the end, clipped syllables enter at double tempo on successive channels around the ring, a very rapid stepped-rotation **(Sound Example 119)**.

---

[194] A random frequency tremulation is applied to a stereo sound such that the loudness peak of any one tremulation is (randomly) different in the two channels. If the sound is a space-filling image (not one image to the left, and another to the right) the tremulations seem to move randomly around the space.
[195] After experimenting with various alternatives the simplest approach proved best – adding tiny slivers of silence in the troughs between syllables, or removing tiny slivers of sound from the same place.

Interlude Act 2: Clouds of Speech

The Properties files were used to find common words and syllables, and relevant phrases containing these automatically retrieved. Words, and sub-phrases containing them, were edited out and grouped (e.g. remember, remembering, memory).

Words were chosen because they were used by many speakers and on many occasions, providing a wide variety of sources; because they contained different sounds to the words chosen in previous clouds (different vowels; use of sibilants or liquids); Sometimes for their meaning (remember", "never").

Event clouds were then assembled based on particular words or syllables. The "Remember" cloud assembles short clusters of very short phrases containing the word "remember etc." **(Sound Example 120)**; strong channel-centred-reverberation (see above) of these phrases, producing a different event **(Sound Example 121)**; the syllable "mem" repeated, rotating around the sound-surround space - several different "mem"s rotate together, but at different speeds, and with different rates of repetition, a prominent motif in the Finale of Act 4 **(Sound Example 122)**; a heavily shredded[196] version of this scattered over the sound-surround space **(Sound Example 123)**.

The "Something" cloud, eventually dissolving in its "s" sound, assembles short phrases starting with the word "something" to form a sound-surround texture - this accelerates, rising in pitch (sample-rate change), with its low frequencies gradually filtered away, and the whole image rotates at a faster and faster rate **(Sound Example 124)**; the reverberated end of this mixed to mono, tremulated rapidly and rotated rapidly, used as a separate strand; the same combined in canon, the two images rotating, in parallel, 180 degrees out of step **(Sound Example 125)**; time-stretched versions of the original phrases; aggregates of the "ss" sounds within the phrases, some time-stretched.

The "ll" cloud combines several strands of material each from an individual voice, using multichannel sequences of "li", "la" "lo" syllables, swapping from channel to channel; the same material with iterated repeats[197] of each syllable, each fading into its own reverberation.

The event based on "Different" works similarly but, as it progresses, focuses on the "diff" of "different ", then just the "ff", eventually using time-extended "ff" sounds with tremulations **(Sound Example 126)**. Similarly, the event based on "good" dissolves into a sea of "g" sounds.

The "never" event stresses the pitches of words or syllables through reverberation, or time-stretching, some extended events pulsing and/or rotating round the space. Others use very long spectral-time-stretches which have a "metallic" resonance **(Sound Example 127)**.

---

[196] Sound is cut into random length chunks, and the chunks rejoined in a random order. The resulting sound is the same length as the original, and can be shredded again, then again and so on.

[197] Exact repetition (looping) of materials has a particular synthetic quality. The CDP process of Iteration adds slight randomly variations to the timing and pitch-shift of each repetition of the sound, producing an output more like a naturally-occurring iterated sound.

Interlude 3: Speech Harmony

Using the Properties Files statistics I searched for pitch-groups common to motifs in several different voices, and containing larger pitch intervals. In addition, as adult male voices are typically lower than adult female voices, and both usually lower than young children's voices, I needed to find the most common useful pitch-groups in each range, and decide how these might be combined into harmonies. Eventually a set of 6 harmonic fields were selected, together with the vocal phrases using their pitches. For the 7th field, the low C which ends the sequence, I took vocal lines which hovered around that pitch, and adjusted all the voice pitches closer to the C.

To focus attention on the pitch content, harmonic field filters[198] were constructed, tuned to all the pitches of a chosen set of motifs, and the motifs passed through the filter bank. The first harmonic area in the first half of the section mixes an array of the original voices, one on each channel **(Sound Example 128)** ; the same material mixed in mono and resonated through pitch-following filters **(Sound Example 129)**; the same mono material filtered in such a way that we hear pitch resonances, but not vocal features (like sibilants), all reverberated **(Sound Example 130)**. The mono variants are projected through every loudspeaker so the harmonic field is everywhere. In the second half of the Interlude, these mono materials, reverberated, are made to rotate slowly around the space.

The second harmonic area adds to the reverberant strand a randomised fluttering[199] over the 8 output channels. In the 2nd pass there are two versions of this fluttering material, one echoing the other, slightly delayed and 180 degrees apart (opposite) in the sound-surround space **(Sound Example 131:** *simulation of 8-channel effect***)**.

Some filtered materials, strongly disguising their vocal origin and each with different filter parameters, were combined by sequential cross-fading to create long, pitch-oscillating pedals. At the very end, the low C material of this type is transposed upwards by various octaves and 5ths and these versions combined so the sound appears to swell across the register, and subside into the bass once more. At the same time another strand on C, strongly filtered but still vocally recognisable, rotates around the space **(Sound Example 132)**.

---

[198] Described in the chapter on *Fabulous Paris,* under *"Developing new instruments"*.

[199] Tremolo is applied to a multichannel sound such that the sound rises in level in each loudspeaker in turn. The sequence of channels used for this can be specified in a regular pattern or as a random permutation of all of them (followed by a different permutation, etc. – this ensures all output channels are used equally often).

The Portraits

(most of the portrait sound examples are from stereo originals)

The Fisherman's Tale

Two key ideas here were capturing and time-extending the Northumbrian burr and developing a recurring motto phrase based on the word "herrn". The burr is a characteristic feature of Northumbrian speech, rolled softly on the arch of the tongue, a little further forward than the French "rr". This occurs in the word "herrn" (herring).

Grain-extension[200] was used to greatly extend the burred "rr" in several occurrences of the word "herrn". Shorter and longer extensions, and (static or time-changing) pitch-shifts up one octave, and down one and two octaves were made (without changing the vowel shape or rate of iteration of the "rr"). Combined, these form phrases which descend to the lowest octave using loudness enveloping to crescendo to the final "..rr-n" of the last event **(Sound Example 133)**. More or less reverberation could be added to the tail of this sound.

In parallel the syllable "he" of "herrn" was combined with a reversed copy of itself ("eh"), and the output repeated to produce an ululated version of the syllable. The process was applied to the syllable in four occurrences of the word "herrn" with different pitches, and the ululating lines combined into short phrases **(Sound Example 134)** used on their own or to precede the octave-descending phrase. This ululating material is decelerated as an anacrusis to the final strong cadence.

In addition "Cos you didn't mek nowt" and "Coming aboot (salmon)" are extended by rhythmically overlaid repetition. In the latter case, the phrases gradually fall in pitch (preserving the vocal vowel shapes). The phrase "years ago" is extended by texturing first "years", and then "ago", with no pitch-change of the sources, so that the 3 pitches of the phrase are foregrounded **(Sound Example 135)**. The "o" of ago is then time-stretched, so that its pitch is sustained. The phrase "was still gan" is filtered with a pitch-following-filter[201] and transposed up two octaves to produce the seagull-like sounds which echo the pitch-contour of that vocal phrase **(Sound Example 136)**.

Childrens Voices I

This portrait combines story fragments told by several small boys, attempting to retain the overexcitement of many of the tellings. Various musical objects are created.

Back-to-back versions[202] were made of moments which step between clear pitches. These pitch-oscillating events were overlaid in various ways to make assemblies of characteristic harmony. The end of this material was then strongly reverberated, and this material used independently **(Sound Example 137)**.

---

[200] See the *Globalalia* chapter, section *"Ma-rrr"*.
[201] The Harmonic Field filter mentioned previously, now confined to a single pitchline, which follows the pitch of the vocal line beng filtered.
[202] A time reversed copy of a sound is made, and the original sound edited onto the end of this.

The "tha..t" at the end of "and that was that" was greatly time-stretched by roughness extension[203], then made to rise in pitch (sampling-rate change) **(Sound Example 138)**. Further variants were made, using spectral time-stretching, spectral-tracing[204], and adding tremolo to the stretched tail. This becomes a musical motto.

The clown story falls over itself in excitement, accumulating one bizarre event after another. This is exaggerated by the musical treatment, mixing a layer of variously time-stretched versions of the story with a layer of start-synchronised copies. The copies in this second layer are placed at different positions in the stereo space and each accelerates at a minutely different rate so that stereo echoes gradually emerge **(Sound Example 139)**. Each thread of the premix also gradually merges into a shredded[205] version of the text. Towards the end of the portrait the clown-story is harmonic-field-filtered[206] with increasingly tight filtering, so the pitches of its harmonic field begin to resonate strongly **(Sound Example 140)**.

In the escaped cow story, overexcited delivery of the word "pump"[207] produced "pfump" (an accidental vocal imitation of the cow's flatulence). "Pf" is developed into noisy extended aggregates which are later greatly extended in the Finale of Act 1 **(Sound Example 141)**.

The breaths in two very breathy voices are selected and some developed by time-stretching. In the Finale of Act 4 this material is further stretched, with time-reversals, becoming more like pneumatic machinery, then trembling and rotating round the space **(Sound Example 142)**.

The Budgie

The principal idea here was to capture and extend the grittiness of the voice. A roughness-extension procedure[208] was used to capture and extend grittiness fragments in the voice. Once captured and extended, the rasp-stream could be panned, and/or decelerated, either without changing the duration of the grains, or with time-stretch **(Sound Examples 143)**. The sibilant "s" was extended using a technique similar to roughness-extension[209]; the extended sounds pan across the space, sometimes with a slow slide in tessitura and/or a slow or rapid time-varying tremulation **(Sound Example 144)**. Individual vowels are emphasized by time-stretching and/or reverberation (e.g. the first "e" of "Peter"). Some syllables or words are stereo-bounce echoed with ("Blue") or without ("Peter") pitch-focusing filtering[210]. Very softly-spoken phrases are aggregated **(Sound Examples 145)**, the aggregates punctuating the main narrative.

---

[203] This is the grain-extension process, mentioned elsewhere, applied to the roughness in a vocal sound.
[204] *Only* the most prominent partials in the spectrum are retained, *on a window-by-window basis*. See '*Audible Design*' for more details.
[205] See Footnote 196.
[206] See footnote 198.
[207] North of England word for "fart".
[208] See Footnote 203.
[209] This process searches for noise-bands, rather than iteratives, in the vocal stream, then extends them.
[210] See Footnote 201.

The Bellydancer

This is the only section of the piece to use any sounds *not* derived from the voice recordings themselves. A small brass ensemble picks up prominent pitched-phrases in the speech-line as the story progresses, and these are folded into a simple rhythmic brass-band accompaniment **(Sound Example 146)**. The brass ensemble was enhanced through changing the spectrum of sounds and by mixing sounds together, to generate a larger (imaginary) ensemble. Other modifications were made for specific moments (reverb, excessively wide vibrato etc.).

The principal sound idea is the capture and extension of the rasp-sonority of 'bloke' in the motto phrase "It's a bloke". The "oke" of "it's a bloke", when first heard, has been shortened (by editing). It next occurs in its original form and later is extended using the roughness-extension process **(Sound Examples 147)**. This extended sound becomes important in the Finale of Act 1, where a sequence of exponentially-falling envelopes counted over wavesets[211] generate a bell-like sequence, itself then dissolved by spectral tracing **(Sound Examples 148)**. At the climax of the story, the original speech is enhanced by echoes, texturing, pitch-shifting by octaves, and time-stretching. Part of the reverberant echoes which spread in stereo behind the time-stretched "I've been over there…" are made by extracting the peaks from the vocal phrase and time stretching them 32 times **(Sound Examples 149)**. The very deep transformation uses multiple processes gradually applied to the source ("it's a bloke") including pitch-following filtering, time-stretching producing pulsations (a phasing artefact of spectral time-stretching) and low-pass filtering.

Teens Gossip

Here the aim was to capture the essence of gossip in a rhythmic musical device, hiding the text-content of the gossip. Examples of exclamatory speech were used as a foil to this rhythmic material. Using peak-extraction the peak of each syllable in the speech is grabbed and these peaks reassembled at a regular tempo[212]. This retains the pitch-contour, vowel sequence and changing expressivity of the speech, while losing the specific words used **(Sound Example 150)**. These rhythmic gossip-lines are articulated in various ways; call-and-response in stereo, repetitions of elements in the line, larger-than-life tremolo, texturing of several strands. One gossip phrase is time-stretched to twice its length (half its speed), a cadencing device just before the portrait ends. And at the end of the finale of Act 2, one line of this gossip material recurs in a repeating cycle, circling rapidly around the 8-channel space.

The Act begins with rising phrases from this rhythmic material, used as echoed snippets with reverberation. These recur in textures which are sometimes octave transposed to higher registers (and correspondingly speeded up). These animate the

---

[211] Wavesets are delinated by zero-crossings in the signal. In a complex sound these are irregularly spaced in time. Hence the envelope-attack onset-times, based on counting these, are slightly irregular.

[212] Using a coarse time-window we track the fluctuations in the loudness of speech which correspond to the individual syllables within words. The envelope peaks tell us where the syllables lie, and this information can be used to slice out a specified-duration segment from each syllabic peak (adjusting the cut-points slightly in time to capture the start of the syllables if possible). These can then be reassembled at some specified tempo (or in a specified rhythmic pattern). The result is a rhythmic stream of events which captures both the melodic contour, vowel content and changing expressivity of the speech, whilst losing the specific verbal content.

eight-channel space around the front-stereo "story-telling" **(Sound Example 151)**. The gossip material is interrupted by blocks of several exclamatory voices in which particular words can be heard. These blocks evolve e.g. rising in octave-shifts with no vowel change. Some exclamatory words (e.g. "whopping!") are vastly extended by time-stretching and panned across the stereo space.

The Dancer's Tale

In this portrait we work principally with the pitch implications of the wide-range vocal line. The hesitations and glossalalia in the voice were also collected together to form recurring assemblies of hesitation, resonated in their own harmonic field **(Sound Example 152)**.

To resonate the pitch of the vocal lines, two types of filter were used, a pitch-following filter (PFF) which is a time-varying filter following the changing pitch of the vocal line[213], and a harmonic-field filter (HFF) which is a bank of filters whose tunings do not change with time, but are tuned to all the pitches used in the vocal line (the Harmonic Field of the phrase)[214].

By using a sequence of PFFed echoes of the vocal line, with increasing tightness (Q), and filtering with decreasing numbers of harmonics, the vocal line appears to dissolve into pure melody as we pass from one echo to the next **(Sound Example 153)**. The tail of the echoes can be extended with reverb or time-stretching, while adding time-varying vibrato and/or tremolo to it. An HFF based on the pitches in a particular vocal line can be applied to that entire line, or to a texture of sounds cut from the line (without changing the pitch, therefore preserving the harmonic field). The filter-resonated events can evolve, as different Q-valued versions merge into one another, perhaps with slight tremulations or randomised corrugation of the envelope[215] as they evolve. In this way the harmonic implications of speech lines can be extended in diverse ways **(Sound Example 154)**. Individual words or syllables (e.g. the "awe" of "awestruck") were highlighted by time-stretching and sustained PFF resonances. Later, these same resonances recur, with variation **(Sound Example 155)**. Each syllable of a word can be extended in different ways **(Sound Example 156)**.

In addition, slightly time-stretched echoes of the (possibly PFFed) phrase, suggest the words themselves linger in the resonant space; sibilants and plosives ("s" and "p") were extracted and used to form textures, lingering around the original text **(Sound Example 157)**; the rhythm of "Bob and I go ballroom dancing" was emphasized by rhythmic repetitions, dissolving into filtered variants **(Sound Example 158)**.

---

[213] See Footnote 201.
[214] See Footnote 198.
[215] A sound like laughter (ha-ha-ha-...) has a loudness contour loud-quiet-loud-quiet- etc. A rolled-rr sound has the same contour at a much faster speed. We can exaggerate this contour by making the area of quietness slightly longer and the loudness correspondingly shorter (we are not time-stretching the sound here, just altering the loudness envelope). This is envelope corrugation.

The travelling butcher amplified his sales patter, powering it from a noisy generator attached to his lorry engine **(Sound Example 159)**. The first problem was to separate his voice from the rumble of the generator. The thin quality of the extracted voice, however, gave it a sonic character distinct from the other portrait voices, and the lorry rumble itself could be used as a distinct musical element.

First of all we use spectral subtraction[216] to remove the generator's rumble from the voice. As the rumble is very loud, the remnant voice has lost all its low-frequency components and is strongly coloured, as if heard through a poor-quality walkie-talkie **(Sound Example 160)**. The transformed voice was then cleaned with the Cleaning Kit (see "Cleaning"). To obtain the lorry, parts of the source where the voice was silent were separated out and joined together, then extended by repetitions to produce a sound of generator-rumble only. A pitch-focusing filter, of low Q and at the pitch (and just 2 harmonics) of the most prominent pitch in the rumble, is applied to focus the sound **(Sound Example 161)**.

The rumble material was then used as a distinct musical strand, pitch-shifted up by 1, 2, 3 and 4 octaves (transposing the spectrum), and these transpositions gradually cross-faded so that the rumble rises in tessitura. The material of the highest transposition was then cut into segments, isolating individual 'plops' of the sound, and these used to form a texture (sounding much like the pre-textured source). The sounds within this were gradually pitch-shifted upwards (sample-rate change) and the texture then cross-faded into the end of the transposing rumble, to extend the tessitura of the complete sound upwards, with variations **(Sound Example 162)**.

The extracted voice is progressively processed, first by spectral-tracing, then spectral-blurring and low-pass filtering, losing clarity as it dissolves. This complete strand wanders slowly away from centre stage. A copy then enters at the centre, taking the opposite route, then a third. The three gradually merge to a mono moving line, and vibrato is added, the verbal content completely obscured. Finally the peaks of the obscured-voice are abstracted and retimed at approximately double the tempo of the transformed-lorry 'plops', just before the original voice-line recurs **(Sound Example 163)**.

In the second half of the portrait the materials begin again at their starting point, but they are progressively time-contracted, and mixed with accelerating vocal lines in an accelerating spin through the stereo space.

---

[216] A portion of the recording with generator sound only (no voice) is spectrally analysed and the maxima, in all spectral channels, are subtracted from the complete (generator + voice) recording. For a very low level noise floor, this is an excellent means to remove unwanted noise, but in this case the lorry is sufficiently loud that, on subtracting it from the voice, we lose most of the voice's low frequencies.

Childrens Voices II

This portrait combines story fragments told chiefly by girls. Harmonic implications of stories and phrases are extended. The various "Do you know?" phrases are used as a recurring refrain, sometimes clustered, leading to the girl's story towards the end of the portrait. Various speakings of "Humpty" and "Dumpty", from the telling of the nursery rhyme, are aggregated, and the aggregates progressively harmonic-field-filtered. The ends of the aggregates are reverberation-resonated. This resonated material is extended and used in its own right **(Sound Example 164)**.

The hamster-tale voice has characteristic rising intonation. This is emphasized in a texture made from these rising gestures. Towards the end this texture is 'plucked' by steep-falling loudness-envelopes (based on counting wavesets) **(Sound Example 165)**. The rising scale of the laugh in the "wishing star" story is time-extended by regular repetitions spread across the stereo space. An abstracted variant is made by harmonic-field-filtering (few harmonics and tight filtering), disguising vocal features.

The rising cry "I went out" at the end of the aeroplane/pushchair story is aggregated with various pitch-following-filtered versions of itself, retaining the characteristic harmonic field **(Sound Example 166)**.

The Farmer's Tale

This voice has very characteristic cross-break articulations. These were used to create a bagpipe-like instrument to accompany the story. The various vocal-breakings were first cut out from the source and then passed through pitch-following filters with the appropriate number of harmonics and Q-value, preserving the pitch-leaps in the voice. The ends of individual notes were extended or contracted by time-stretching, and more or less of the start-articulation included, depending on the note's position in the 'bagpipe' phrase. In this way enough individual bagpipe-articulated notes were generated to create a virtual instrument which could be used to accompany the original spoken voice **(Sound Example 167)**. These articulated notes are further developed in the Finale of Act 3 **(Sound Example 168)**.

In addition the phrase "round and round and round" is extended by rhythmic repetition, later combined with a similar treatment of "as you go round". The principal pitches of the two phrases lie on a pentatonic scale and this material, itself rotated in the stereo space[217], is used to accompany the storytelling **(Sound Example 169)**. The occasional 'fluttering' of syllables in the original voice is quietly extended, a sound feature used in the Finale of Act 5 **(Sound Example 170)**; a harmonic field resonance from a phrase lingers, and so on.

---

[217] See footnote 134 in the *Imago* chapter.

Heathcliffe, come here!

In this portrait several extended narratives are presented, all pushed nearer to the same regular moderato tempo, close to the original, with repetitions of individual phrases, spatial antiphony etc. used to underline this, increasingly so as the portrait progresses.. As the tales unfold, individual words or phrases are sonically developed, becoming recurring musical elements, articulating the musical flow.

Individual FOFs[218] within the phrase "Heathcliffe, come here!!" are captured and time-frozen on their particular pitch to generate several variants of the phrase. Variable vibrato is added to the sustained FOFs to give a more plausible sung quality. Further variants are made by panning across the stereo space. Later, some of these have part of their spectrum spectrally pitch-shifted up or down by octaves producing chords in the voice, or events in higher registers. All these variants become "recurring" musical elements in the portrait **(Sound Example 171)**.

The mainly unvoiced "..cliffe" part of this phrase and, later, various speakings of the word "pencil" (with strong plosive and unvoiced elements) are elaborated through the repetition of tiny different-sized chunks within the sound, selected by counting specific numbers of zero-crossings (waveset repetition). "Pencil" is also elaborated by textured repetition, superimposing different speakings of the word, mixes of all of these with the waveset-repetitions, time-stretches of the tail of "pen", aggregates of "pe", and random shredding of the word itself **(Sound Examples 172)**.

A patterned extension of the word "democracy" is created by chopping it into random chunks, then repeating these in a regular permutation sequence (defined by an English bell-ringing pattern). This is then cross-faded into a version of the same sequence of events, with each event pitch-focused-filtered at its own pitch **(Sound Examples 173)**. This is further developed in the Finale of Act 3 (hear **Sound Example 191**).

Other words and events ("afternoon", "look", the laugh on "had ") are elaborated in various ways, "afternoon" being sung as a chord by superimposing pitch-shifted copies which retain the vowel-character of the original, then gradually adding a pulsating tremolo **(Sound Examples 174)**.

The Stories I Hear

Sylvia uses many different voices to tell her stories. I decided to use expressive snippets from the stories, juxtaposed with developments of various growls, yells and break-crossings from the voice. The phrases "then all of a sudden, it's dangerous..." and "the stories I hear" are repeated to give the portrait a song-like structure. The audience's "oo" and laugh responses were gathered into stereo groups, and become recurring musical elements **(Sound Examples 175)**.

The growling voice of "have you had a go(rr) an em", was developed, creating stereo mixes out of repetitions of part-phrases; textures of the growly element "had a" at regular intervals and increasing densities; and differently engineered roughness-extensions of "go(rr)" which are then rapidly panned. The last of these morphs briefly

---

[218] The voiced sounds in speech are produced by a sequence of small wave-packets or FOFs

into a watery sound (using tiny displacements of the pitches of the grit particles during roughness-extension[219]) **(Sound Examples 176)**.

For the high-pitched yell of "are you still using that thing", several individual FOFs[220] from the vowels are extracted. Then each is used as a very bright "instrument" playing at the original pitch-line of the voice (sometimes transposed down an octave). Several such instruments are combined into a squawking aggregate **(Sound Examples 177)**. Several variants are used. One spins round the stereo space, accelerating and rising in pitch as it fades.

In the yelled phrase with break-crossing "Three years on the bloody trot", individual syllables or words which jump the break in pitch (and some time-reversed versions) are aggregated into a stereo texture, preserving the pitches. A variant of this transposes the texture up an octave, preserving the vowel shapes **(Sound Examples 178)**.

The Soldier's Tale

In this portrait, the sub-phrase "so close" is used as the source of both pitched and unpitched materials to be developed, especially during the Finale of Act 3. The "s" sounds from "so close" are extracted and assembled into a stereo event with a regular pulse, repeating like a shaken sand-filled rattle. This is made from the two syllables with their low frequencies filtered out, hence focusing on the sibilants. The resulting pulse streams are corrugated (see earlier) **(Sound Examples 179)**. In the finale of Act 3 this stereo materials returns, faster and more focused.

The falling minor 3rd of "so close" is developed. Very long reverberation added to the "o" of "close", greatly extends the lower pitch. This extended phrase is also transposed down a minor 3rd so the lower note of the original is in tune with the upper note of the transposed phrase – and also with the "o" of "ago" in "a long time ago". The rhythmic repetition of the two pitches (with randomised sequencing of pitches, and their accentuation) occurs half way through this portrait, becoming a key feature of the Finale of Act 3. This is made in the same way as the sibilant stream but with the sibilants filtered out, hence focusing on the pitched vowels. It is then corrugated **(Sound Examples 180)**. Towards the end of the portrait, the stream is pitch-shifted up an octave plus a 6th.

In addition, some phrases (e.g. "there was a ditch at the side") are echoed by soft brass-like sounds (pitch-following filtering of the vocal line), and a final variation of "a very red mark that's all" is transposed down an octave (without changing the vowels). The pitches of the vowels of this phrase are resonated by a harmonic field filter and extended in time and tessitura to generate the chord which swells over the end of the portrait.

---

[219] See also the end of section *"Ma-rrr"*, in the *Globalalia* chapter.
[220] See footnote 218.

These rapidly delivered narratives go gradually "out of focus" as they are told, and sounds mentioned in stories (e.g. duck quacks, the toast) are elaborated. Each narrative is synchronised to the same regular pulse, slightly faster than the original. The stressed syllables in each word are slightly exaggerated (loudness contouring), then the phrases synchronised to the beat by subtly retiming the syllables. The rhythmic regularity is underlined by repeating elements and by echoes, playing across the stereo space, all synchronised with the pulse. As each narrative begins, two further copies of the story are introduced, each at a very slightly slower speed, so that the story becomes first reverberant, then echoed, then "muddied".

In addition, sibilants (especially the "ts" ending "pourin through mi texts") are extended, panned and trembled, articulating the rhythm, like percussion instruments **(Sound Examples 181)**. The phrase "travelling poet" becomes a repeating element with variations **(Sound Examples 182)** made variously by strongly reinforcing the "t" of "travelling" and the "p" of "poet"; isolating syllable peaks (with surrounding silence) then superimposing these on the original sound, emphasizing the rhythm of the phrase; resonating the two pitches with a pitch-focusing filter using a high Q and few harmonics, to focus on and extend the pitches, which become pedal points for the tales. One of these pitches is echoed by similar treatment of "(a bit of a) do".

Sound events mentioned in the stories are picked up and elaborated. Keith's imitations of duck quacks are developed as an assembly of (human imitations of) duck quacks **(Sound Examples 183)**. The toast "To the Cosmos", related in the story, is echoed by a pre-recorded male chorus **(Sound Examples 184)**.

The Best Thing That Ever Happened To Me

The principal feature of this vocal material is the rising melodic shape of the ends of most phrases, some rising to the 5th of the scale, and some (as in "I just loved it") to the sharpened 4th. The various rising phrase-ends in the voice were collected together and used to form a texture. This was filtered through a harmonic field filter based on the (tempered scale) pitches of the vocal lines which rises to the 5th. The filtered version is added to the unfiltered version in the mix, and as it enters, the tuning of the texture is pushed upwards towards the 5th. Another process was used to extract all the vocal FOFs from one of these phrases, and the pitch-line of the phrase was pitch-tracked[221]. Several versions of the pitch line were then resynthesized, each using a single FOF, and these enveloped with the loudness contour of the original voice. These string-like sounds were then textured together (heard most clearly towards the end of the portrait) **(Sound Examples 185)**.

---

[221] Speaking (not whispering) voices, use pitch in the vowel sounds, and in many consonant sounds. The pitches are not restrained to any scale and generally slide about (rather than step carefully). This (real, sliding) pitch of speech can be tracked by first extracting the time-changing spectrum of the phrase. In each spectral window (time-frame) we search for peaks, and compare their frequencies. If these are (roughly) whole number multiples of the lowest peak's frequency, then the spectrum is said to be 'harmonic' and corresponds to a clear pitch. Complications occur with sounds which are pitched but noisy (e.g."zz"), unpitched elements (e.g. "s") and silences. So we need to deal with these (e.g. by interpolating between the real pitches on either side of these pitch-free events, or by inserting markers to indicate that no pitch is present) when generating a pitch-line equivalent of the speech phrase.

The phrase "exciting life" also has strong pitch contours. The same "strings" procedure is applied to this phrase, and variants are constructed by forcing the final glissandi to rise to a note an octave (or 2 octaves) above the original goal pitch, or to rise from a register to the original pitches from an octave below. The various versions are combined to form a texture around the original vocal phrase **(Sound Examples 186)**.

The Finales

(Sound examples are stereo reductions)

Finale Act 1

In the Finale of Act 1 many sonic events from the Act are extended, elaborated and spatialised. Here are a few examples.

The descending "herrn" phrase creates a recurring pedal, which now descends to deeper octaves and, at the very end of the finale, slowly pulsates.

The "f" of "pfump" is time-stretched by roughness-extension and rotates slowly around the space. Many "pf" sounds are massed in an extended sound-surround texture. On its final appearance, this gradually becomes very-dense **(Sound Example 141)** and crosses over into the Voicewind with which the Act had begun, and now ends. Another thread of this extended texture rises slowly in tessitura. In a further strand, the two (adjacent) pitches of the text, which tune with the "herrn" event, are focused by a harmonic field filter (the vocal character disappearing) and pulsed, the pulse rotating around the space.

The rising tail of the transformed "And that was tha.....aat" is greatly time-stretched, with tremolo added, rotating around the space, leading to an explosive end. Sometimes 3 (or more) rotations chase one another, spatially 120 degrees out of step **(Sound Example 187:** *reduced to stereo***)**.

The "...oke" of "It's a bloke" is vastly time-stretched by roughness-extension. In one variant this sound is harmonic-field-filtered, and rapidly zigzag-panned[222] over the 8 channels, creating an illusion of "everywhereness". In another, waveset-counted steeply-descending loudness envelopes transform the sound to a stream of 'plucked' pitches **(Sound Example 148)**. The tail of this sound is elaborated variously, in the strand in the example by gradual spectral tracing crossing into a watery texture of the traced elements, whilst in another strand, pitch-rising and pitch-falling copies are superimposed on the original. It is combined with a slowly rotating extension of the extended "grit" sound from the Budgie Tale, gradually pitch-resonated through tight filtering.

---

[222] Zigzagging reads a sound file back and forth at random (or in a user-specified way). Zigzag panning pans each zig or zag between output channels in a randomly permuted order. With rapid panning the sound seems to be everywhere at once.

Finale Act 2

The Finale begins with the fluttering material with which the entire Act begins, and ends with a long extension (by repetition) of one of the "Gossip" phrases, now rotating around the surround space and cadencing inconclusively, as in its original appearance. Harmonic field extensions of materials previously used in the Act are extended in time and animated in the 8 channels space, juxtaposed and variously transposed, to form a harmonically evolving web. The butcher's voice contrasts with this tempered scale material as it is approximately a quarter-tone out of tune, and spectral hold[223] is applied to some of its syllables producing strange inharmonic resonances. Meanwhile the high-pitch fluttering, derived from the lorry rumble, rotates.

Finale Act 3

This finale is in ternary form. In the first and third parts, the rhythmic pulsed materials derived from "so close", from The Soldier's Tale, are developed. The "s" based material is now faster, and more regularly and incisively pulsed. It is introduced by a quickly rotating and tessitura-descending crescendo onto an explosive attack, a stack[224] of reverberated versions of one impulse (**Sound Example 188:** *stereo reduction*). This then tremolos into the tempo of the Finale, and recurs later (or is implied) as the Finale proceeds. The pulsating "ss" then wrap-pans[225] across the space, eventually leading to successive impulses being assigned to random permutations of the output channels. Other strands of this material are fed through pitch-focused filters where the Q value slowly increases, gradually focusing each strand onto a different pitch or pitch-pair. Meanwhile, the two-pitch stream also derived from "so close" is also panned around random permutations of the channels, at its original pitches, and a minor third lower.

"Heathcliffe" derived events are extended in time (FOF-extension or long reverb), some rotated with a slowly rising and falling pitch like a siren, others rising in pitch and pulsating at the basic tempo of the music, and so on. The "Three years" material from "The Stories I Hear" is time-extended, while the "are you still using that thing" event is elaborated by layering variously time-stretched copies animated by their own stereo delays. This creates short and long versions of a recurring phrase with a vibratoed middle note. The "gorr" material becomes an extended aggregate with a long derived rasp at the end, juxtaposed with the above (**Sound Example 189**). Horn-like vocal sounds, which step upward, derive from the voice in "The Farmer's Tale", (**Sound Example 190**) while deep pedals from the "Herrn" event recur beneath all this material .

The central section develops the "democracy" bell-ringing event from "Heathcliffe, Come Here". As the pattern repeats, the word chunks are increasingly pitch-focus-

---

[223] The spectrum in a single analysis window is sustained. With noisy, inharmonic or modified spectra (like the Butcher's voice) this produces a sustained inharmonic sound (we hear several unrelated pitches not lying on the tempered scale).
[224] Sample-rate-changed transpositions of the source (lower sounds being longer) are superimposed on one another. If the attacks of all copies of an attack-resonance event are precisely synchronised, the stacked events merge into a single new sound (we do not hear the result as a chord of several sounds).
[225] See *A Sound-Surround Working Environment* earlier in the chapter.

filtered at their own pitches, creating a bell-like resonance. The sequence is punctuated by increasingly deep stacks of these pitch-resonated sounds, deeper "bells" (**Sound Example 191**: *stereo reduction and contraction*). The horn-like vocals float above, some direct extensions of the voice in "The Farmer's Tale", some pitch-following filtered and more "instrumental" but with voice-like vibrato at their tails while other sounds deriving from this voice read back-and-forth across the break in the voice producing a rapid soft ululation (**Sound Example 192**).

Finale Act 4

The finale of Act4 brings together and reworks many of the materials previously heard in the Finales of Acts 1, 2 and 3, leading to a tolling of the biggest of the "democracy" bells, each toll anticipated by a long anacrusis (a very long time-stretch of the opening of that same sound). Over this the speaking voices begin to sing. Some voices extend single notes by long reverberation; others use vowel-preserving spectral pitch-shifting on a time-stretched note. But most are extended by freezing the voice on a specific FOF impulse within a vowel, and using this to recreate a vocal line of designed pitch[226]. Time-varying vibrato of various (slightly randomised) depths and frequencies is added to the recreated line to produce a more plausible singing quality (**Sound Examples 193**).

At the end of the piece, there are two strands of many voices, each strand filling all 8 channels in the surround-sound space. One of these strands appears to dissolve the voices in a patina of high frequency mouth-crackling. This is itself made up of two 8-channel mixes, each with 1 voice placed on each of the 8 channels. Both strands were fluttered[227], causing fragments of each voice in turn to be heard in its own channel. The entire sound-surround image was then set in rotation at an accelerating rate. Waveset omission[228] was then progressively applied to the sound end, giving it an increasingly gritty quality. The tail of this sound was passed through a pitched filter-bank, a slowly rising bank of 4ths, and the output progressively high-pass filtered (so we hear only unvoiced or apparently unvoiced constituents) and reverberation gradually introduced as it fades to nothing.

The other 8-channel strand is slowly dissolved, through increasing density and shuddering, into the Voicewind sound, mirroring the opening of the entire piece.

---

[226] The voiced sounds in speech are produced by a sequence of small wave-packets or FOFs. The speed at which these FOFs come past determines the pitch of the voice, whilst the particular shape of the packet defines the sonority we hear e.g. an "aa" as opposed to an "oo". In the real world, when the pitch goes up, the FOFs are truncated (rather than squeezed) without altering too much their basic shape. We can emulate this by the simpler process of slightly overlapping the FOFS, again *without* changing the length of each packet. (If we overlap the packets too much we produce a kind of reverberation effect as the sound is effectively echoing itself). In the real world, when the pitch goes down, the FOFs are extended (rather than stretched) continuing their basic shape in some coherent way. We can emulate this simply by spacing out the FOFs, leaving silence in between them. Despite the artificiality of this approach, the results (vocal sounds transposed down in pitch while preserving their vowel character) are convincing.

[227] Tremolo is applied to a multichannel sound such that the sound rises in level in each loudspeaker in turn. The sequence of loudspeakers used for this can be specified in a regular pattern or as a random permutation of all of them (followed by a different permutation, etc. – this ensures all output channels are used equally often).

[228] A proportion of wavesets (delineated by counting signal zero-crossings) are replaced by silence.

Diffusion
of stereo works

DIFFUSION OF STEREO WORKS

Most of the pieces described in this book are in stereo, intended to be expanded to multi-loudspeaker performance by diffusion. For diffusion, the stereo signal from the source is fed to several stereo-pairs of loudspeakers positioned appropriately around the auditorium. Usually the left channel of any pair is on the left of the auditorium and the right channel on the right, but some loudspeakers may be positioned differently (see *Diffuse* and *Close*).

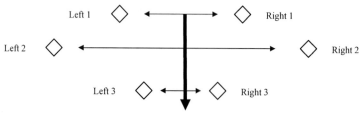

Where the performance space is long and narrow, in order to maximise the number of audience members receiving a stereo image, and if the loudspeakers are of identical type, the rear loudspeakers can be exchanged, giving a set of different stereo images at the front of the space and at the sides.

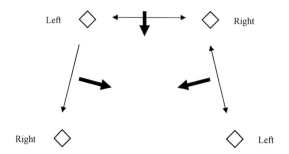

However, this is an exceptional situation and we'll assume that loudspeakers are assigned in the normal way, left channels to the left of the auditorium, right channels to the right.

During the performance the balance of the signal between these different stereo pairs can be altered, dynamically, by using faders on a mixing desk controlling the level on individual (pairs of) loudspeakers. In some situations, this control can be extended by forms of fader-automation. However, some kind of manual override should always be retained as the presence of the audience will alter the acoustic of the performance space, so an ideal diffusion achieved in rehearsal may sound quite different once the audience has filled the space.

155

The aim of diffusion is to underline or enhance the gestures in the music, or the character of contrasting sections. To achieve this, loudspeaker pairs need to be positioned in the space to produce contrasting but compatible sound images. How this is done will depend on the number and type of loudspeakers available and the nature of the space. As the aim of stereo diffusion is to ring the changes on the musical material, the loudspeaker pairs need not be of identical type. Decisions usually need to be made on the basis of the room characteristics and the loudspeakers available at the venue, cutting one's cloth to best suit the circumstances.

Subwoofers (carrying just the lowest frequency content of the signal) are anyway distinct and their positioning in the space is not so critical, as the spatial location of the source of low sounds is difficult for the human ear to determine. Speakers used for a *Diffuse* or *Far* signal (see below) need not be of such a high quality as those used for the principal stage projection - foldback monitors for example, if sufficiently powerful, may be used for this. As high frequencies convey more spatial-location information to the ear, grids of tweeters
suspended above the audience, can be used to enhance spatial information, if they are available.

The structure and acoustics of the room are also important. Performance spaces should be acoustically dry, rather than the lively acoustic preferred by chamber groups. Drapes or material-faced screens, carpets and soft-furnishings (as well as the audience itself) will all help to dampen the acoustic of the space. There are many possibilities for positioning loudspeakers, and these will depend to some extent on the geometry of the performance space. I will discuss only a few typical positionings - *Stage, Wide, Very Wide, Far, High, Diffuse, Close, Punch* and *Rear*.

The minimum setup for diffusion would be a *Stage* pair of loudspeakers giving a front stereo sound image, and a *Wide* pair of loudspeakers positioned wider than the first pair. Adding the wide pair to the stage pair, produces a panoramic stereo spread appropriate for an audience in a medium to large auditorium. (Stage means only the area in front of the audience and does not necessarily imply a raised stage area in the auditorium).

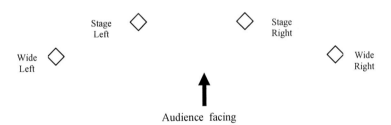

The loudspeakers should be at the same height, and each pair should be angled to give a stereo image near to the centre of the audience, and the audience should be encouraged to sit centrally in the space (rather than on the peripheries).

This basic setup can be extended to wider and more lateral positions, and as more of these loudspeakers are brought into the mix the audience is wrapped in the sound.

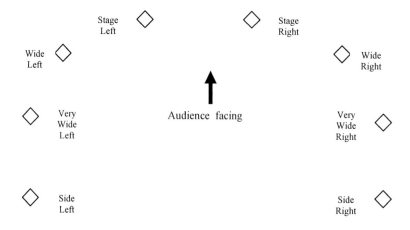

With this arrangement it is also possible to make elaborate diffusion moves, for example cross-fading between a pairing of Very-Wide-Left with Stage-Right to a pairing of Very-Wide-Right with Stage-Left, via a paring of Wide-Left with Wide Right (see diagram) causing the stereo image to rotate clockwise, but such moves would need to have some very specific relation to the evolution of the musical material being presented.

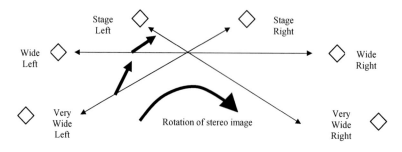

Depth or distance, in front of the audience (*Far* loudspeakers) can be achieved simply by positioning loudspeakers a long way back from the front of the stage, where the stage area is sufficiently deep. In more typical situations, far loudspeakers can be placed at the rear of a shallow stage, and facing away from the audience, into drapes if they face a solid reflective wall. If necessary, high frequency roll-off can be applied to the sends to these loudspeakers to mimic the high-frequency-loss-with-distance of sources in the real world.

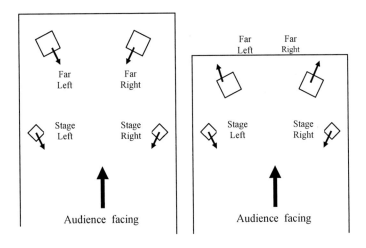

Audience facing

Audience facing

A *High* position can be used to project sound over the heads of the audience. This can underline particular sound gestures, or place a whole section of material in the upper plane. Mixing between the *Stage-Wide* plane and the upper plane can gradually lift the image. Balconies can be used to position high loudspeakers, or speakers can be hung from a grid, but such high loudspeakers must project over the heads of the audience, rather than being angled down towards the audience (the usual positioning of overhead loudspeakers in clubs and other venues, where the aim is to achieve a consistentcy of sound projection, rather than the diversity of possibilities required for good diffusion). High positioning does not always have the intended effect, especially in very reverberant spaces.

Diffuse projection aims to bounce the sound from the walls or ceiling of the space, to fill the space with sound for particular gestures or, for example, to throw the sound upwards where it can be taken up by any set of *high* loudspeakers. I use this diffusion sequence in the projection of the *Fugu-Sea* events in *Imago*. A diffuse option is always useful in any diffusion configuration. Diffuse speakers can be placed by the side walls of the auditorium, angled at, say, 45 degrees so that they play sound towards the walls, bouncing it upwards to the ceiling (the walls must be reflective). Or a pair of loudspeakers may be placed on the stage, pointing sideways (at right angles to the direction the audience faces) and angled upwards to bounce sound off the ceiling.

Projection at lower level but nearer to the audience on *close* loudspeakers, can help differentiate a more intimate section of musical material. The second movement of *Two Women* is often diffused first from a set of close loudspeakers, gradually adding other pairs, including the diffuse, as the musical material becomes more elaborate so that the sound image gradually fills up the space, returning to the intimate projection for the end of this movement. Close loudspeakers can be smaller studio monitors placed near to the audience, in a lower plane than the Stage-Wide principal pairs and, where sufficient small matching loudspeakers are available, possibly paired Left-Right-Left-Right-etc around the space to give a clear stereo image to as many audience-members as possible.

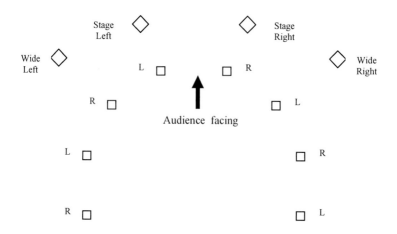

A pair of loudspeakers may be positioned together at front centre stage to add *Punch* to significant percussive attacks in the music.

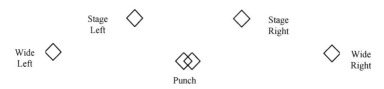

Rear loudspeakers may also be placed behind the audience. I use *Rear* loudspeakers only sparingly when diffusing stereo pieces, as hearing sound from behind is intrinsically more disturbing than hearing sounds from the direction in which you are facing. In a multichannel surround-sound situation, the rear perspective is integrated into the total panorama, but in a stereo piece, there needs to be some good reason to project the stereo image from behind the audience. However, at the end of the first area of *Tongues of Fire*, about 10 minutes into the piece, a quiet clock-like ticking sound slowly decelerates, leading to a pause, followed by a strong restatement of the theme. I sometimes slowly migrate this ticking sound to the *Rear* loudspeakers, switching rapidly back to the normal frontal configuration (during the pause) for the theme restatement. So, in a sense, the sound-image drifts off to another place (which could also be *Far*) so as to enhance the impact of the restated theme.

In larger systems, extra loudspeaker sets may be available. The example diffusion of *Red Bird* included in later pages used the BEAST system at Birmingham University. Here *Desk* refers to loudspeakers positioned at the mixing desk in the centre of the audience, and facing outwards. *V.Dist* are faraway speakers, even more distant than *Far* (e.g. these might be speakers positioned outside the auditorium). The BEAST system has a great number of loudspeakers, so that *High* is represented by a whole layer of loudspeakers on an upper balcony (so *High-Rear* is mentioned), while *Side-Fill* loudspeakers are of a type and positioning to provide a filling-out of the image without being prominently present in the mix.

During rehearsals it's important to listen from various different seating positions in the auditorium, paying particular attention to the most peripheral seats (those furthest removed from the ideal centre of the stereo image). A projection may sound perfect from a mixing desk placed at the centre of the stereo image but underwhelming if sitting on the periphery so compromises may have to be made to provide a good experience for the majority of the audience. The presence of the audience will itself alter the venue acoustic, but this should not drastically alter the main features of the rehearsed diffusion - in general, the overall level may need to rise slightly, perhaps slightly differently on different loudspeakers.

For each piece I create a rudimentary graphic diffusion score blank. Any names given to sound-events in these scores are merely for purposes of easy event recognition, and do not represent the way in which the sound-materials were thought about during the construction of the piece. The scores for later pieces have more precise timing information. Diffusion-score blanks for several of the pieces described in this book will be found at the end of the book, and may be copied for use in further performances.

For a particular event in a specific venue with a specific set of loudspeakers, the diffusion instructions for the performance are written onto this diffusion-blank. These specific instructions are determined during rehearsal of the piece in the space, and act as a guide or reminder for the performance proper. In the following pages you will find some examples of worked diffusion scores from particular performances, some of which are more detailed than others.

DIFFUSION EXAMPLES:

Worked Examples of Diffusion Scores

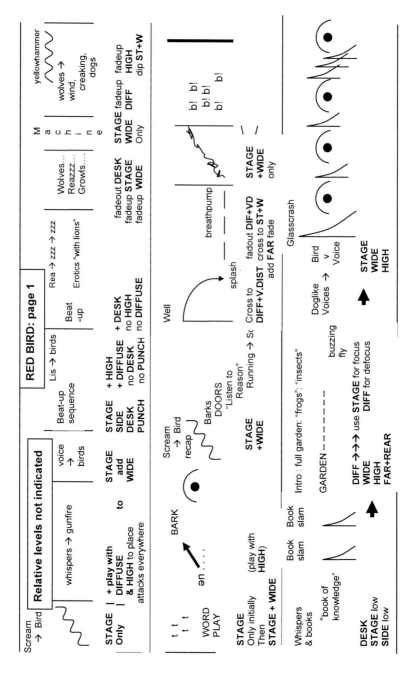

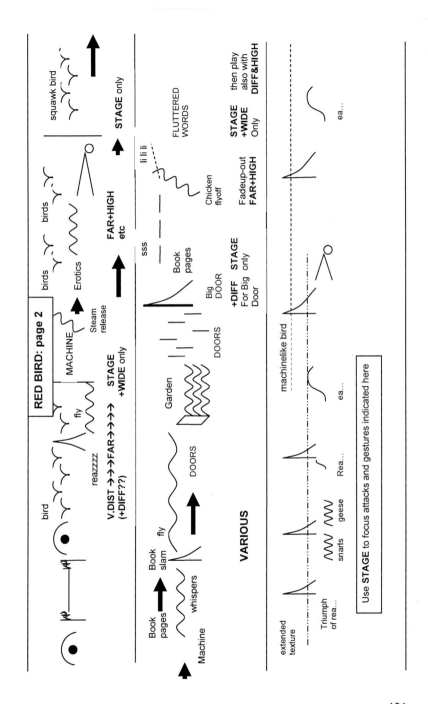

RED BIRD: page 2

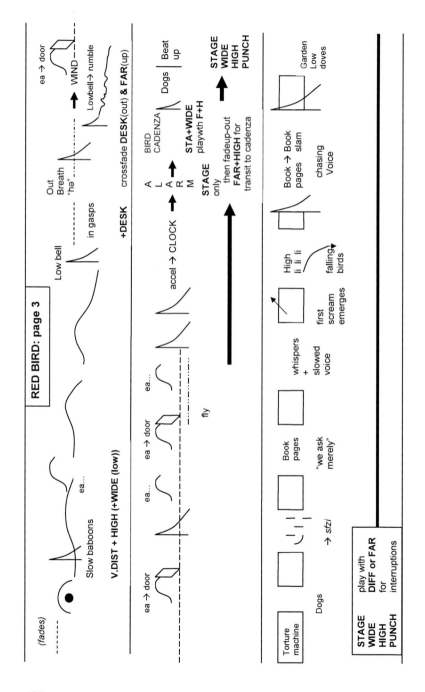

RED BIRD: page 3

165

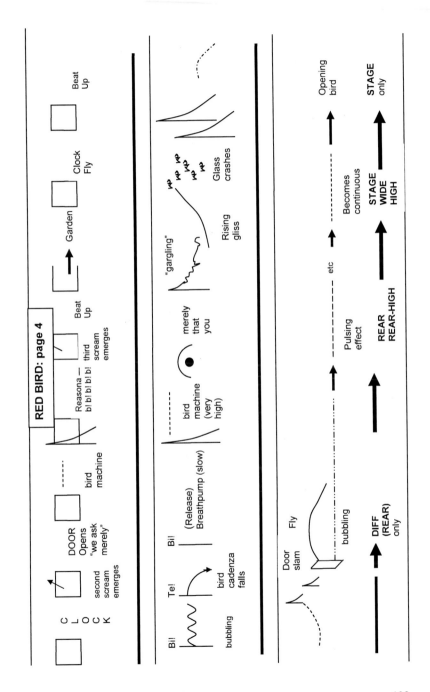

RED BIRD: page 4

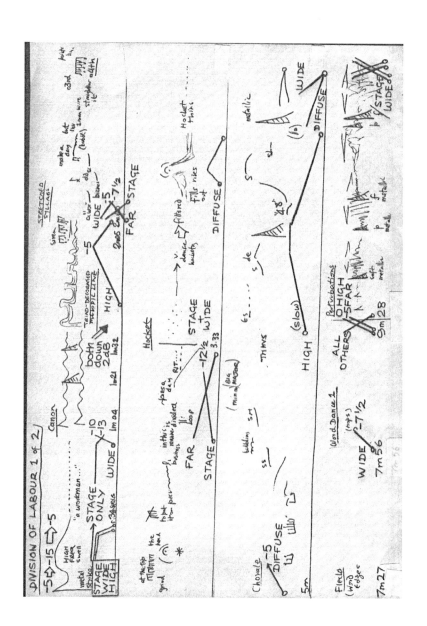

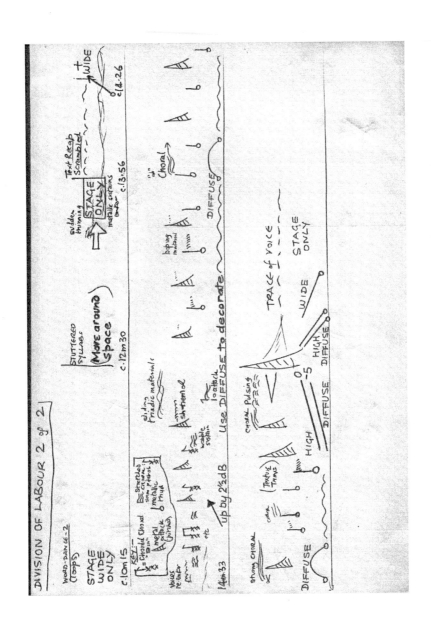

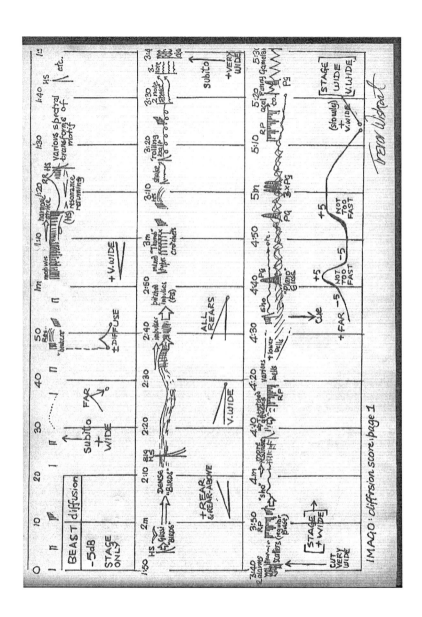

IMAGO : diffusion score : page 1

Trevor Wishart

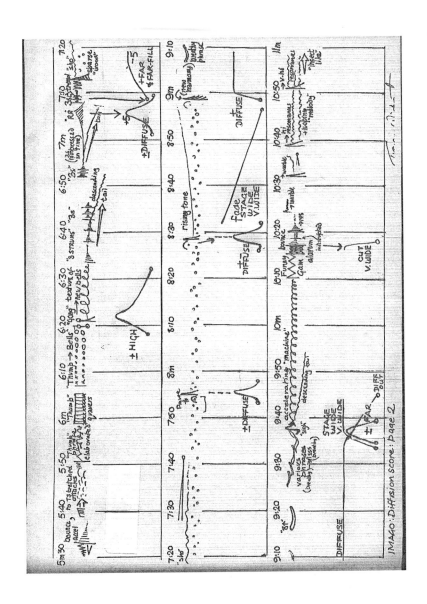

IMAGO: Diffusion score: Page 2

170

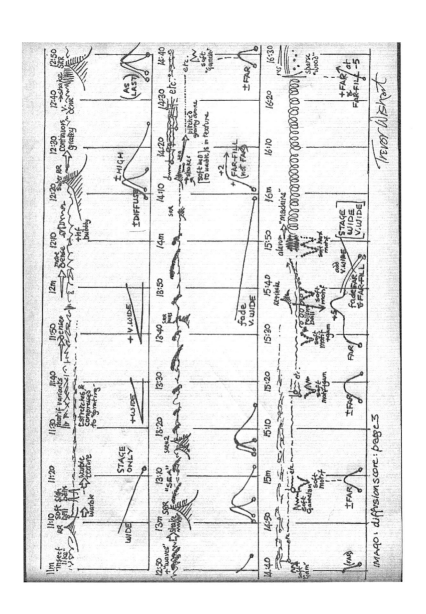

IMAGO: diffusionscore: page 3

171

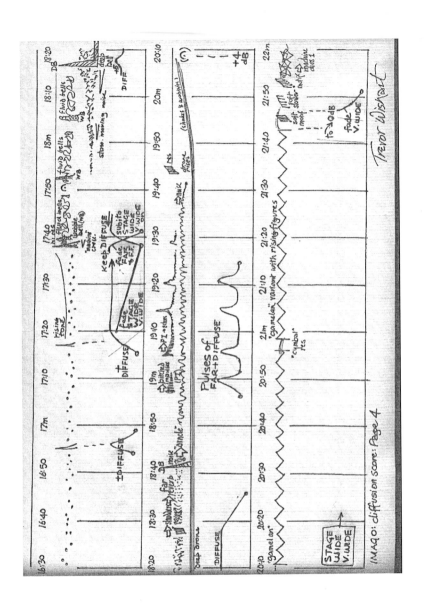

IMAQO: diffusion score: Page 4

Trevor Wishart

172

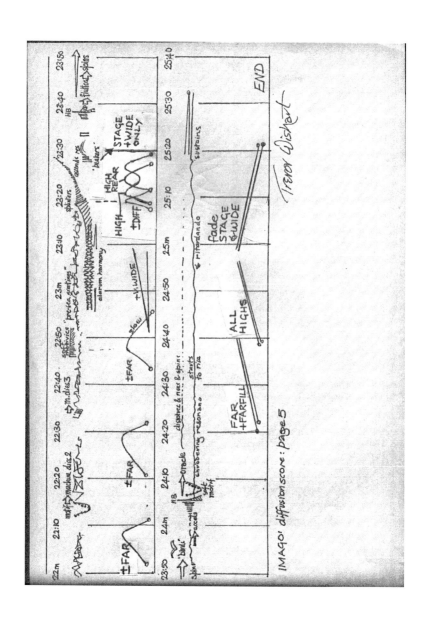

IMAGO: diffusion score: page 5

Trevor Wishart

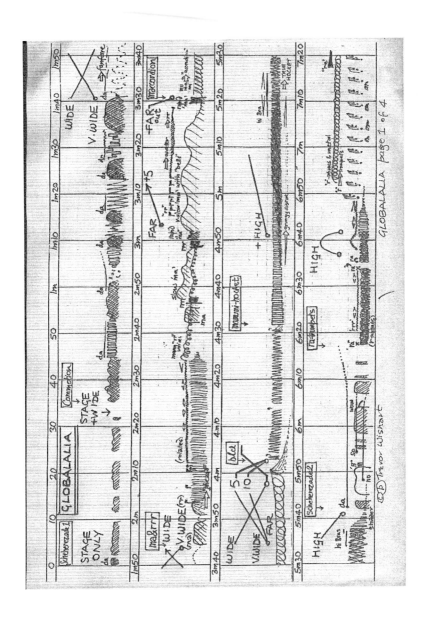

GLOBALALIA page 1 of 4

© Trevor Wishart

174

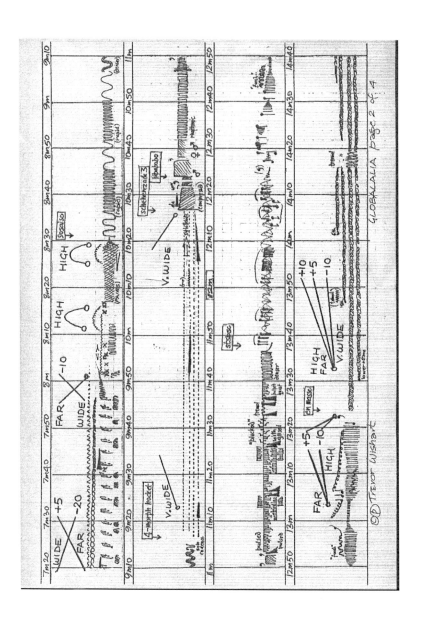

GLOBALALIA page 2 of 4

© Trevor Wishart

175

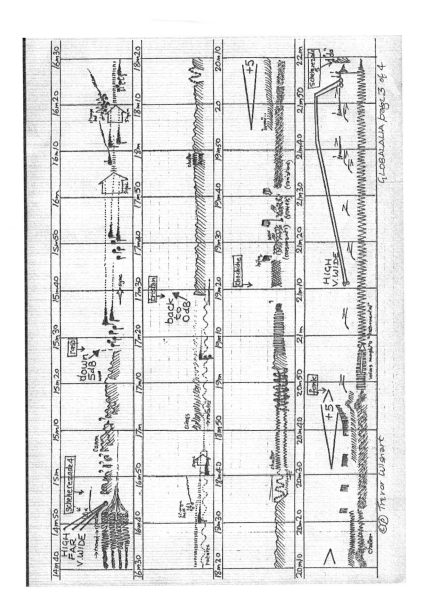

GLOBALALIA page 3 of 4

©® Trevor Wishart

176

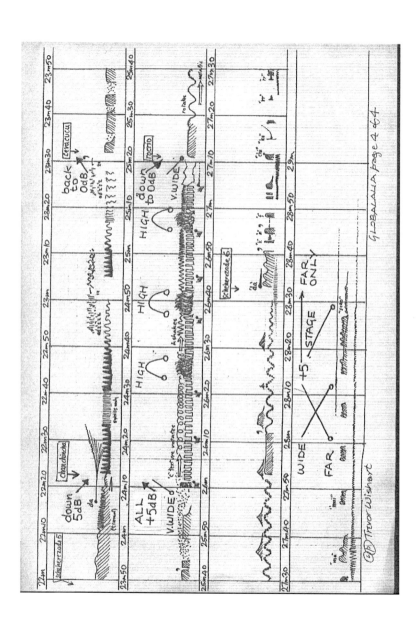

© Trevor Wishart

GLOBALALIA page 4 of 4

177

DIFFUSION SCORES:

Blanks

(the following pages may be freely copied)

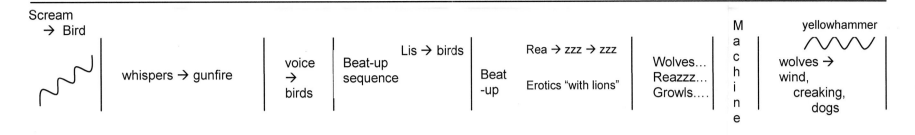

Scream
→ Bird

whispers → gunfire

voice
→
birds

Beat-up
sequence

Lis → birds

Beat
-up

Rea → zzz → zzz

Erotics "with lions"

Wolves...
Reazzz...
Growls....

M a c h i n e

yellowhammer

wolves →
wind,
creaking,
dogs

RED BIRD: page 1

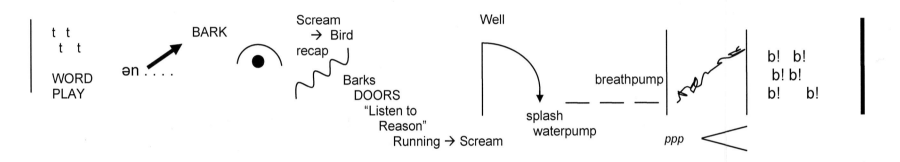

t t
 t t

WORD
PLAY

ən . . . .

BARK

Scream
→ Bird
recap

Barks
DOORS
"Listen to
Reason"
Running → Scream

Well

splash
waterpump

breathpump

ppp

b! b!
 b! b!
b!   b!

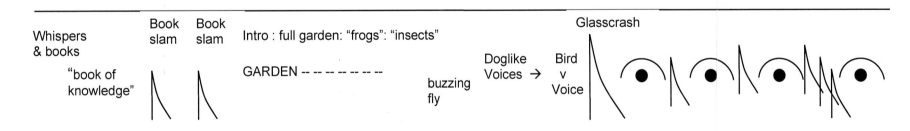

Whispers
& books

"book of
knowledge"

Book
slam

Book
slam

Intro : full garden: "frogs": "insects"

GARDEN -- -- -- -- -- --

buzzing
fly

Doglike
Voices →

Bird
v
Voice

Glasscrash

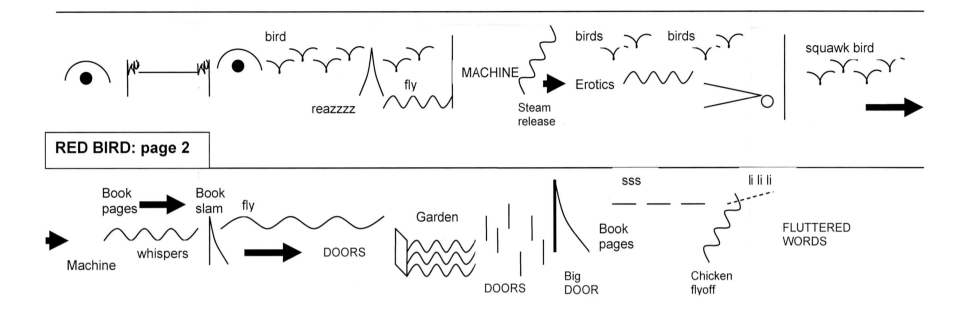

RED BIRD: page 2

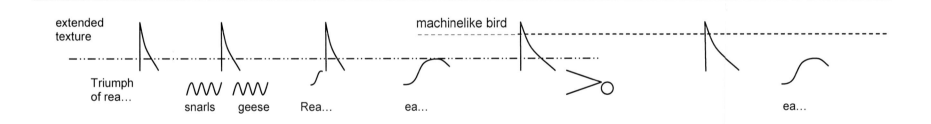

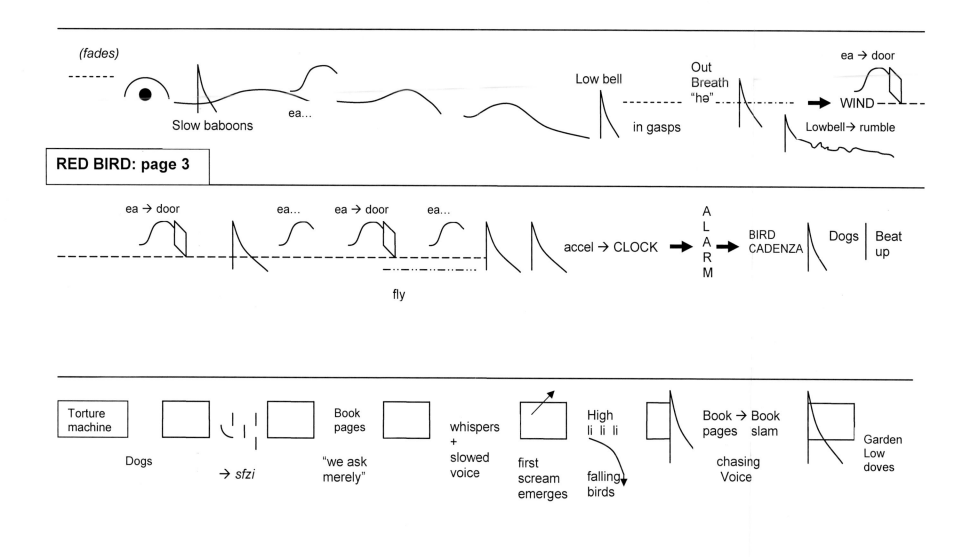

RED BIRD: page 3

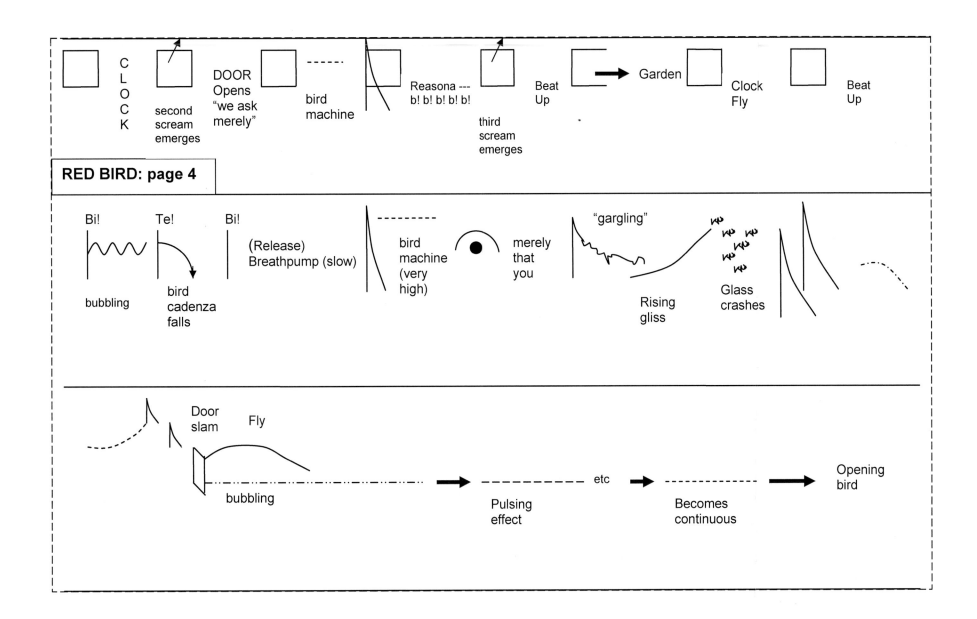

RED BIRD: page 4

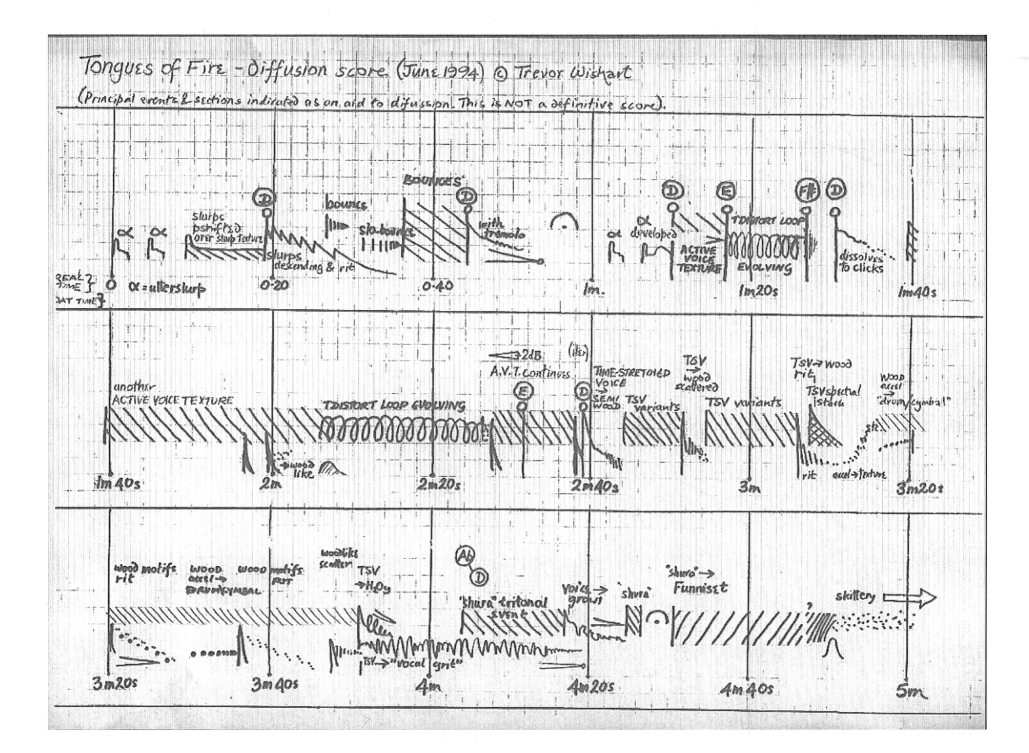

Tongues of Fire – Diffusion score (June 1994) © Trevor Wishart

(Principal events & sections indicated as an aid to diffusion. This is NOT a definitive score).

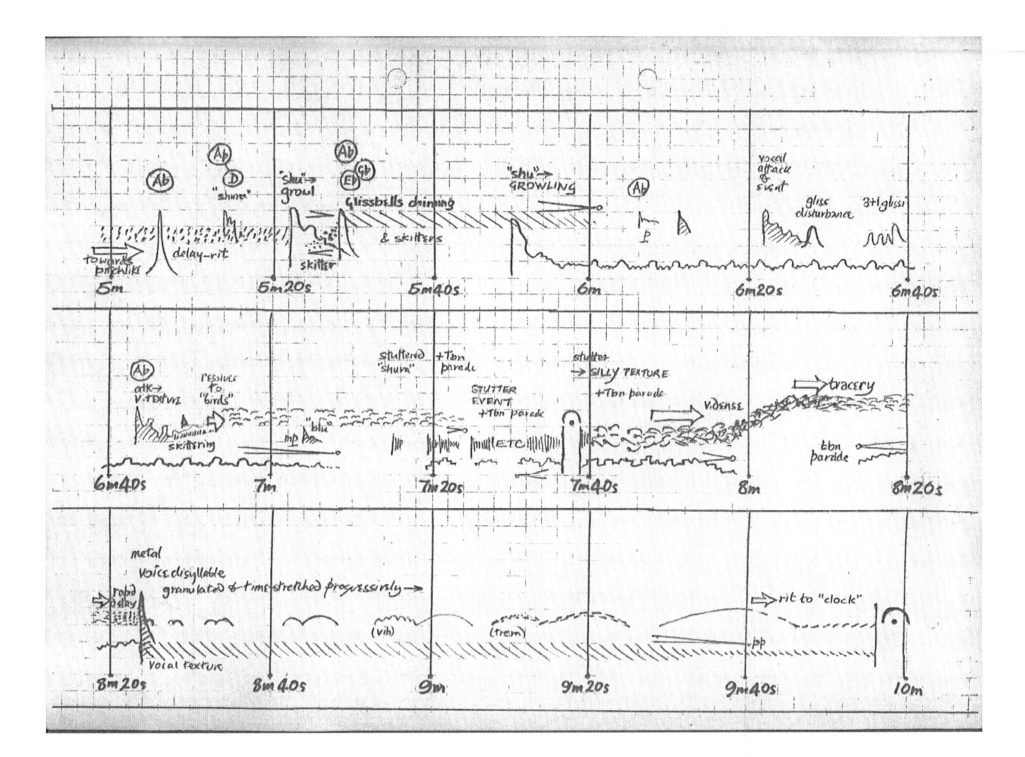

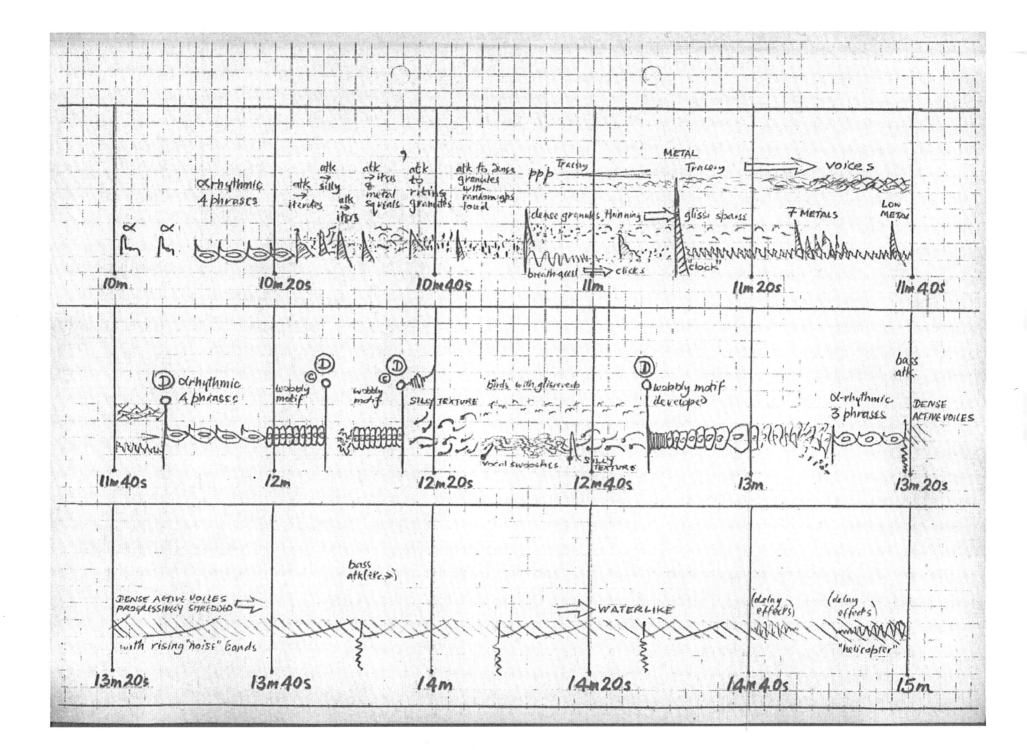

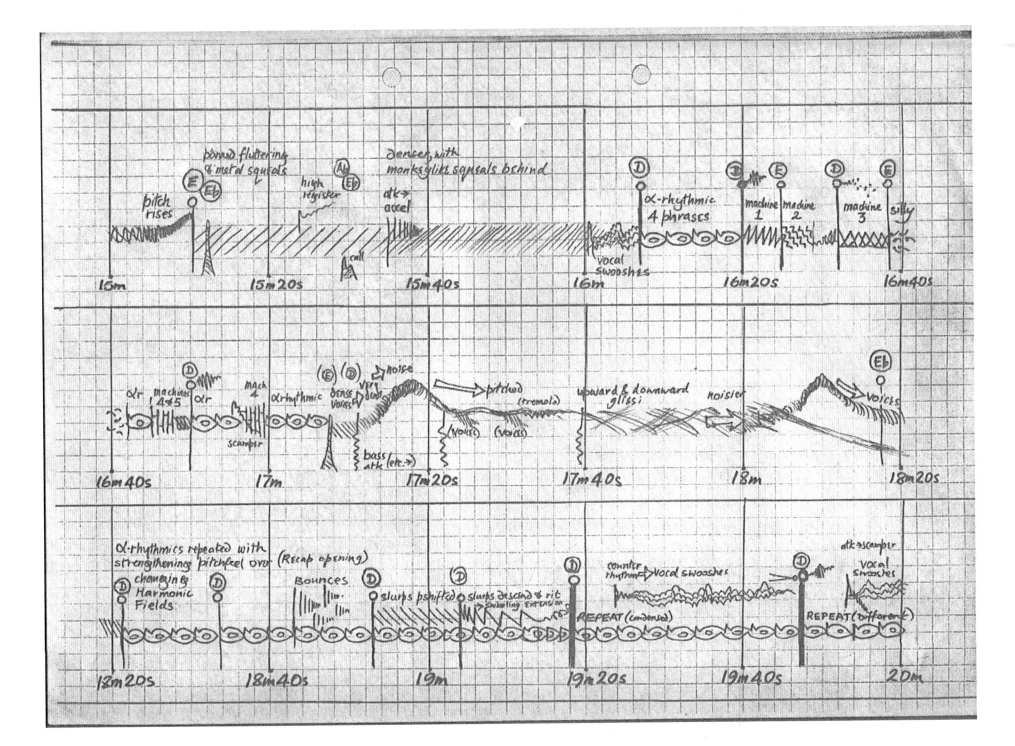

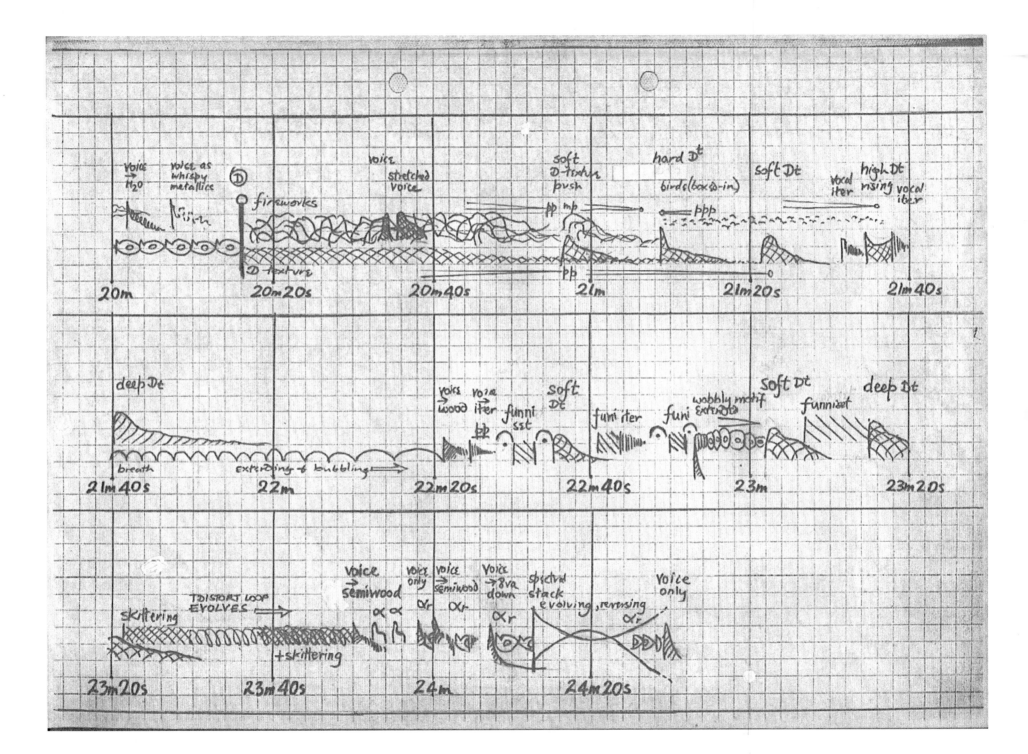

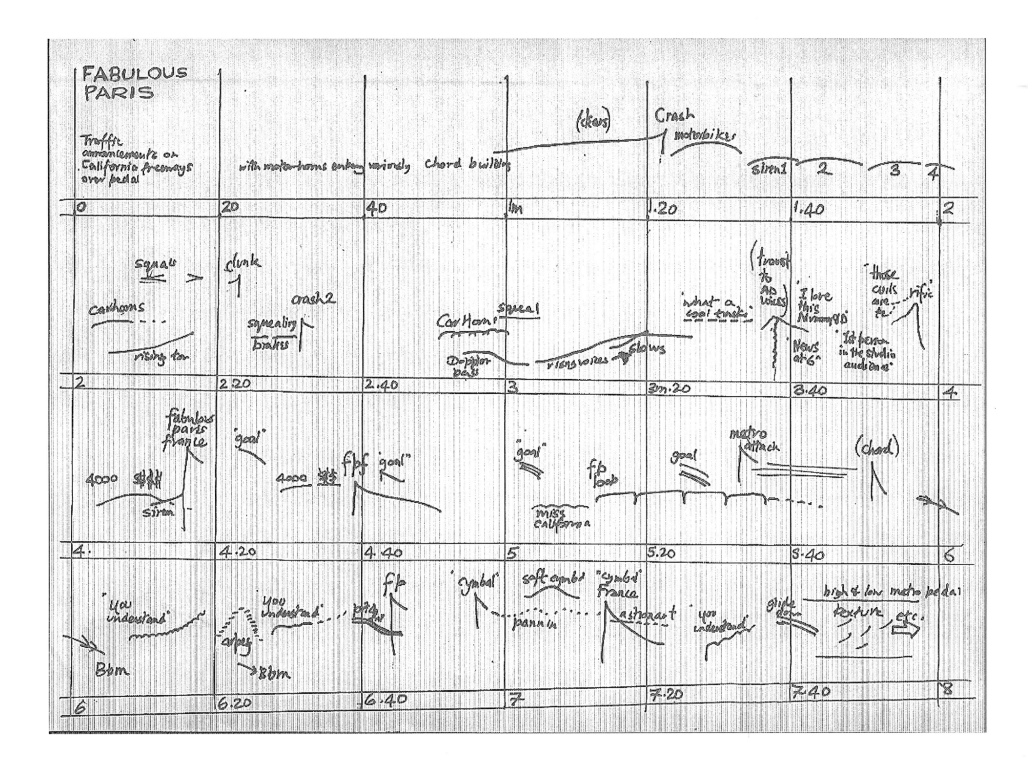

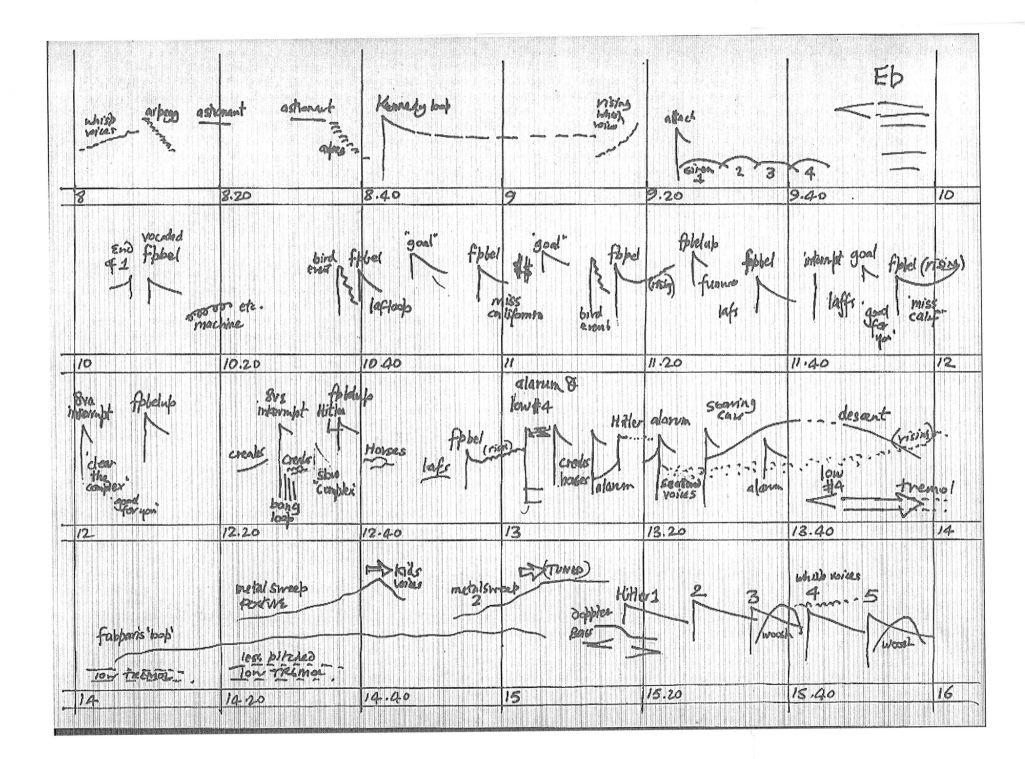

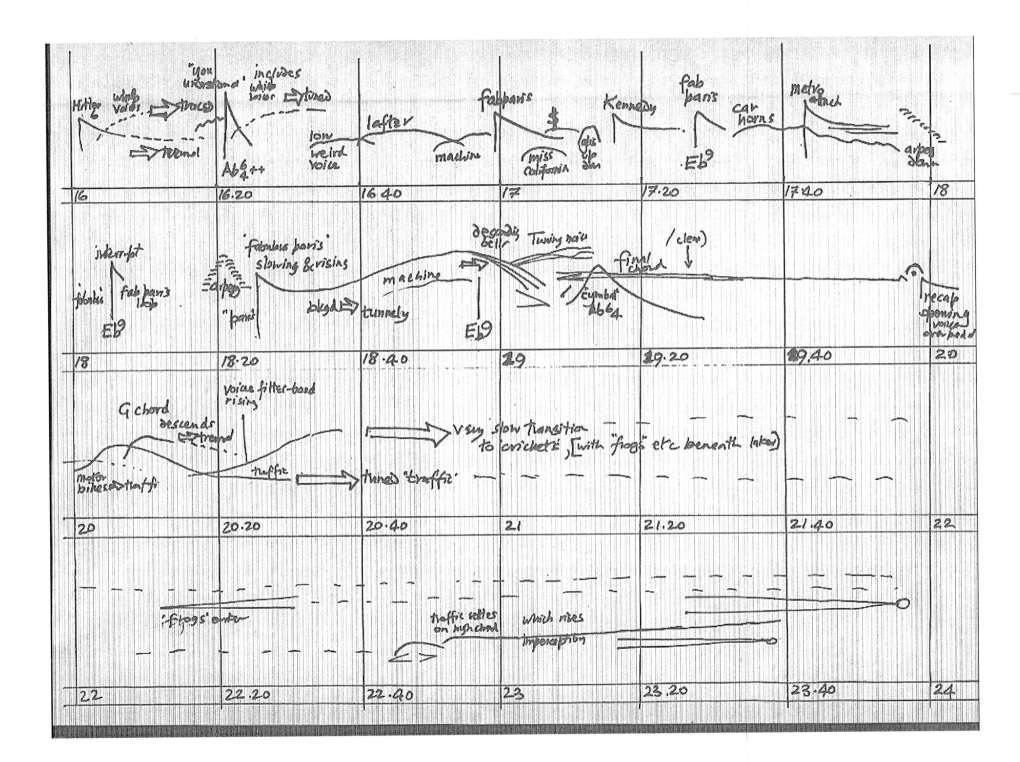

"ANGEL" : Trevor Wishart

0 **10** **24** **37** **42** **46** **50** **1:05** **1:17+** **1:29+** **2:07** (15)

Now6	Now6	Now6	Now6	Oh Oh!	Aunty	Now 6	Now6	Concerts	OH! and…

Now this is me | Oh well \ | Sally, | | This is when we | This is…
When I was 6 | Now then \ | Dolly | | used to go out | used to be in
| | | | | COOP
| | | | | Choir

2:15 **2:23+** **2:51** **3:07** **3:39** **3:49** **4:02+** **4:10** **4:18+** **4:27** (38)

You on the sands	Now 6	Now 6	This Is You → Tpt →This is You	Asleep	Irene	she was a	charm the

Whitley Bay | Cadenza | lovely | apples
| Hey Look, | | You on sands | had   she | person   from a tree
| this is you! | | asleep | something radiates
| TRUMPETS,PIANO | | | special   …lovely

4:38 **4:57** **5:00** **5:15** **5:25** **5:31** **5:37** **5:43** **5:50** **5:56** **6:05+** **6:13** **6:23** (29)

| Funny | Maybe got it wrong | Now6 | Now 6 | Now 6 | Now6 | I've been more your | |
| Little | very, very | |\ |\ | |\ |\ | |\ |\ | |\ |\ | Godmother | Godmother|

Quiet Way | Oh well | oh look
| |\ | |\ | | \ | |\ | |\ | |\ | |\ | Angela's in America
Glasses | | | | | | | Went to
| | | | | | | Whitby

6:29 **6:52** **7:00** **7:08** **7:38** **7:47** **7:50** **8:06** **8:20** **8:27** **8:30** **8:34** (37)

That's yr dad's Mother's sister| now that's | | That | beautiful
| Years in Bed | An earlier one | That dress | dress | dress
| | Somedy gevit to me | beautiful | beautiful | that
| | | mellow ------------ | | oh it
| Plucked | S-s-s-s-s-s-s-s-s-s | that's that --- | | was
| | | flat → bells--- | | beautiful

8:37 **8:49**/51 57 **9:02** 05 **9:13**/15 21/22 26/27 30 32 34 37 **9:39+** **10:43**

Now6	Now6	Now 6	Now6

laf   laf | laf   laf | laf | laf | laf
never | never   never   never | never,   never | never again
again | again   again | | again

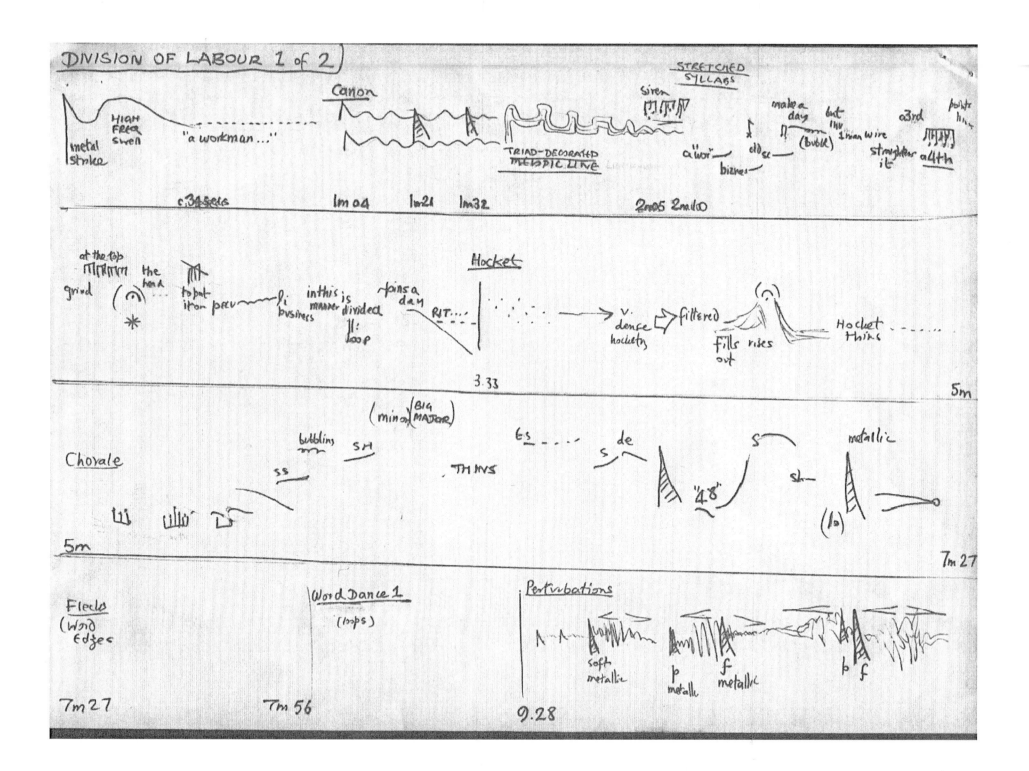

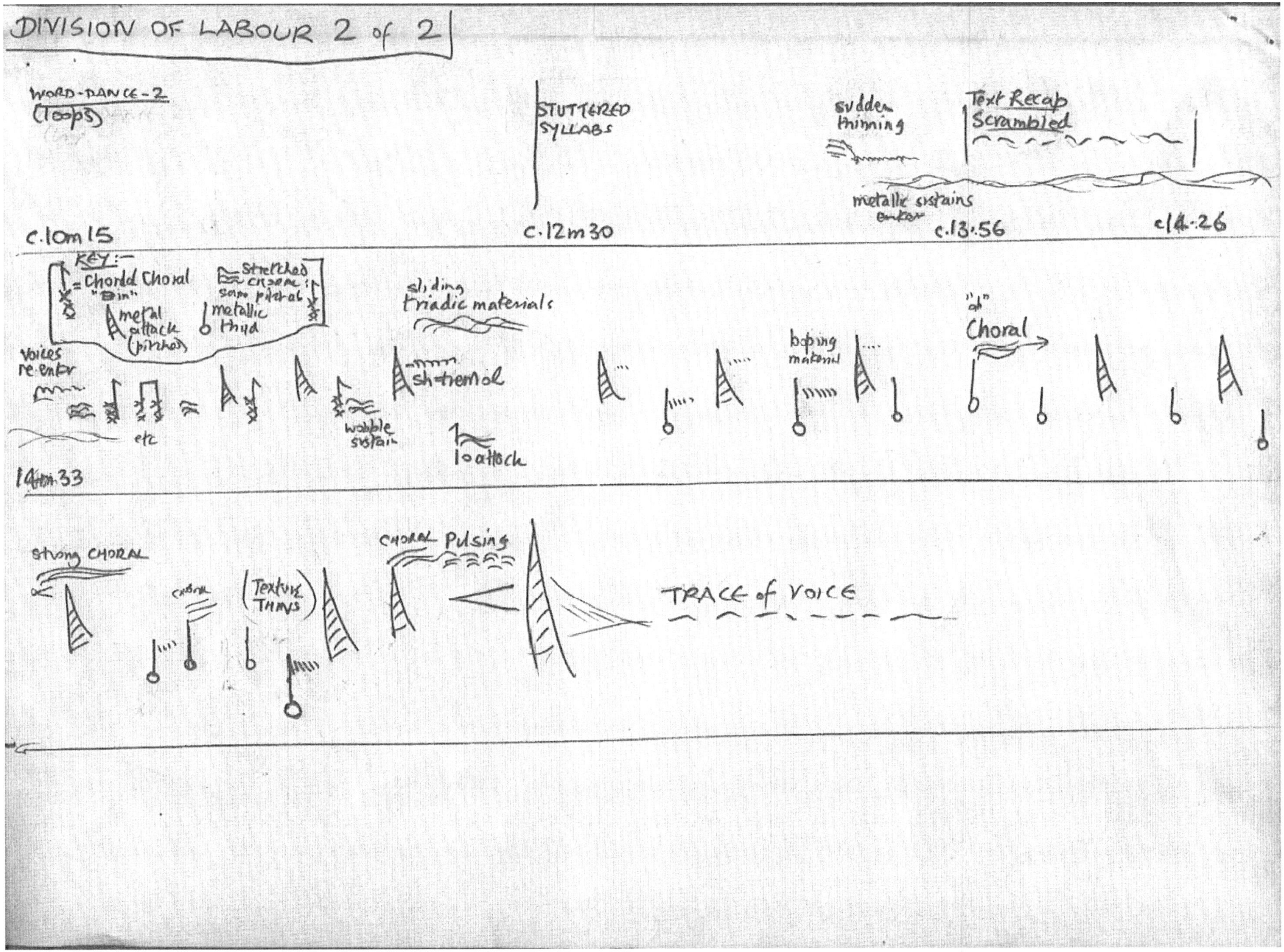

DIVISION OF LABOUR 2 of 2
WORD-DANCE-2
(Loops)
STUTTERED SYLLABS
sudden thinning
Text Recap Scrambled
metallic sustains enter
c.10m15
c.12m30
c.13.56
c14.26
KEY:-
= Chordal Choral "Bin"
metal attack (pitches)
metallic thud
Stretched choral: same pitch at
Voices re-enter
etc
wobble sustain
sliding triadic materials
sh-tremol
lo attack
looping material
"ah" Choral
14m.33
strong CHORAL
CHORAL
(Texture Thins)
CHORAL Pulsing
TRACE of VOICE

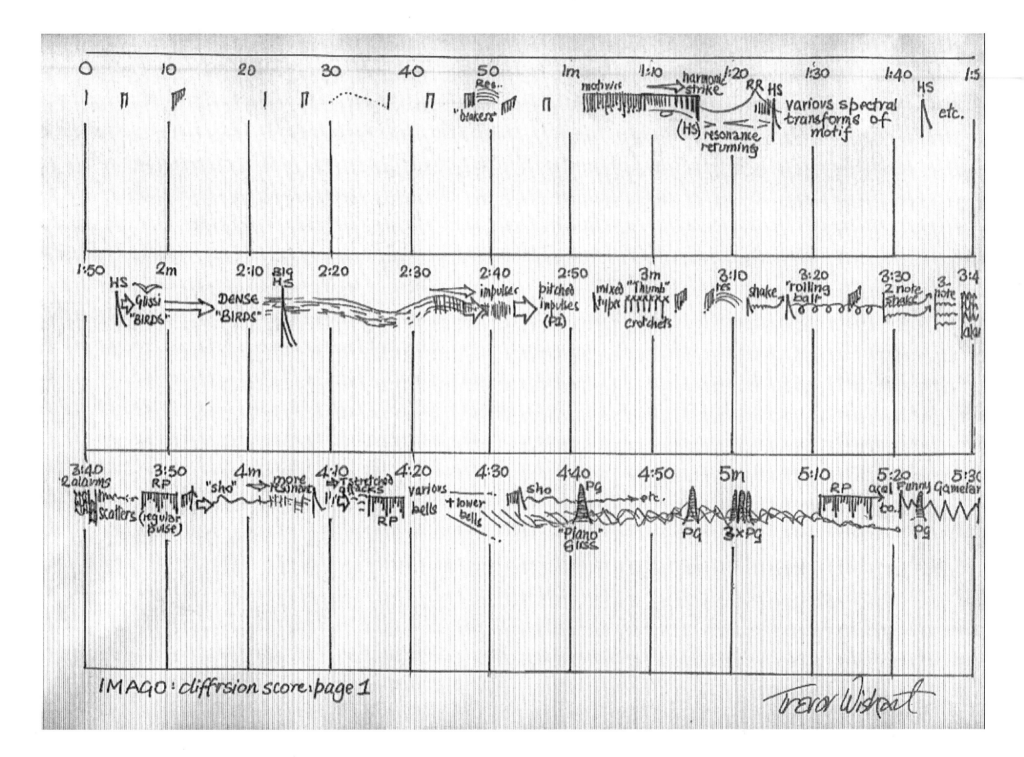

IMAGO: diffusion score, page 1

Trevor Wishart

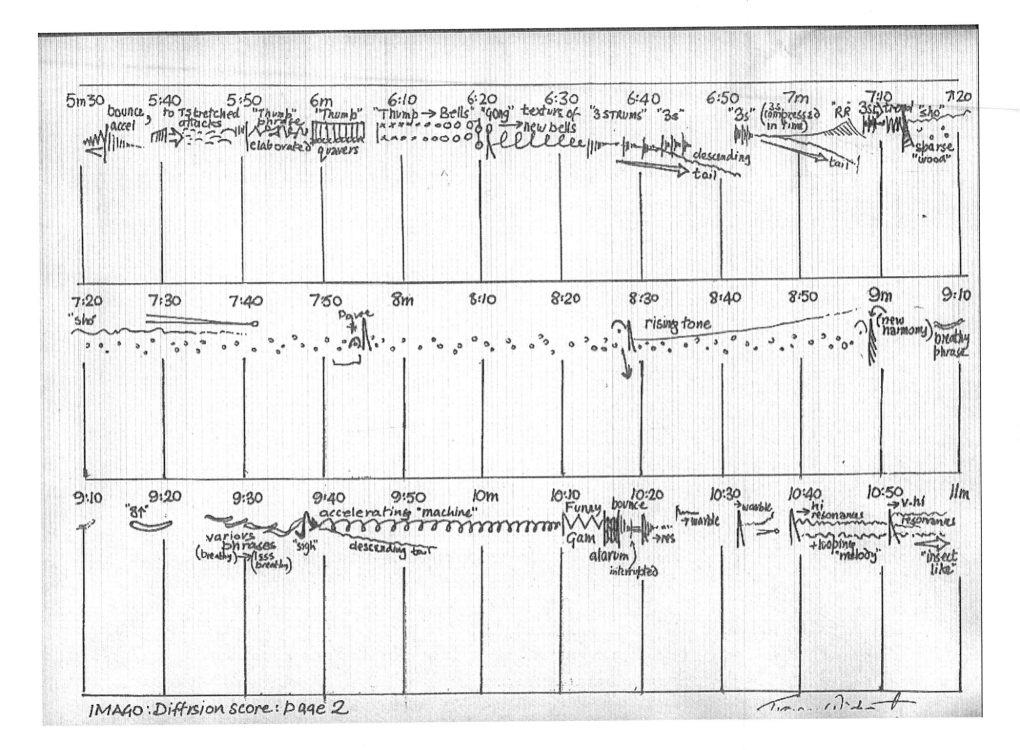

IMAGO: Diffusion score: page 2

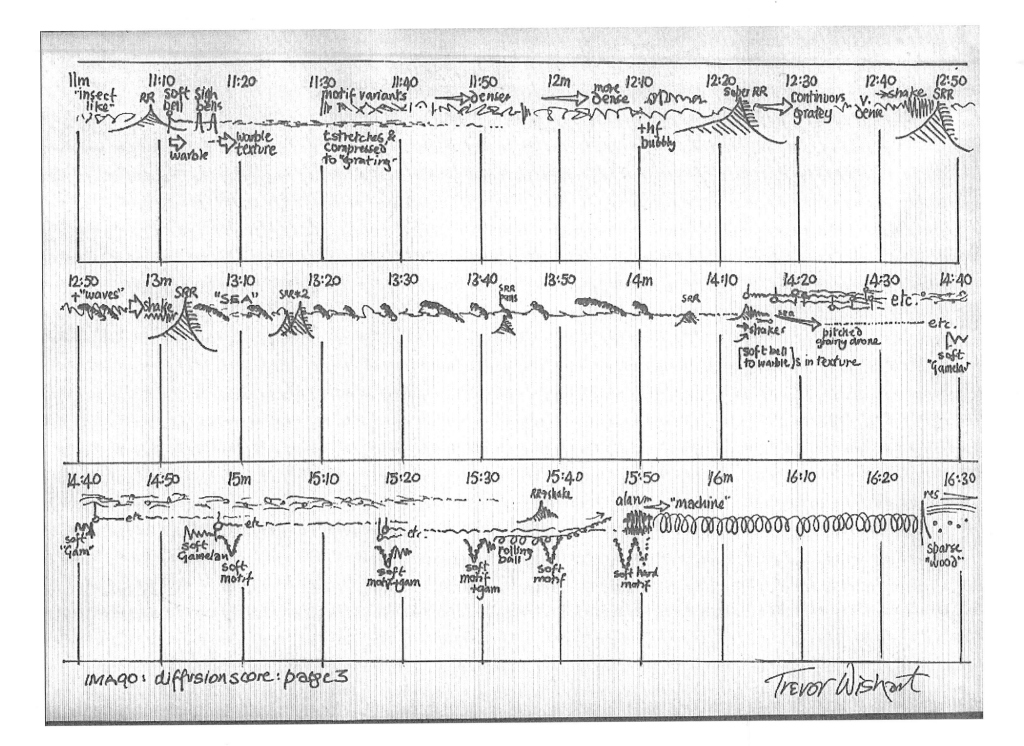

IMAGO: diffusion score: page 3

Trevor Wishart

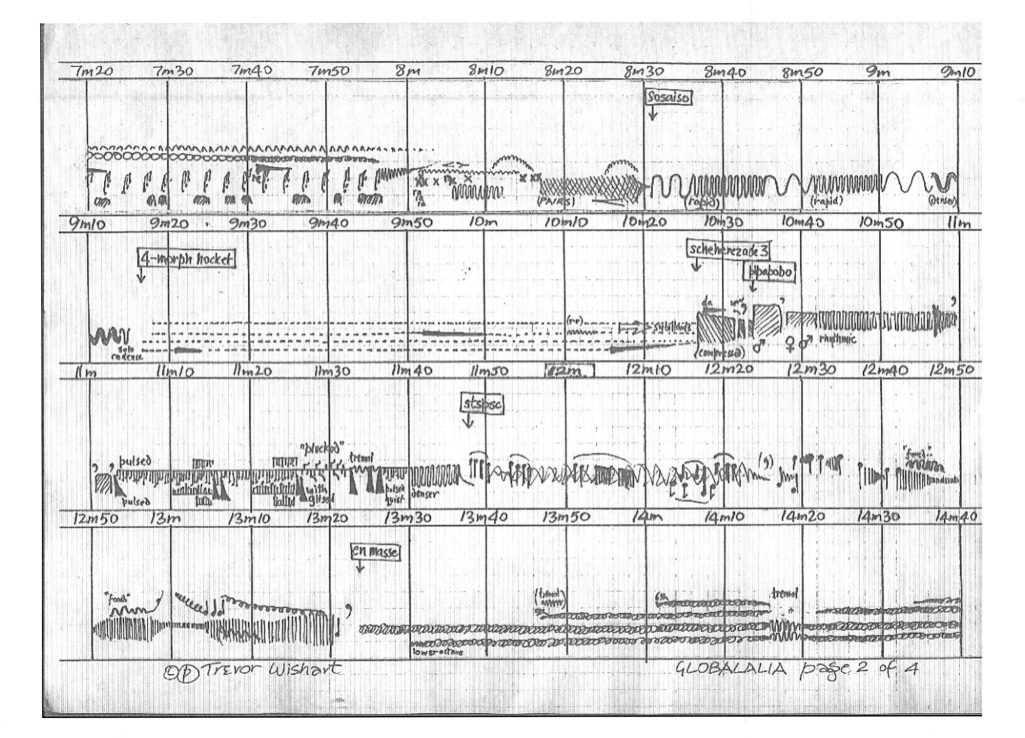

GLOBALALIA page 2 of 4

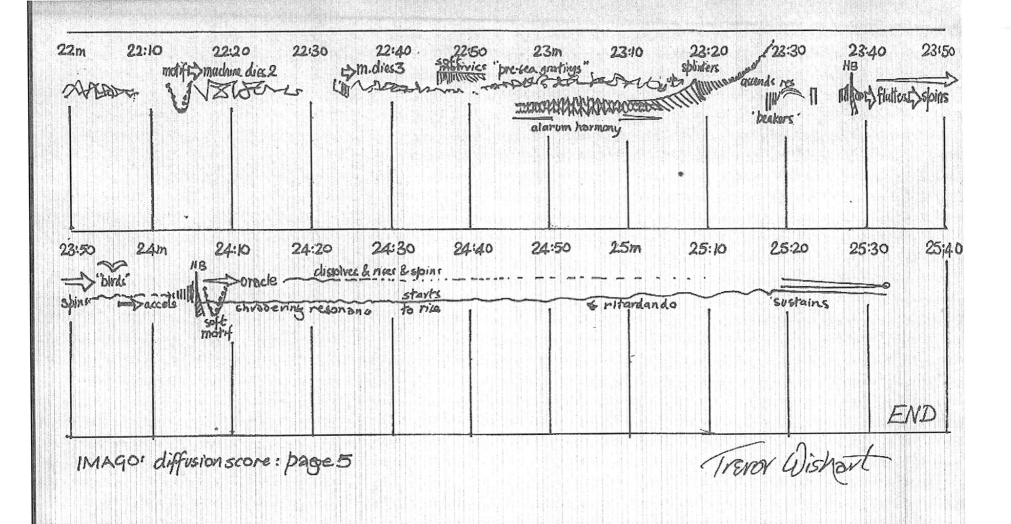

IMAGO: diffusion score: page 5

Trevor Wishart

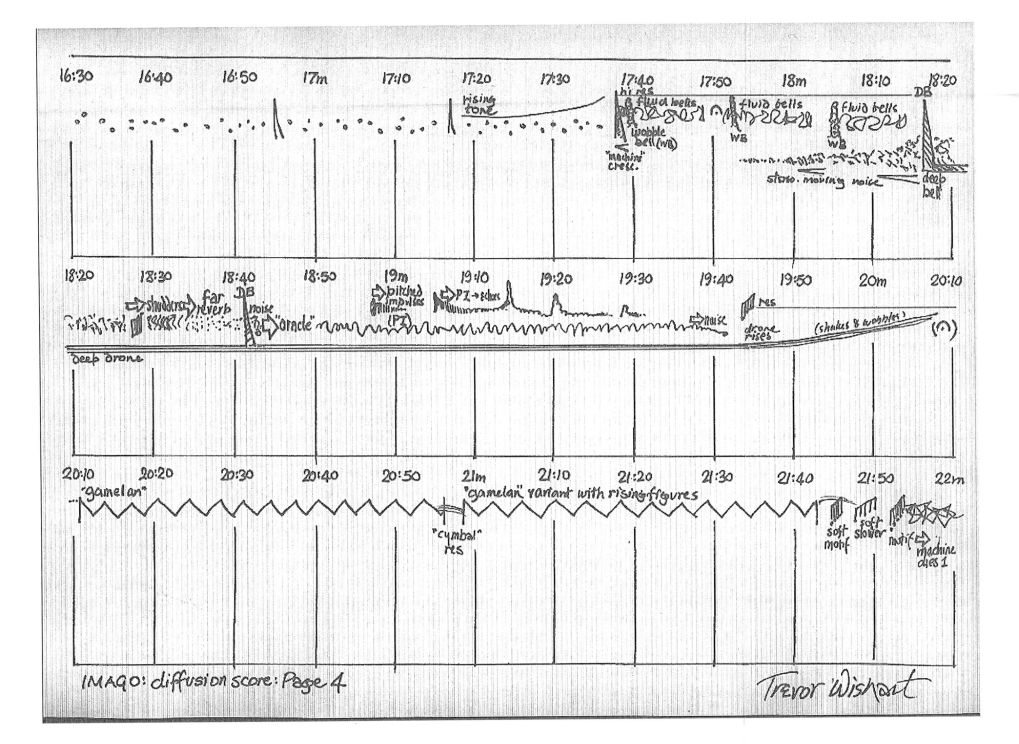

IMAGO: diffusion score: Page 4

Trevor Wishart

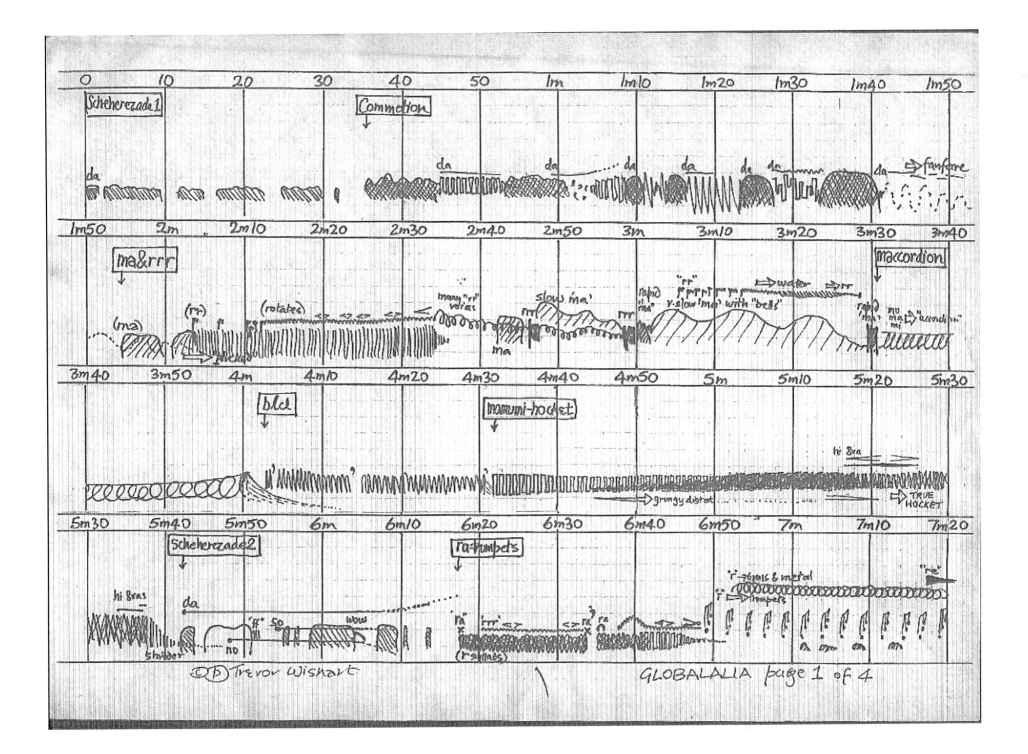

GLOBALALIA page 1 of 4

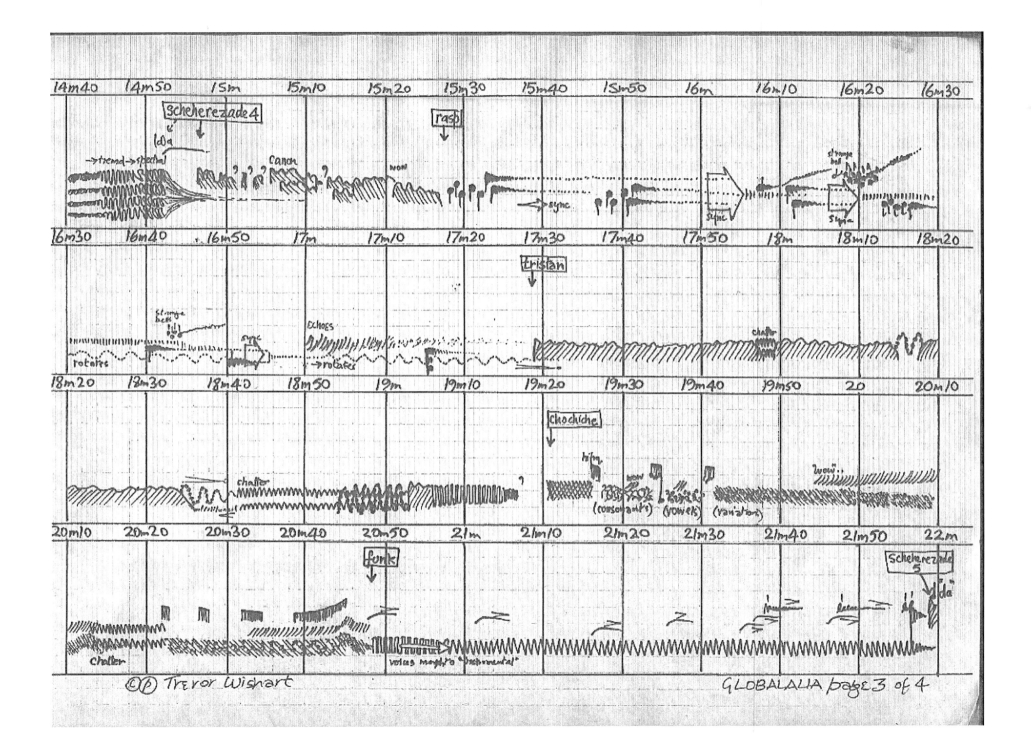

GLOBALALIA page 3 of 4

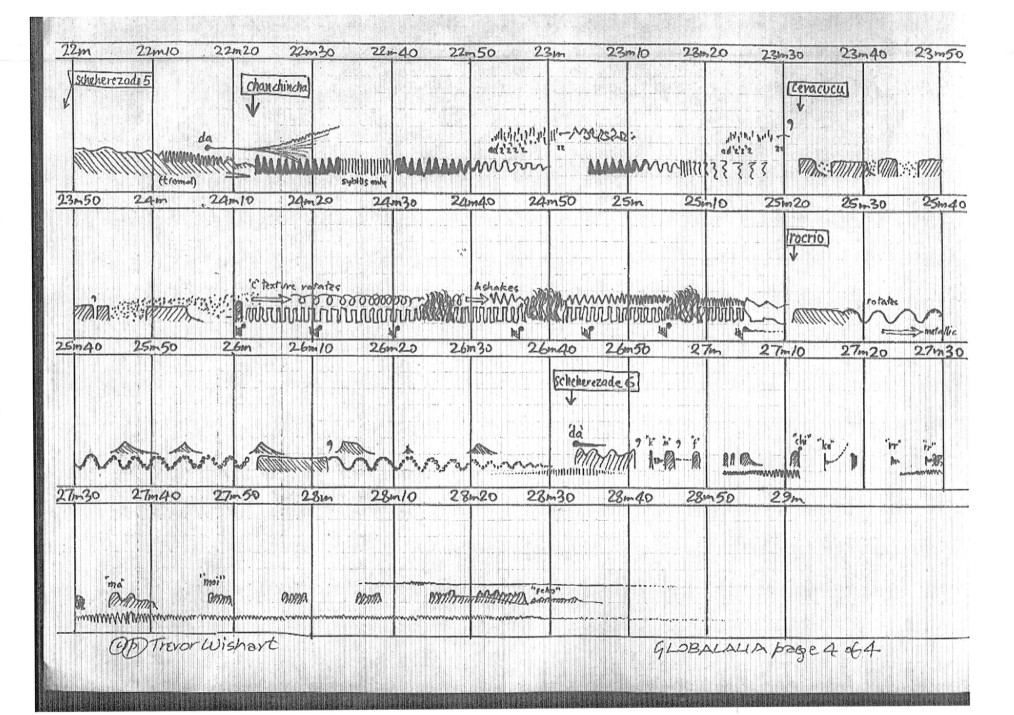

© Trevor Wishart

GLOBALALIA page 4 of 4